OLD MAN
FOG

SMITHSONIAN SERIES IN ETHNOGRAPHIC INQUIRY
William L. Merrill and Ivan Karp, Series Editors

Ethnography as fieldwork, analysis, and literary form is the distinguishing feature of modern anthropology. Guided by the assumption that anthropological theory and ethnography are inextricably linked, this series is devoted to exploring the ethnographic enterprise.

Advisory Board

OLD MAN FOG

and the Last Aborigines
of Barrow Point

John B. Haviland with Roger Hart
Illustrations by Tulo Gordon

Smithsonian Institution Press
Washington and London

Copy editor: Jean Eckenfels
Production editor: Jack Kirshbaum
Designer: Linda McKnight

Library of Congress Cataloging-in-Publication Data
Haviland, John Beard.
    Old man Fog and the last Aborigines of Barrow Point /
    John B. Haviland with Roger Hart ; illustrations by
    Tulo Gordon.
        p.   cm. — (Smithsonian series in ethnographic inquiry)
    Includes bibliographical references and index.
    ISBN 1-56098-913-0 (cloth : alk. paper). —
    ISBN 1-56098-803-7 (pbk. : alk. paper)
        1. Australian aborigines—Australia—Barrow Point (Qld.)—
    History.   2. Hart, Roger.   3. Australian aborigines—Australia—
    Barrow Point (Qld.)—Biography.   4. Mythology, Australian
    aboriginal—Australia—Barrow Point (Qld.).   I. Hart, Roger.
    II. Title.   III. Series.
    GN667.Q4H38   1998
    305.899150943—dc21   98-38563

British Library Cataloguing-in-Publication Data available

Manufactured in the United States of America
05 04 03 02 01 00 99 98   5 4 3 2 1

∞ The paper used in this publication meets the minimum
requirements of the American National Standard for Information
Sciences—Permanence of Paper for Printed Library Materials
ANSI Z39.48-1984.

For permission to reproduce illustrations appearing in this book,
please correspond directly with the author, John B. Haviland. The
Smithsonian Institution Press does not retain reproduction rights
for these illustrations individually, or maintain a file of addresses
for photo sources.

Frontispiece (page vi): Detail from *King Harry thrown overboard* by
Tulo Gordon (figure 6)

To two cousins, Tulo *Wunba* Gordon,
thawuunh, bubu-gujin, binaal-gurraay-baga, and
Lizzie Confin Jack, *ngathu warra ngamu,*
both present throughout,
but gone too soon to see the book itself.

Contents

Contents

FOREWORD

I was six years old when this tall American who everybody said was "half Chinaman" or "half Filipino" came to stay in Hopevale. John and Leslie Haviland were staying at old man Billy **Muunduu's** place, two doors away from our house. John was learning **guugu,** our language.

When I went next door to my **yumurr**[1] Mary McIvor's house every day to play cards or marbles under the mango tree, to listen to her daughter Amy's Charlie Pride records, or to pretend to look for **wuugul,** lice, in my old daughter Mary's head, I wondered why this white couple next door chose to live among all the black fellas, instead of with the European staff and school teachers at the top side of the mission.

Like the rest of us, they were using an outside bathroom with no hot water, the outhouse toilet, and they were eating black people's damper and **mayi,** food, all the time. What was the matter with them? Maybe they were the hippies the elders at church and Sunday school were warning us about.

John soon became formidable in his grasp of 'true Guugu Yimithirr' —as my old friend Roger would later say, *"Alu uwu mindiir."*[2]

In testimony to his mastery of the language, they used to tell a story (I don't know whether apocryphal) about Haviland standing with a group of men around the old curio shop (now, tragically, demolished) when a Hopevale man, newly arrived from down south, and not knowing who John was, joked to the locals, *"Ganaa ngayu yii wangarr bagal?"* (Is it all right if I just beat this white fella up?) The joker got the fright of his life when this six-and-a-half-foot American said in perfect Guugu Yimithirr: *"Nyundu nganhi baadala, ngayu warra mangaalmul!"* (Just you have a go, (and see if) I have no hands!)

I knew old man *Urwunhthin,* as Roger Hart, father of Janice and Bernard and that mob, since I was a kid. He was one of the many people who formed the social universe of my childhood and upbringing at Hopevale. I didn't see him much during the 1970s when he was out working in the cane fields at Mossman, but I knew who he was and he would have been able to tell that I was Glen Pearson's son, Charlie's grandson, and old **Arrimi's** great grandson. It's like that when you live at Hopevale. He would have known more about me than I knew about myself.

I grew up thinking that Roger Hart was just another mission man who spoke Guugu Yimithirr and, like my grandfather Charlie, was removed to the Cape Bedford Mission as a child. It was when I began to tape some oral histories of older people for my history thesis at Sydney

University in late 1985 and 1986 that I was surprised to be told by my
father that I should go and talk to Roger Hart, who spoke his own language. I had known from an early age that Roger's country was **Gambiilmugu**—northern neighbors to my great grandfather's country **Bagaarr-
mugu** at Jeannie River. But I knew nothing about the **Gambiilmugu**
language. I only knew about the language of Hopevale, Guugu Yimithirr;
my mother's language, *Kuku Yalanji;* and a couple of old people who
spoke *Lamalama* languages. I had not heard of the Barrow Point language being spoken by anyone in the mission.

I went to see old man Roger and there began our friendship. Our
friendship started on the veranda of the Old People's Home in the company of another newly found mate, and Roger's childhood friend and
relation from Cape Melville, the late Bob Flinders. It turned out that a
number of the old people—including Bob, the late Leo Rosendale, and
Lindsay Nipper—could speak snippets of Roger's language. I decided to
learn Roger's language so I could converse with him.

Athirr wulu, alcohol, and **matheermul,** brainless, were early gains to my
vocabulary. Appreciating my desire to learn, Roger generously taught me
so that we had our own secret language to observe and mock those
around us.

Sitting with the old men on the veranda overlooking the village,
watching the mission life, we would spend hours and days yarning
about language, history at the mission, history before the mission, customs, hunting, birds, animals, plants, the weather, the past, the present,
the future, Christianity, the church, politics, and land rights. Roger and
I would spend days under his mango tree. Like John Haviland's talks
with Roger, **lipwulin,** Barrow Point, obsessed our conversation.

John's account in this book of getting to know Roger Hart, his life
and that of his people and his country, resonated for me. I was greatly
privileged to find this friendship, because it came at a time when identity and history and land rights were utmost in my thoughts. My long
hours and days and weeks of talking with my mates, Roger, Bob, and the
other old people, turned into years, during which time Roger and I
mourned the steady passing of our friends.

Roger's history here is the best evocation we have of life in the wake
of the devastation wrought by the violent invasion of the Cooktown
hinterland after the Palmer River gold rush, that is, life on the fringes,
outside of the mission. In the period from the turn of the century to
World War II, remnant Aboriginal groups lived an itinerant traditional
life when they could, caught between frontier cattlemen, miners, and
fishermen, who inhumanely exploited them, and the government and

missionaries, who wanted to take their children away from their families and to eventually bring this camp life to an end. The government and missions eventually succeeded, and a handful of lonely old people ended their days on the reserve at the edge of Cooktown.

My great grandfather **Arrimi,** who appears in Roger's stories, inhabited my childhood dreams. He was an outlaw bushman who evaded the police and could only surreptitiously bring **mayi,** food, to my father at Cape Bedford Mission. I often wondered how he and the people who still lived the bush life managed to survive. Roger's book tells us about the last days of the bush people.

In many respects, life in these circumstances—occasional work, hunting and traveling around the countryside—might have had possibilities. If only they could have been left free. If only they had some land for themselves. If only the whites weren't so inhumane and there was no exploitation. Maybe they could have kept their families and remained in their country.

If there is much sadness and loss in Roger's story about the removal of the people from their homeland, and his eventual loneliness as the last survivor of the mob born in the bush, the land claim won by Roger and other **Yiithuuwarra** people before the Queensland Land Tribunal in the early 1990s tells a hopeful story of reunion and the fact that the **Gambiilmugu** people are alive and well, and they have a future.

Work by Roger, through diligent accumulation of knowledge about his people and patient recording of this knowledge, and by other old people like the brothers Bob and Johnny Flinders, made it possible for his descendants to reclaim *lipwulin* under the land rights opportunities that have arisen in the twilight of his life.

As well as his strong memory and sharp mind, Roger is the most gracious and generous of men. My affection, which grew instantly, remains steadfast for *athunbi anggatha,* my friend, from *lipwulin.*

Noel Pearson

NOTES

1. This classificatory kinship term puts Mrs. McIvor into the category of Noel Pearson's "child" (on the patrilineal side), despite the fact that she was already an elderly woman when he was a little boy.
2. Literally, "he's a real champion for the language."

Figure 1. Tulo Gordon's story map of Barrow Point

ACKNOWLEDGMENTS

Any project that, like this one, spans nearly two decades of work spread over three continents manages to reach its conclusion—this book—only by virtue of the efforts of many. These are some of the people I would like to thank for their help. To others, whose names time has erased from my memory, Roger and I send wordless thanks.

At Hopevale, many people have welcomed me and other members of my family and helped us to learn about **bama** ways. For this book, most important have been Roger Hart himself and his family, especially Allen Hart, Bernard Hart, and Patsy Gibson, their families and children, along with the widely extended family of the late Tulo Gordon and his late wife Gertie, especially Helen Michael and family, the late Noeleen Michael and family, and their brothers, especially Willie, Godfrey, and Reggie. For their constant teaching, friendship, and hospitality over the years I am especially indebted to Walter and the late Lizzie Jack and all their children, my brothers and sisters; to Pastor George and Maudie Rosendale; and to Roy and Thelma McIvor. For support, encouragement, help, and company on our last trip to Barrow Point I am grateful to Merv Gibson and to Noel Pearson. Of many members of the Hopevale Council who have eased practical affairs and opened Hopevale to me, I wish especially to thank Gearhardt Pearson, Lister and Leonard Rosendale, and Peter and David Costello.

For their hospitality and kindness when Roger, Tulo, and I visited the south, I would especially like to thank the late Bendi Jack and his family in Melbourne, Conrad Keese and his family in Sydney, and Fred, Joan, Michael, and Leonie James at Lake Tabourie and Sydney, N.S.W.

My academic debts in this work are many. I am especially grateful to Bob Dixon, for first introducing me to North Queensland and its languages; to Bruce Rigsby and Peter Sutton for generously sharing their notes and knowledge of Queensland languages, genealogy, and geography, and for their unflagging encouragement. I offer special thanks to Elinor Ochs and Sandro Duranti for first inviting me to put some of this material into a semi-academic form. I owe a special debt of gratitude to Elisabeth Patz, for her translations of many German archival materials, most of which were kindly provided by the Bavarian Missionary Society at Neuendettelsau (courtesy of its archivist Konrad Rauh), and by the Lutheran Church of Australia, in Adelaide. I am also indebted to Nona Bennett, for her computerized annotations of these early archival records, and to Kathy Frankland of the Queensland State Archives. Many people have helped with removing some of the awkwardnesses from the texts; I especially thank Sharon Larisch, Dick Bauman, and anonymous reviewers for Smithsonian for their suggestions.

Over the years of work represented in this project, we have enjoyed financial support from many sources. Initially, Haviland, Hart, and Gordon had research grants from the (then) Australian Institute of Aboriginal Studies, often including loans of vehicles as well as other practical help. Institutional funding of Haviland's research came from the Department of Anthropology, Research School of Pacific Studies, Australian National University, from Reed College, from a fellowship from the John Simon Guggenheim Memorial Foundation, as well as from the Cognitive Anthropology Research Group of the Max-Planck Institute for Psycholinguistics and from the Centro de Investigaciones y Estudios Superiores en Antropología Social (CIESAS)-Sureste (with funding from CONACYT-Mexico) which partially supported writing the manuscript. The Cape York Land Council, through the generous offices of Noel Pearson, also supported the final stages of the research itself. Finally, The Body Shop (Australia) and generous support from Mr. Barrie Thomas made possible the publication of the color plates that accompany the book.

For their hospitality (not to mention, cheese, fish, and prawns) during the main writing of the book, I am indebted to Arno and Ino van Ooyen of Elst, Gelderland, the Netherlands, to David and Nona Bennett of Potato Point, N.S.W., and to Jonathan Kelley and Mariah Evans, of Queanbeyan, N.S.W.

At a more personal level for their encouragement, love, and enthusiasm despite my many fits and starts while working on this project, and also for sharing many parts of the work itself at various stages of research, thinking, and writing, I wish to thank (and send my hugs to) Lourdes de León, Isabel Haviland, Maya Haviland (who was one of the earliest critics of my renditions of Roger Hart's stories into English), Sophie Haviland, Leslie Knox Devereaux, Patsy and Alex Asch, the late Roger Keesing, Shelley Schreiner, Bruce and Barbara Rigsby, Stephen Levinson, and especially the late Tim Asch for his company and inspiration on one of our last trips to Barrow Point.

INTRODUCTION:
"WILL YOU WRITE DOWN MY LANGUAGE?"

There once was a reasonably large tribe of people who laid claim to the area around Barrow Point, on the coast south of Cape Melville and north of Cape Flattery in far north Queensland, Australia. Roger Hart, probably the last surviving member of the tribe to be born in the bush, came into the world sometime between 1914 and 1916 just west of Barrow Point at Ninian Bay. In this period a good-sized group of nomadic Aborigines still lived around Barrow Point. They traveled between different seasonal camps and relied for their livelihoods both on their own hunting and gathering and on government-supplied provisions or occasional work on stations or boats. Earlier in the century the area had become one of the last refuges for Aborigines north of Cooktown who had been hunted off or deported from zones where Europeans had established mines, farms, or settlements. Many people in Roger's world, including his mother, had spent time working for white settlers and farmers. Although Roger Hart's biological father was probably one of these settlers, Roger's Aboriginal father—his mother's recognized Aboriginal husband at the time of his birth—was the person who gave him his language, his traditional land, and his tribal identity.

By the early 1920s, the Barrow Point people were under attack, from police, settlers, and commercial fishermen who plied the coast in search of inexpensive Aboriginal labor. Within ten years, the Aboriginal camps at Barrow Point had been burned by government officials and the people relocated to a different area farther north. By the Second World War, most of these people too were dead, and only a few of the traditional owners of Barrow Point people survived, mostly scattered through Aboriginal communities elsewhere in Queensland.

I met Roger Hart in 1979 when he asked me if I had any "spare time" to help him "write down" his Barrow Point language, a cousin of the Guugu Yimithirr language I had gone to Queensland to study. Over the next few years we worked sporadically on the material in this book. Our collaborator was Tulo Gordon, an artist and storyteller from an area called **Nugal,** on the Endeavour River. Tulo had been one of my teachers of Guugu Yimithirr when I first went to Hopevale, an Aboriginal community north of Cooktown, in 1971. He was also one of Roger Hart's childhood friends from early mission days. Our idea was to combine Roger's autobiography, the history of his people, and the traditional stories he remembered from his childhood. Tulo Gordon, before he died in

1989, painted the illustrations that accompany the text, based on our conversations and Tulo's journeys with us to Cape Melville and Barrow Point in 1980 and 1982.

Biography, in the narrative fragments of Roger Hart's story, is equivocal, ambiguous, and interactive. The process by which we jointly induced Roger to assemble his "life history" begins with what Tulo used to call Roger's "strong memory" and continues in Roger's invention of himself, his evolving self-knowledge and sense of identity. Even the stories about old Fog that serve as the central intellectual property of the Barrow Point people are our own patchwork of conflicting versions, contested elements, themes, and morals. They derive from authoritative but contradictory retellings, using different words and, indeed, different languages —fragments of the original Barrow Point tongue, mixed with the fluent Guugu Yimithirr of Roger, Tulo, and others, and punctuated throughout by the elegant, archaic English many Hopevale people command. The story of old man Fog is legitimated by the undisputed fact of Roger's ownership, but it is also undermined by the treachery of time and memory. Roger's stories, about mythic times, about the history of his tribe, and about his own life, were richest as we approximated the contexts of old: when he and I, sometimes with Tulo's company, sat around the campfire talking about former times on our visits to Barrow Point itself.

Roger Hart's story is thus formed from little pieces of narrative that range from autobiographical remarks, slipped in over tea and biscuits in the midst of linguistic elicitation, to consciously performed historical or biographical reminiscences. Of the latter, some were filmed and others tape-recorded. They are examples of an invented genre—"telling my life story"—that people at Hopevale have become practiced at delivering. The most important source has been conversation about past life and adventures, routinely tape-recorded in the course of our visits to Barrow Point and its environs, as well as to other sites in Queensland, where Roger Hart has spent his life. Supplementing this are the haphazardly preserved archival sources that record a European view of Aboriginal affairs in the far North. Writing down the resulting "texts" belies their dependence on the particular interlocutors in each of these conversations, on the circumstances and activities of the moment, and on the momentum of history—even recent history, as claims on land and language have come to be of central importance in modern Queensland. Indeed, any account of customs, traditions, and events involving Aboriginal people in far north Queensland is likely to appear more coherent and less riddled with gaps than actual knowledge warrants. Interested parties

often want facts to be neater than they are, and recording even fragments tends to knit them together and give them form and consistency
that perhaps they do not merit.

For example, one sometimes thinks of a "life story" as a sequence of
events, a chronology of happenings, experienced by an individual moving through time and space. Some parts of such a story may survive only
in memory; others may be inscribed in documents; others may be lost.
However, in theory the absolute trajectory of events is fixed, frozen by
the facts of the past. The Barrow Point lives that Roger Hart and I have
managed to reconstruct are not like this. Instead they are sketchy
glimpses of biography, fashioned by us in a way that perhaps resembles
how people once talked about their kinsmen's exploits, around cooking
fires, in wet season cave shelters, in canoes, or in the long weeks of initiation. The protagonists of such narratives are not strictly individuals,
not easily separable from their kinsmen nor, indeed, from their countries. A single named man or woman may actually stand for a whole
chain of relatives, defined by how they 'bite' (as one says in Guugu
Yimithirr) or 'eat' (as one says in Barrow Point language)—that is, 'call'
by a kin relationship term—other people in the social universe. Thus, in
different tellings, the adventures of one person may merge with those of
another, still remaining essentially equivalent in all the ways that matter, that is, that define who the person was. For another thing, happenings and their moral character are fused in the biographical reminiscences Roger and I gathered, which are thus not mere chronologies or
sequences of events, but tales, **milbi,** 'news, stories,' usually with strong
if implicit moral resonance.

As life changed with the arrival of European and other foreign invaders, the lives (and accordingly the "life stories") of people from Barrow Point became at once more complicated and more fragmentary. Kin
chains were broken and their links scattered, leaving each individual
both more isolated and more important than he or she would have been
as part of a coherent social whole. Ways of understanding people's actions changed. Even the languages changed, as people lost their own
words and began to use instead those learned from strangers. There was
also a change in who one's interlocutors could be for narrating lives. As
the social world was reduced and distorted by invasion, sickness, dis-
persal, violence, and death, the company of one's kinsmen gave way to
the company of fellow displaced persons, other survivors and refugees.
Their interests and abilities to assimilate and evaluate 'news' and 'stories' were radically different from those of the kinsmen who once shared
a campfire or an initiation ground.

Two themes recur in Roger's story that merit special comment. The first is the massive and pervasive intervention in Aboriginal life—one could almost say its deliberate dismantling—by European society in the first half and particularly the first twenty-five years of this century. The second is a special dilemma of identity, felt most acutely by Aborigines of mixed descent, manifest in a deep personal ambivalence people like Roger Hart experience about who they are in the world. The effects of the first were already apparent, and the seeds of the second had already been sown, in Roger Hart's childhood at Barrow Point.

Words and expressions in Guugu Yimithirr, the language of Cooktown and the area north to the Starcke River, are written in **bold** when first introduced. Words in Barrow Point language are rendered in ***bold italics.*** A potentially confusing array of kinsmen and other characters will march across the pages that follow, and some genealogical notes about what Roger calls "relations" appear in the endnotes. In keeping with the customary practices of Aboriginal people, many references are made to places, territories, and clan estates—the traditional "runs" of different Aboriginal families and groups—and these, too, are sometimes amplified in notes. Contrary to customary etiquette, on the other hand, I have made more use of the names of people now deceased than Aboriginal propriety would ordinarily permit.

I moved away from Australia in 1985, and work finishing our book was postponed again and again. Our collaborator Tulo Gordon died in 1989, and in the following year Roger Hart began to invest his energies and his knowledge of tradition in efforts to regain his lands and those of his kinsmen under new Aboriginal land rights legislation in Queensland. Now, almost twenty years after we began, we finally bring Roger's story and Tulo's pictures to publication. It is perhaps ironic that we assembled the materials for this book in an era when the very idea of "land rights" for Queensland Aborigines was remote. Even though the book itself remained unfinished, some of the materials gathered for it were already serving as evidence in the highly charged arena of land claims in the 1990s. Let me apologize to Roger, my cous', for the fact that "writing down" his "language" has taken considerably more "free time" than any of us could have imagined when we first met on a rainy morning at the Hopevale store in 1979.

Part One

THE STORIES OF BARROW POINT

Hopevale and Hope Valley

The Hopevale Aboriginal community is the descendant of a Lutheran mission, called Hope Valley, established in 1886 in the aftermath of the Palmer River gold rush.[1] The original mission was located at Cape Bedford, north of Cooktown in far north Queensland. People now use the name Hopevale for the modern town, reopened inland from the original site in about 1950, when the residents of the old mission, who had been evacuated south during World War II, returned to their homeland. Hopevale people speak of the early Lutheran mission on the coast as Cape Bedford, sometimes referring to the main settlement on the southeastern tip of the cape by its original name Hope Valley. There were also important settlements on the north side of Cape Bedford at Elim as well as outstations farther north on the McIvor River.

The people living around the Endeavour River spoke a recognizable form of the Guugu Yimithirr language in 1770, when Lt. James Cook and members of his crew collected a few words from Aborigines they met in the area.[2] About one hundred years later gold was discovered inland on the Palmer River, and the port of Cooktown was opened at the mouth of the Endeavour to supply the diggings. The town served as the point of entry for thousands of gold miners, both European and Chinese, frantic to reach the Palmer.

The resulting devastation of Aboriginal life was total. Aborigines who lived by the rivers that were to be panned for gold or who occupied territory between the coast and the Palmer were rapidly dispossessed of their lands and often of their lives as well. Other Aborigines were driven from their homelands as European settlement extended outward from the gold routes. Surviving groups of Aborigines fled farther into the hinterlands or took up a parasitic existence on the fringes of newly sprouted towns.

Within ten years, by the mid 1880s, the scattered remnants of the original Aboriginal tribes from the Cooktown area were in a sorry state. Both church and civil authorities began to take steps to organize Aboriginal lives on lines more amenable to European hopes and plans. In 1886 Bavarian Lutheran missionaries, with support from local police and the Queensland government as well as from missionary societies in South Australia and in Germany, opened the mission at Cape Bedford. The original purpose was to educate and protect the remnants of the Aboriginal tribes who lived on barren coastal land north of Cooktown.

As early as 1881 the Cooktown police magistrate had been looking for ways to induce people from scattered Aboriginal camps around Cape Bedford to come into Cooktown, where they might be put to some use about the town.[3] (The "use" the Cooktown citizens had in mind turned out to center on unpaid domestic and bush labor and sexual abuse.) The early missionaries, on the other hand, intended to set up a permanent and ultimately self-sufficient station at Cape Bedford, where they could insulate their charges from what they saw as corrupting influence from heathen bush Aborigines and "civilized" Europeans alike.

By the turn of the century, when the missionaries at Cape Bedford had been working for some fifteen years, a new government bureaucracy was installed to oversee Aboriginal life throughout Queensland. Cooktown's gold boom had waned and the economy of the north had settled into an indifferent mixture of mining, cattle, sugarcane, and fishing. The remnant Aboriginal population had long since ceased to be seen as a menace. It was regarded instead as a nuisance and an offense to public morality and civilization. The government gradually enacted legislation to allow police, through the bureaucracy of the protectors of Aborigines, first to control the movements of Aborigines, to shift them from place to place, to deport them to distant parts of the state, and ultimately to incarcerate them and to break up families by institutionalizing children.

Because of a policy of isolating young newly Christianized Aboriginal women in the mission dormitories, and by serving as a ration depot for government Aboriginal relief, the Cape Bedford Mission became a seasonal focus for the visits of otherwise seminomadic groups of heathen Aborigines, many of whom were interested in securing proper marriage partners from among the mission inmates.[4] By the first years of the century, the Cape Bedford missionary, Rev. Schwarz, was reporting visits from groups of people to the northwest, including previously unknown bands from as far away as Barrow Point and Cape Melville.[5] Out of these early contacts there grew a complex interaction between government, mission, and tribe that would ultimately bring about the demise of the Barrow Point people.

In the second two decades of the 1900s, at an accelerating rate, children in nomadic Aboriginal camps were taken from their families and bundled off to reformatories and missions. At first these were "neglected" children (a euphemism for children of mixed descent), and later *any* children found by police in Aboriginal camps, who were by law to be placed in institutions for education and training. Because the Cape Bedford Mission depended on government funds, it was to some degree controlled by the official bureaucracy for administering Aboriginal lives. Thus, when children were removed from their families in the bush, the

Lutheran missionaries were obliged to accept some of the "waifs, orphans, and strays" into the previously isolated Hope Valley community. The ranks of Hope Valley's inmates swelled from a certain proportion of such children. Roger Hart, whose life and memories of a childhood at Barrow Point form the basis for this book, was one of them. His relatives brought him from Barrow Point in about 1923 and deposited him at the Cape Bedford Mission.

The influx of children from outside the mission continued through the 1920s and into the 1930s. During this time, Hope Valley suffered from pressing financial problems. The mission opened several outstations where families of adult Aborigines tried to subsist on their own farming efforts.

The first years of World War II were even more difficult times at Cape Bedford. Resources were scarce, and the needs of the mission community were growing. Relying heavily on a few favored Aboriginal families, the missionaries tried to establish a succession of new stations and farming operations on the limited terrain of the mission reserve. Roger Hart, who had by then married the daughter of one of the missionary's most trusted Aboriginal helpers, was part of the plan to create an autonomous and self-sufficient Aboriginal community in the Cooktown hinterlands.

The events of World War II drew closer to northern Queensland, however, and in 1942 the entire population of the Cape Bedford Mission and its outstations was evacuated without warning and transported south to an Aboriginal settlement at Woorabinda, inland from Rockhampton. The mission superintendent Rev. G. H. Schwarz, who had arrived in Queensland from Bavaria in 1887 and who had lived at Cape Bedford ever since, was interned in a camp for German aliens. He was thereafter not allowed to return to his Guugu Yimithirr congregation of, by then, more than half a century.

The experience of the next eight years in exile in the south was both traumatic and liberating for the people from Cape Bedford. Their numbers were dramatically and suddenly reduced by disease. (Roger Hart and his wife lost three children during the first months of their stay in the colder climate of the south.) Woorabinda left them disoriented and exposed, for the first time in their lives, to unmediated contact with the "outside world." People attended ordinary schools, held paid employment, traveled on "manpower" gangs to agricultural labor throughout southern Queensland, and made a wide range of new acquaintances, both black and white.

At the same time the Cape Bedford people, both at Woorabinda and on work gangs away from the settlement, remained a close-knit group.

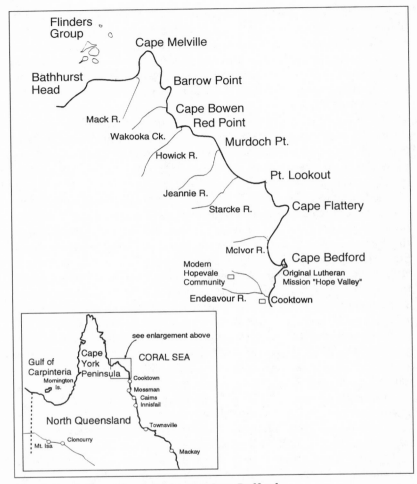

Map 1. North Queensland, Cooktown, Cape Bedford

A few influential elder people (including Roger Hart's father-in-law) struggled to hold the community together[6] and to keep alive the possibility of returning to their own country in the north. With help from Lutheran authorities, at the end of the 1940s they ultimately succeeded in reestablishing an Aboriginal reserve in their homeland. The new site—50 kilometers north of Cooktown and about 25 kilometers inland

6

from the original Hope Valley—was named Hopevale. Roger Hart was a member of one of the groups of workers who returned from Woorabinda in the early 1950s to clear the bush and build houses, gardens, streets, and a church, in preparation for the return of families to the new community.

Most of the oldest Hope Valley people had died in the south during the war, and many families had been, if not entirely destroyed, reduced to only one or two members. Exile thus left the community's social resources radically altered. Because of a serious shortage of marriageable women, groups of young men left Hopevale periodically during the fifties in search of wives. Many women from Palm Island, Bloomfield, Yarrabah, Weipa, and even Woorabinda returned with their new husbands to raise their families at Hopevale. The community was further augmented by scattered Aboriginal people from southeastern Cape York Peninsula who had Hopevale kin. Roger Hart came once again in contact with people from the Barrow Point tribe who had managed to survive the war.

Since the 1950s, Hopevale has been a fluid community. Some people have spent long periods in "the south"—that is, in Brisbane and other Queensland towns—as part of Lutheran efforts to relocate Aboriginal families from Hopevale in the wider context of Australian society. Children and young adults began to study and work away from the mission, and people from Hopevale now participate in statewide networks of Aboriginal social life, travel, and political activity. The early missionaries' carefully constructed isolation for their Hope Valley congregation was irrevocably dismantled at modern Hopevale.

The sense of identity, however, was not. When I first arrived at Hopevale in 1970, people had no hesitation in sending me to learn from the best speakers of Guugu Yimithirr and from those who had the clearest legitimate claim to both the language and the territory. The disparate origins as well as more recent history of many people who had been brought to Cape Bedford from other parts of Queensland meant that although virtually all the residents of Hopevale spoke Guugu Yimithirr as their first language, the great majority of them did not actually claim Guugu Yimithirr as their *own* "tribal" language. For this they deferred to the experts, whose genealogies derived from true Guugu Yimithirr–speaking families and their associated clan territories. The oldest members of such families were the expert teachers to whom, all agreed, I ought to apprentice myself. These teachers—predominantly old men— were determined to teach me not only how to speak acceptable Guugu Yimithirr, but also about kinsmen past and present, about clans, totems, places, tracts of land, plants both useful and dangerous, fish, fishing spears, and fishing spots, about how to keep directions straight,[7] and also how to behave with grandfathers, sisters, and mothers-in-law.[8]

In the 1970s and 1980s, Hopevale was in the throes of modernization. The community was beginning a transition from an externally administered Lutheran mission, dependent on church and government not only for finances but for direction and control, to the semi-autonomous Aboriginal settlement envisioned by the Queensland legislation of the era. It would still be another decade before changes in Queensland's Aboriginal land laws offered Aboriginal communities some measure of autonomy and inspired young people to revive "tradition" as a strategy for regaining control over Aboriginal lands. Instead, divisive local and family politics were the order of the day. Who controlled the community council and the government resources that funded it? Who occupied the scarce jobs at the store, office, and workshop at Hopevale? Who was entitled to employment at the lucrative silica mine at Cape Flattery, located squarely on mission territory but sending its royalties to Brisbane and its profits to Japan? Who was able to launch "private initiative" on the mission, to raise pigs, butcher cattle, operate a taxi, sell fish and chips, fishing line, or petrol? And if *your* family had some sort of power or resources, what about *mine*?

I had been trying to understand the evolution of the Guugu Yimithirr speech community, where matters of genealogy and social history were entangled with nearly every detail of social life, especially speech. My research[9] had concentrated on the era in mission history when the oldest people still alive had arrived, mostly as young children. However, events at modern Hopevale had drawn me into questions at opposite ends of the chronology of the community: on the one hand, fragmentary "traditions" of land and language that could be reconstructed from a time before Europeans invaded and, on the other, transformations of social life that followed the disintegration of the missionaries' planned utopian isolation, after World War II.

As the centenary of the founding of the Cape Bedford Mission approached, the social history of the mission community came more and more to permeate daily conversation. Celebrations planned for the anniversary of the arrival of Rev. Schwarz at Cape Bedford drew several of the oldest men, with me tagging along, back to the old mission site to clean up some of the ruined buildings, to label them for a commemorative visit, and to fossick[10] around for mementos of the early mission days. In the company of these community elders, on expeditions to sites throughout the mission reserve and beyond, history was always in the air, and talk traced ambivalent trails. Old-time superstitions were juxtaposed against up-to-date Lutheran dogma and then against "real" fears and dangers in the bush. Newly learned words turned out to be vulgar, impolite, or taboo; others were revealed to be sacred, deferential, and "deep." The respect and propriety of the past were both mourned (as expressions of now-lapsed tribal law and authority) and condemned (as oppressive, sexist, and venal). The missionaries were portrayed with Janus faces: enlightened saviors one moment, intolerant racists the next. Old stories told yesterday as vulgar tales of the old men were today potent moral lessons and tomorrow would be quoted as ancestral territorial charters.

Elderly people at Hopevale found the turmoil in the community distressing and confusing. They mourned the loss of order and authority once imposed by church and missionary. They lamented the fading of respect for kin and Aboriginal custom under the conditions of modern life: too much grog, too many motor cars, neighbors too close. Tradition demanded that one treat one's mother-in-law with respect, for example, but at modern Hopevale, with houses lined up cheek by jowl and many young people eating from their relatives' old age pension checks, one might actually be living in her house, sitting down face to face to eat at her table. Elderly people were scandalized. "These younger people can swear or curse their mothers-in-law, but we [old folks] just *can't!*"[11]

It was into this heady atmosphere of learning and teaching, memory and discovery, that Roger Hart stepped one day at the Hopevale store. It was a rainy morning in June 1979, a payday, and people were flocking to use their pension, welfare, and salary checks to buy flour, tea, sugar, meat, bread, tinned milk, prawn bait, fishline, and other staples of Hopevale life. Children clamored for ice blocks and bags of chips. Adolescent boys begged cigarettes off their better-heeled kinsmen. Cousins borrowed banknotes to fill their petrol tanks. Competing with this morning socializing, an unseasonable storm blew sheets of rain up under the shallow verandah. I had joined a few old men clustered in a corner where a large mango tree offered partial shelter.

A trim gentleman approached, with bare feet, khaki pants, a baseball cap, and a short-sleeved shirt whose pocket bulged with tobacco. He was reserved as he greeted me in Guugu Yimithirr.

"**Wantharra, thawuunh.** How you, mate?"

I had been working at Hopevale, by then, off and on for about nine years. During that time I had met most of the oldest people at the former mission, and it was known that I was trying to write down what they could teach me of words, kin, and custom from the area around

Cape Bedford and Cooktown. Roger Hart had been absent from Hopevale during most of the time I had been working there.

"You getting on, **thawuunh** [friend]? **Ngayu** [I am] Roger Hart. You ever heard about me?"

I did not recognize the face, but I had heard the name mentioned many times to refer to the genitor of one of the large and important families on the mission. I used to spend evenings playing country music with a couple of young married men in the community, and one of them, an eager guitarist named Alan Hart, had earlier that month spoken about his father, Roger. The old man, he told me, was living off the mission, working somewhere on the coast around Mossman, north of Cairns. He had his own language, and he knew a lot of stories.

Now here was Roger, shaking my hand, and rattling off the names of anthropologist acquaintances, much the way he might compare kinsmen with an Aboriginal person from elsewhere in Queensland.

"You know Peter Sutton? He learned a bit of my language."

It turned out that just as I had heard about him, Roger had also heard about me: the American who hung around the old people and who could speak some of the Hopevale language. He knew I had been writing down stories and asking people about the past. He already knew all about the old people who had been teaching me Guugu Yimithirr.

"That old fellow, your 'father,' I call him **mugay** [uncle].[12] And your friend here—you're making a book with him[13]—he's my **thuway** [nephew]."

Roger Hart explained why he had sought me out. He was not really from around Cooktown at all. He came instead from Barrow Point, to the north near Cape Melville. He had only recently returned to Hopevale after having lived for some years "on the outside," cutting sugarcane near Cairns, where he had gone to escape the protected but confining life of the Aboriginal mission. It was true, he announced, he did have his own language. Indeed, he was beginning to fear that perhaps he alone could still speak it, since all his other childhood friends were, he thought, dead. Roger's proposal to me was pointed and straightforward.

"You think you might have some time, when you free, to write down my language?"

This was an offer that no one interested in Australian languages could refuse.

As I quickly learned, Roger had much more to teach than his language. That morning there began a conversation that continues to this day, touching on topics that range from the structure of the Barrow

Point language to the history of the Barrow Point people, from the stories Roger heard as a child to the stories he himself could tell about growing up as an Aboriginal in Queensland. Roger's desire to have his language written down was bound up with a whole history to be recorded.

When I returned to Hopevale in May of the following year, I came armed with what materials could be found about the Barrow Point language. Among these was a copy of a cassette tape recorded in Mossman in 1970 by the linguist Peter Sutton in which Roger and his old mate Toby Gordon,[14] jointly and in several different languages, recounted parts of a traditional story from Barrow Point about the exploits of the trickster hero **Wurrey,** or "Fog." During three months that year, and sporadically over the next four years, Roger and I worked first through Sutton's wordlists of the Barrow Point language and then on a corpus of reconstructed linguistic forms growing out of our conversations.

Far from the political squabbling, in the shade of mango trees they had planted or under verandas they had built with their own hands, elderly Hopevale men routinely engaged me in anachronistic conversations. Sitting for hours immersed in old words and stories, from Hopevale's past and sometimes from distant country like Barrow Point, about which almost no one any longer seemed to care, we had been left behind by modern Hopevale.

A few younger people were occasionally attracted by the exotic words of Roger's Barrow Point language. Many Hopevale residents retained an ancient Aboriginal preoccupation with language as a marker of identity. Although teenagers might joke and flirt in English and rarely speak "language," all the same they knew that Guugu Yimithirr abounded with alternate names for the same objects. Some words were "seaside" (coastal), others "outside" (from inland dialects), others from different languages altogether. Although young people frequently claimed not to understand the words their grandparents used, they still recognized some words as "deeper" than others: words that sounded like they were for "kings or chiefs" or that showed more (or less) respect for one's interlocutors.[15] My tape recordings and halting conversations with Roger in his virtually incomprehensible northern tongue were thus curiously fascinating, if a bit irrelevant, alongside their cassettes of Australian country music, American soul, and Jamaican reggae.

To people like Roger our conversational combing of the past was more than mere nostalgia. It was part of the oldest residents' search for origins and order. Roger Hart shared his memories of childhood at Barrow Point with the Hopevale artist Tulo Gordon, a friend from his earliest days at the mission, painting in words an image of Aboriginal bush life as Tulo painted it in acrylics. Roger's re-creation of the past was also an exploration of who he was here and now. How had he, a Barrow Point man, come to live out his life in Tulo's country? Why had he, light-skinned and abandoned by his Aboriginal father, alone of his tribal playmates survived? Where did he belong? For sixty years Roger's Barrow Point childhood had been set aside. He had received a mission education and raised a family premised on his part-European ancestry in the mission hierarchy of caste and color. Now he was trying to reconcile his earliest memories with the texture of the bulk of his life, and Roger's preoccupations began to infect both Tulo Gordon and me.

Tulo Gordon, always a restless, inquisitive, and critically minded man, wanted to make sense of his life on the mission and to understand in retrospect the events of his childhood from the perspective of Aboriginal life throughout north Queensland. As an immediate practical matter, he was fighting for a pension and needed to establish his exact age for bureaucratic reasons; he was thus fascinated by remembered events and their dates. More globally, he wanted to resolve contradictions in his feelings about the missionaries, the church, race, traditional law, territory, ownership, and modernity. These were issues about which he thought, spoke, painted, and wrote with great insight and passion until his death in 1989.

In 1982, Roger Hart, Tulo Gordon, and I made the long walk back to Roger's birthplace at Barrow Point, a spot Roger had not laid eyes on for six decades. Roger and I trekked in again in September 1984, and we returned once more by vehicle in 1989. On our trips to his birthplace as in the course of daily life, questions of origins and biography were a background as tangible as the sand, the trees, and the weather. The more we walked in Roger's memories, the more his life as a member of a now vanished "mob" of people came to dominate our conversations. Gradually his and other older peoples' recollections, as well as archival research, allowed us to sketch an interconnected series of histories that I have tried to weave together in this book.

Let us begin where Roger and I began, with the first episodes of the story of old Fog, **Wurrey,** trickster hero of the Barrow Point people. Fog's adventures trace the boundaries of the known and owned world of Roger Hart's ancestors, and at the same time they illustrate, largely in the breach, how one was supposed to behave while within those boundaries. Roger, Tulo Gordon, and I rehearsed these episodes many times. They never ceased to entertain us, but as Tulo commented, they "make you think." Meant to be heard by initiated adults, these were not mere fairy tales about a time when animals were men. They were moral lessons about an Aboriginal world.

~~~~~~~~~~
Wurrey

This story is about **Wurrbal,** old man Fog. He is called Wurrey in Barrow Point language. The story begins at his home at **Yida-mugu,** Red Point.

One day he set out on a journey to the west.[1] He traveled until he came to the Jeannie River. There he met old lady Curlew. I call her **Yimbaarr.** She lived by herself just near the river.

Old Wurrey was carrying his fishnet with him, slung across his back. He knew that old lady Curlew had lots of fish, but she kept them all to herself. She raised many kinds in a big lagoon near her camp at the Jeannie River. (The lagoon is still there, too.) You could see their fins sticking up out of the water and their tails splashing about, sending ripples all across the surface. Old Fog had come up there to catch some of them.

As he approached Fog could see the fish down in the lagoon. He didn't say anything, though. First he hid his net in the grass so that Curlew wouldn't see it. Then he went up to the old lady.

"I am very thirsty," he told her. "Please give me some water. Perhaps I could get a drink from this lagoon over here to the east?"

"No, no, don't go over there," replied Yimbaarr. "You can have a look in my well, up there on the north side. Get a drink from there."

Fog went up to the north side of her camp where he found the well. It was a spring, what we call **athiirr thuyu.**

First he had a look back to the south where the old lady was sitting. She was paying him no attention. Then he stuck his hand down in the water and stirred it up, making the water so dirty you couldn't drink it. When the well was good and muddy he went back to old Curlew's camp.

He sang out, "**Gaw!** I can't drink that water, you know."

"Why not?"

"Because it's all muddy." He lied to her, you see.

The old lady got up and went to look in the well for herself. Sure enough, the water was full of mud.

Figure 2. Fog throws old lady Curlew down among her fish

"How did this water get so dirty?" she asked.

"I don't know, what do you suppose?" he replied.

"Oh, well, come with me then." She led him down to the south side of her camp, to the big lagoon.

"Don't make a sound," she said. "Just go down slowly and quietly, and then you can drink *that* water." She was afraid Fog might frighten the fish and make them jump about. She thought he didn't know they were there.

Then the old lady went back to her camp and sat down again, paying him no more mind.

When she was gone, Fog walked down to the lagoon. He didn't bother to have a drink, you see, since he wasn't really thirsty. He only pretended to drink. Then he went back and said to old lady Curlew, "I think I'm going away now. I'll see you next time." He kept on telling lies.

Fog went back toward the east and picked up his net from its hiding place. Then he sneaked back to the lagoon. He looked around again to make sure that the old lady wasn't watching.

He took his net and started throwing it into the lagoon, pulling up heaps of fish. They were great big fish, and they splashed about in the water.

The old lady heard the noise. She jumped up and ran to the lagoon to find out what was wrong. What could be causing the splashing?

When old lady Curlew saw Fog throwing his net and stealing her fish, she began to curse and swear at him. She called him all kinds of awful names.

It made Wurrbal angry. He left his net and ran over to the west. The old lady was standing there swearing at him. He picked her right up off the ground. He carried her back to where the fish were thrashing around in the net, and he heaved her right into the middle of them.

"**Ngaanhigay!**" she shrieked, "Ow, ow ow!" She howled with pain.

The fins on the fish had jabbed her in both knees. Well, those Curlew birds today have big lumpy knee joints. That's how it happened. Old lady Curlew's knees swelled up after being jabbed by the fish spines. Curlews carry that mark right until today. They still have swollen knees.

She kept on howling: "Ngaanhigaaay!"

Even now you sometimes hear Curlew sing her sad cry at nighttime. She's weeping because of the pain in her swollen knees.

That's where old Fog's story starts, at the big lagoon by the Jeannie River.

Old Fog left Curlew where he had dropped her. He was in a hurry to take his fish away. He started pulling the net, dragging it down the river. The Jeannie River never used to dry up. It used to have water all the time, although it wasn't very deep even in those days.

Well, now there were two **Duburrubun** brothers, two magpies. They used to camp with old lady Curlew. The old lady looked after them. When old Fog came around, the two brothers had gone out hunting to bring the old lady some meat.

While old Fog was dragging the fish down the river, the two Magpies came back to the old lady's camp. They heard her singing out, crying and wailing.

"What's wrong?" they asked.

"Oooh, that rotten old Fog threw me down among the fish," she said, "and their spines jabbed me in the knees."

"Where is he now?"

"He's gone down that way. He's taking my **minha** down the river."

15

The Magpie brothers jumped up and started after old Fog. The older brother ran down the west bank of the river, and the younger brother ran down the east bank. After a good way, they stopped, hoping to catch old Fog. But Fog was dragging his net downriver, and it caused a great flood where he passed. He was still going.

The brothers rushed farther downriver. They pulled up again to have another look. Wurrbal had already gone on, turning north now.

Off they went again. But every time they stopped to look at the water, it was still. The big flood had already passed. Old Fog was still ahead of them, pulling the fish along in his net.

Finally the two Magpies came right to the mouth of the river. They looked around. Where was he? They looked north, and they saw that Fog had tied his net to a rock just north of the river mouth. He had released all those fish into the sea. That's how some of the freshwater fish species from Curlew's lagoon got out into the sea in the first place.

Old Wurrbal had disappeared, heading inland. He was off, on his way.

"Oh, well, there's nothing we can do." The two Magpie brothers couldn't catch up to him before he got to the sea.

They didn't give up, though. They just headed inland, following his tracks, and you may as well know that they met Wurrey again by and by.

That was Fog's first adventure. That was when he started telling lies.

Fog Visits Guraaban

After he released the fish, Wurrey headed west, back inland. He traveled a little bit west and a little bit north. After a while he came close to a mountain called **Guraaban,** Brown's Peak. There was a big mob of people living in a camp there.

Old Fog marched up from the south and right into camp.

"Here I am! I've come," he said. Then he added, "I have a terribly hungry belly after walking all this way."

The people in the camp were glad to see him. They thought he might have brought some news.

"**Ma,** you sit down." They showed him where to rest. "Go over there in the shade."

Once Fog was seated comfortably, straight away they started asking

Figure 3. Wurrey eats honey at Brown's Peak

him for news. "What's happening in the east," they asked. "How is everyone out that way? Are all the people well? How's my uncle? How's my grampa?"

Well, Fog had to give them an answer. He started to invent some news.

"Ah, everyone over there is well. They're all right," he began. "Only this one's Granny died," he went on, pointing at one of them. "Your grandmother died over there to the east."

He started telling lies now.

"Yes, she died, only yesterday it was."

People started wailing and crying now.

Wurrey was just getting started. "Yes," he said, "and this fellow's father died, too."

He spoke to him: "Your father died yesterday, I am sorry to tell you. He was speared to death."

So all that lot started crying, too. They smeared themselves all over with white clay to mourn for their dead relatives.

"You should head east, mourn them there," said old Fog. "But don't start crying yet. I'm really very hungry now."

He sat down in the shade again.

"Get me something to eat."

The people in the camp had to forget about their dead relatives for a while. They went to find some food to give Fog. They had robbed some wild honey, *u:lgal,* from a native bees' nest. They mixed that in water.

"Here, drink this!" They handed the *u:lgal* to old Fog.

Well, Fog was a sly trickster. While they were mixing the honey for him, he was digging a hole in the ground. He dug and dug, but secretly, you know, so nobody would notice him. When the hole was deep enough, he moved over until he was sitting right on top of it.

They brought the honey to where he was sitting, and he started to drink. But this was his trick, you see: the honey went in his mouth and ran right through him into the hole.

The people kept on mixing more and more of their honey. "Here, drink this! Is your belly feeling better now? Are you full yet?"

"Not yet, **guya.** Bring me a bit more, eh?"

They kept mixing honey and taking it over to him where he sat on the east side of the camp. He still wasn't satisfied, so they had to make more and more.

"What kind of stomach does this fellow have, anyway?" they asked each other. "Uncle Fog has been eating and eating. He should be satisfied by now, but he keeps clamoring for more honey."

The people from the camp began to feel suspicious. They went up to old Fog, sitting in the shade, and they pushed him over.

"Hey, **dagu,**[1] this old man has been sitting with his rump over a deep hole. The honey is running right through him into the hole!"

They sent some kids off to fetch some **bayjin** grass. They plugged old Fog's bottom with a wad of the spongy stuff so the honey wouldn't run out anymore.

"But I'm still hungry," said Fog.

They mixed up the last of their honey and gave it to him. He drank it down, and this time his belly swelled up full.

"Ah, now I feel satisfied. I've eaten enough. I guess I'll be going," said old Fog, standing up.

When the people in the camp saw he had finished eating, they remembered their dead relatives. Again they started to wail and to smear themselves with white clay. They started to plan a trip to bury their kinsmen.

"We'll go east tomorrow to take care of the dead ones," said some.

"Let's start now," said others.

Old Fog didn't pay them any more attention. He just got up, with a belly full of honey, and set out again toward the west.

~~~~~~~~~~~~~~~~~~~~~~

The Giant Dingo Dog

Fog left Guraaban and kept going west. When he got halfway to where he was heading, he pulled up to camp for the night.

Now, you remember the two Magpie brothers. They had started to follow old Fog when he was still in the east, before he let all those fish go. From the mouth of the Jeannie River they had followed his tracks west. But they always stayed a little to the south of him, never getting too close.

The Magpie brothers were now camped at a place just north of Jones's Gap, a break in a high range of mountains. They were staying at the camp of old lady Carpet Snake. Since they were just young fellows, they camped with her, but not too close. That old lady had a big dog, you see, a very big dingo dog.

The two brothers had been planning to ambush old Fog, but in the meantime they had gotten very hungry. They set out hunting. By and by they began to smell something good to eat. They began to look around to see what it was. The smell was coming from the north. They searched and searched, and pretty soon they found a Leichhardt tree.

"Ahh," they said, "it's the fruit that the old lady eats."

They began to eat what they found lying on the ground. They ate and ate and ate. When they had finished all the fallen fruit, they still weren't satisfied. So they climbed the tree and began to eat the ripe fruit, just quietly. They ate and ate and ate, until late in the afternoon.

Old lady Carpet Snake came back then, from the west. The two Magpie brothers could hear her as she moved along, talking to herself.

"I'll just go and get that **mayi**.[1] I'll go and eat my fruit," she was saying as she came closer and closer.

The two Magpies didn't say anything. They just sat silent in the tree.

The old lady came up to her Leichhardt tree. She started hunting all around, looking for her fruit. She searched everywhere.

"Where's that **mayi?**" she said. "Maybe it hasn't fallen down yet."

Figure 4. The Magpie brothers throw Leichhardt fruit down onto the Carpet Snake

She kept looking and looking. Nothing.

The younger Magpie brother picked a piece of raw fruit from the tree, and he chucked it down at her. It hit her on the back, as she was bent over searching for fruit on the ground.

"Ngaanhigay!" She cried out in pain. "Something hit me on the back! The fruit is just now falling off the tree!"

So she picked up that fruit and gulped it down.

The younger Magpie brother broke off more fruit and threw it down. It was the younger one's idea, see? He kept throwing unripe fruit down. The old lady would pick it up and eat it.

Then she said, "Where is that **mayi** falling from?" She looked up. At that very moment, he threw another piece of fruit, and it hit her right on the nose.

"Ngaanhigay! Now it hit me on the nose!"

In fact, the fruit hit her so hard that it flattened her nose right out. If you see a carpet snake nowadays you'll see that she has a flat head. Well, it's for that reason.

Anyway, she recognized the two Magpie brothers up in the tree. She sang out to them, "So, it's you two larrikins![2] Come on down from there! Oh, my poor nose!"

The two Magpie brothers climbed down from the tree.

Then the old woman made them a promise. She said, "Tomorrow I'm going to send you my puppy. It's a really nice little dog." But she was tricking them. "I'll bring you my little dog, and you can train it for hunting."

"All right, bring it to us," they said.

She let them go, and they headed south again.

They started to talk it over. The younger brother asked his older brother, "Is that old woman telling the truth? She says she's going to give us a nice puppy dog."

The older brother answered: "Puppy dog? Why, that's a huge dog. We'd better run away from here. Otherwise, the dog will eat the both of us right up! Let's go!"

So the two of them ran off. They ran and ran, **di di di di**,[3] toward the south.

Meanwhile, old lady Carpet Snake went back west to her camp. She fetched her giant dog and sent it after them. The dog headed down from the north, barking and whining, on their trail.

The Magpies could hear the dog coming, so they kept running farther south, farther south. Well, nowadays Jones's Gap is fairly wide, but in those days it was just a narrow passage through the mountains. That was many thousands of years ago. The two brothers split up. One climbed up the south side, and the other climbed up the north side. They had decided to try to save themselves by spearing that giant dingo.

Meanwhile the huge dog came along below. His tongue was just coming into view.

The younger brother spoke up. "I'm going to spear him now." The younger brother was left-handed, you see.

His older brother told him, "No. You might miss. Better leave him to me."

Meanwhile the big dingo came closer still. His head sprang into view, as he moved along to the west. The older brother picked up his spear and threw it from the north down toward the south. At the same time the younger brother threw his spear from the south. The two of them kept throwing their spears from opposite directions.

There used to be a big flat plain down below, to the east. It was on that big flat area that the two brothers finally killed that giant dingo dog. It thrashed around and knocked down all the trees.

Once they had killed the dingo, the brothers began to cut the animal up. They cut and cut and cut. All right. When they had finished, they lifted up the meat and carried it west. They carried it a long way, until they came down to the Wakooka Creek.

Somewhere above the river people reckon that even today there is a big hollow place. That's where they dug out a hole for an earth oven. They built a big fire in the hole and covered it with rocks. The two brothers singed off the giant dingo's fur. They stuck the pieces of meat into the oven.

Then they waited. First they had a bath. They found some good shade and lay down to sleep, while the meat cooked. The sun started to go down. They slept and slept and slept.

Finally they got up.

"Okay, let's take the meat out."

They opened the earth oven. They took out all the meat, letting the hot steam escape. Then they set the pieces down one by one in the open air to cool.

At the very moment they were picking the minha out of the earth oven, old Fog appeared from the south. The two of them saw him coming. "Oh, so he's here. He has come up here," they said.

They greeted him. "Our grandfather, you've appeared," they said. "*Adhi-dhu imbwirrin*. Our grandfather has come."

"Yes, I have come. It is me." He was very hungry again.

The Magpie brothers said, "Well, come over here. Come see this meat."

Fog came over and sat down.

"Grandfather, what sort of meat do you want? Do you want the leg?"

"Uh-uh."

"What sort of meat, then? Do you want the arm?"

"Uh-uh."

"Well, then, what meat will you take? The back?"

"Uh-uh."

Then the older brother said to the other, "I think he's asking for the head part."[4] The other brother asked Fog, "What sort of meat do you want, then? Do you want the head?"

"Yeah, give me that."

So they had to give him the head. Then they picked up all the rest of the meat and started back down to their camp.

Old man Fog took the head of that giant dingo, and he set out straight east, up and up, until he got right to the top of Jones's Gap. There he set the meat down and began to work a spell. He decided to give eyes to that animal. (See Pl. 1.)

You see, in those early days, all the animals were blind. Emu, wallaby, kangaroo, and all the rest couldn't see. When people went out hunting,

22

they had only to walk up and hit their prey with a stick. The poor things were blind, and they wouldn't run away.

Fog took the dingo's head and cleaned it off. He spoke to it: "These are your eyes. **Ssuuuuu!** Use these eyes to watch out for people. And this is your nose. **Ssuuuuu!** If **bama**[5] are coming up on the windward side of you, use your nose to smell their sweat, and run away."

You see, he changed everything. He didn't bother to eat the meat. He gave eyes and a nose to the dingo's head. He dug and dug and dug, until he had a deep hole. He took the head, and he put it in the hole and covered it up. He put big stones all over the top of it. People who go to that place now can still see the stones. He transformed all the animals by burying the head there.

After Fog had covered up the giant dingo's head, he set out again. He disappeared.

The Stories: Owners and Morals

Roger Hart and Tulo Gordon were laughing about the Wurrey story. The three of us sat on the verandah of the old hospital at Hopevale, preparing to record several episodes of the stories on film. Down in town, we could hear the whistle that signaled afternoon tea.

As was our custom, we spoke that day in a mixture of Guugu Yimithirr and English, peppered with occasional expressions from Roger's Barrow Point tongue. Tulo Gordon had been one of my Guugu Yimithirr teachers, and he still took pains to help me improve my skills in the language. Roger Hart had taken me on as nearly his only interlocutor in Barrow Point, and it seemed to tickle his fancy to be able to share its virtually secret words with someone else.

One thing I learned from Roger Hart is that one can construct history or reminisce without ever mentioning the past, but simply by talking with certain words. Barrow Point language was, for us, inherently linked with former times, endowed with a strong evocative power in the discourse of remembering. The mere sound of a Barrow Point word could redefine an interaction and redirect a conversation.

Roger Hart had arrived at Hope Valley as a native speaker of the Barrow Point language, with a working knowledge of other "northern" di-

Figure 5. Fog enters his cave at Bathhurst Head

alects, especially the Flinders Island language spoken around Cape Melville. He knew neither English nor Guugu Yimithirr, the language of Cooktown. The one Cape Melville boy already living at Cape Bedford had largely lost his own language, so Roger had to learn to communicate all over again. In school at Hope Valley he learned a slightly old-fashioned schoolbook English and became fluent in Guugu Yimithirr, still today his most comfortable modes of expression.

It was clear that, as he put it, Roger had in many ways "forgotten about" his own language. Once he had entered the mission school, when his Barrow Point relatives visited Cape Bedford, he was afraid to approach them. For the little mission boy, educated into a select group of part-European Lutherans at Hope Valley, these heathen Aborigines had now become visions of danger and the un-Christian life.

When Roger was a young adult, one of his uncles, a man he remembered from Barrow Point, came to Cape Bedford as a boatman and taught fragments of the Barrow Point language to the young men of the boat crews. Roger made a conscious effort to reacquire his native tongue and with it bits of Barrow Point history and tradition. He also began to reconstruct life histories for his Barrow Point kinsmen, now mostly dead or scattered across the Aboriginal landscape. After the war, the exile in the south, and his return to the reconstructed mission community, in the late 1960s and early 1970s Roger Hart lived away from Hopevale mission, sharing a house with his childhood playmate Toby Gordon, by then elderly and in poor health but still fluent in the Barrow Point language. This friend had lived all his life "on the outside," on stations, in Aboriginal camps and settlements. Never having experienced the institutionalization that was Roger's lot as a result of the color of his skin, Toby Gordon was able to spark Roger's dormant memories of a Barrow Point childhood.

The more we probed Roger's knowledge of the Barrow Point language, the more his linguistic intuitions proved to be intertwined with a vast collection of memories and stories. Dredging words out of the past became an obsession. Often we would be stumped by a Barrow Point equivalent for some familiar Guugu Yimithirr noun or verb. At the crack of dawn the next morning, Roger would be knocking on my door.

"*Anggatha*," he would exclaim in triumph, "it came to me in a dream!"

The lexical problems were compounded by the environment itself. Around Hopevale, even the plants and animals seemed to speak their names naturally in Guugu Yimithirr, the language of the place. But what was the name of that particular fruit or tree that Roger could picture from his childhood at Barrow Point but was nowhere to be found here in the south? After we began to work on his language in the late 1970s, Roger's linguistic reconstruction gradually gave way to a full-scale autobiographical excursion. Looking for the name of a tree or fish brought back memories of the places where one had seen such trees or caught such fish. "Remembering the past" and "telling about the past" collapsed into a single activity. Recalling a fragment of a story or the name of a kinsman set off chains of recollections: a man who had acted like old Fog, a woman bitten by a snake at a particular spot, or a forgotten relative whose name flashed to mind at the mention of a long ago event. The past began to pervade the present.

As our conversations stretched over several years, Roger, Tulo, and I began to share a repertoire of Roger's stories. His vanished kinsmen became our companions, and their doings became our gossip. Tales were told, retold, refashioned, and reinterpreted, often altering but never completely abandoning the original voices—usually a polyphonic, multilingual chorus—of our first hearings.

"Everything in that story," Tulo observed that afternoon at Hopevale, "really fits together properly, when you come to look back at it. Old Fog was truly a troublemaker."

"**Wuurbal,** old Wurrey, now," mused Roger. "He's my totem, *anggatha athu.*" Roger claimed kinship not only with the trickster himself but also with the places Fog traveled and with the people who owned his stories. "That story about the giant dingo dog belongs to us," he went on.

The Barrow Point people were once divided into two large groups, one living on the coast at Barrow Point itself, the other clustered inland around mountain ranges to the south. It was in those mountains, at Jones' Gap, that Fog buried the head of the giant dingo dog. The Fog story not only belonged to both of the Barrow Point "mobs," but, indeed, it united the whole region that Fog's adventures traversed, from the Jeannie River to Bathhurst Head. Roger commented, "We all belong together. We all one for that Devil Dingo story."[1]

The socially embracing affiliation between story, place, and tribe has as well its darker, modern side: the loss of knowledge. Roger continued, "I got no relations left from Barrow Point. The younger ones wouldn't know the story anymore. Even my own sons—I used to tell them every night, but I think they've got it all mixed up."

Roger remembers that he once quarreled with his elder son, who had wanted to add an element to the Jeannie River episode. "You see, he wanted to find fault with the story. He wanted me to put into it that the **murrabal** 'baramundi' comes in two species: one belongs to salt water and the other belongs to fresh water.

"I told him it wasn't *my* story. I said, 'Look, the old people didn't tell me the story that way. I don't want to make up my *own* stories; they belong to the old people. What I heard, I'll put it down that way, too.'"

The Barrow Point word *yimpal* 'story' (or *uwu yimpal,* literally, 'word story') like its Guugu Yimithirr gloss **milbi,** denotes a range of storytelling activities, encompassing everything from "tales" or "myths" to simply "news," "gossip," or just "talk." People at Hopevale accustomed to a whole collection of different kinds of stories in English—"anecdotes," "histories," "Bible stories," "fairy tales," and "yarns," among others—do not apply such terminological distinctions to **milbi** or *yimpal.* Roger Hart instead keeps separate "stories" about times past when things happened to distant but traceable kinsmen, from "stories" from a much earlier era when animals walked, hunted, talked, and ate like human beings, and when the present conditions of life were established. One knows what is **manu buthun** 'true' about the first kind of story from the testimony of people who saw and later recounted the events in question; the events have passed from one witness's mouth to another. By contrast, one knows about stories of the second kind not because of someone's direct testimony, but because someone with the right and knowledge to tell the story—a grandfather, an uncle, or perhaps an elder at one's initiation—has confided the details. You know the story because you have been authoritatively and appropriately informed.

There is also an important similarity between the two kinds of story. The moral rules that concern life for Aboriginal people underlie all *yimpal,* just as they underlie one's understanding of events in the present or in the recent past, before "bama way" began to fade from view, as many people of Roger Hart's generation lament. Even more, all of these "stories"—like language, land, or knowledge in general—are owned. They belong to people and places. A story can be mine not (merely) because I was there to see it happen, or because I heard it first, but rather because it happened to someone (or in some place) that belongs to me—my kinsman, my country—or because it is a story my kinsmen told me. That gives me, too, a special right to laugh over the funny parts, to shake my head at the denouement, and, indeed, to tell the story myself. It concerns me. Little wonder that Roger Hart should claim old Fog as his kinsman, his "friend" or mentor.

Fog himself is not, of course, a particularly admirable character. In the first few episodes of his story, he moves from his home at Red Point to the Jeannie River—once a fairly important boundary between the Gugu Yimithirr speakers to the south and the speakers of a group of distinct but interrelated languages to the north—and then starts back through the territories of these northern tribes, marking out notable spots along the way through adventures in which he tricks people. We have already seen him lie, steal, cheat, and work mischievous magic. Things will only get worse.

Fog is a classic trickster hero: he stands for certain precepts of Aboriginal life, sometimes by virtue of his own contradictions. True, he steals old lady Curlew's fish, but then she was hoarding them in the first place. True, he throws her down onto the fish spines, but then again it was indecorous and unwise of her to curse him. He does lie to the people of Guraaban about their dead relatives, but oughtn't they to go visit them anyway? There is also the complicated and ambivalent issue of food: on the one hand, it takes serious effort to find what one needs to eat, and the common resources of the bush must be conserved; on the other, what one has one must share. Fog insists on his right to share other folk's food, but he also takes steps to protect easy prey from human-kind's voracious hunting appetite.

"Those stories were supposed to remind us of something. They were for teaching people, for 'admonishing' them." Roger uses the Guugu Yimithirr expression that means, literally, "poke the ears." "The stories set an example for people to follow. You see how old Fog behaved. The stories taught bama not to do the things he was doing. Our people used to have a very strict law—not like now, when people no longer follow the good way of living."

Roger recounts an almost dreamlike memory of the last time he saw his Aboriginal father. The little boy had been left at Cape Bedford to be brought up by white missionaries. Although Roger had at first tried to run away, he was by now used to mission life. Some months, or perhaps even a year after they had left him at Cape Bedford—Roger's memory is uncertain—a few Barrow Point men visited the mission to pick up supplies, blankets, and tobacco before returning to their own country in the north. Among them was Roger's father. He took the little boy aside, Roger remembers, and used the bad example of old man Fog to exhort Roger to behave properly.

"'Don't be like Fog,' he said, 'don't chase around after women, or play with girls. Keep well away.'"

"'Don't be cheeky,' he went on. 'And don't cause bad feelings or anger among other people.' He told me to follow the law, not to do silly things. He told me everything about how to behave. He said, 'I'll come back.' Then he left, and I never saw his face again."

Roger likens other morals from Fog's story to biblical commandments. "It reminds us not to steal **mayi** that belongs to someone else." Roger laughed. "What you'll get, if you do, is a spear for your troubles."

"All those stories have the meaning on them, down there deep. They help us keep in mind the old ways, even in the face of what is going to happen in later years, in our own times."

As we recorded the stories and talked about writing them down, we faced a new problem. For whom were these stories intended? Roger Hart expressed reservations. Although Tulo Gordon's Guugu Yimithirr tales, published some years before, had been presented as stories for children, the adventures of Wurrey have a very different character. The lessons implicit in Roger's stories were the serious stuff of Aboriginal law, in-stilled in young men at initiation. More problematic still was the frag-mentary nature of the stories as Roger was able to recollect them: surely there were parts missing, or misremembered, perhaps told "back to front." Roger could be no more certain about some episodes than he could be about some of the Barrow Point words scattered anarchically through his memory.

Despite his father's final visit, Roger thinks the stories were inappropriate for children. They were not openly and publicly told, but instead could only properly be passed on between people of certain relationships. Roger himself remembers hearing a full version of Fog's story only as an adult. Old Yagay was an elderly Barrow Point man who had survived World War II and was still living around Cooktown when the Cape Bedford people returned to the north after their exile at Woorabinda. The older man came to stay with Roger for a few weeks, and Roger asked him about the story.

"Later I asked old lady Mary Ann[2] about it, and she told me, poor old thing. She was my **gami,** my same side grandmother.[3] It is quite all right for my **gami** to tell me that story. Only what we call **bama binthu**[4]— someone who is not sacred for you— can tell it. That old lady could tell me anything, you know, use bad words, curse, make jokes."

Instead of speaking openly about Wurrey's adventures, the old people would make infrequent allusions to the story. When the weather was fine, near the mouth of the Mack River, the old men might point at a prominent rock on the top of Bathhurst Head. "'*Wurrey ayila uwer,* look at Fog there to the west, *thurrgu agelu,* standing up straight facing east,' they would cry. 'Fog has appeared over there, looking for fish. There he stands fishing.'"

"That's the only time they would mention the story. That part of it they used to tell. Might as well say they worshipped old Fog."

Another important story tells of a terrible punishment meted out to evildoers in the great camp at Pinnacle.

"That story, you know, was very sacred. They wouldn't tell it to *any*body.

"I never heard it when I was living up in Barrow Point myself. They would never tell it to youngsters. When Yagay came to stay with me, that's another story he told me.

"'Come here. You listen,' he said. 'They didn't tell you children about this. But now you're all right.' You know, I was a full-grown man then. 'Well, I'm going to tell you a story,' he said. And that's when he told me how the earth opened up and swallowed all the people."

Swallowed by the Earth

This is not a fairy tale.[1] This is a fair dinkum story. Who knows how long ago it happened. Perhaps it was back in the 1800s. It is not an ancient story but more recent. One old lady was the only person to survive the events, and she was Toby Gordon's **babi,** his grandmother. She was only a small girl at the time. (See Pl. 2.)

Toby's grandmother saw everything. If the earth had swallowed her up, too, then there would have been nobody left to tell this story. Through her it was handed down to us.

There used to be a big lot of **Gambiilmugu-warra**[2] people living there to the south. On my side toward the coast were the "older brothers." Those from the inland half of the tribe near the area they call Pinnacle were the "younger brothers." They might have had a boundary to divide the two groups. It would have been somewhere west of Wakooka Station. Although our side was to the north and theirs to the south, it was really all the same **Gambiilmugu.** All of us from Barrow Point, and all the **Wuuri**[3] people, too, share the same Devil Dingo story. We all spoke one language, too.[4]

They were a terribly hard-headed, stubborn lot of people. They wouldn't listen to anybody or take advice or orders, that Pinnacle mob. They were fierce as well as terrific hunters. No game could ever get away from them.

It wasn't only minha they hunted, either. They used to go out at night and sneak around other people's camps. The houses they used to have in the old days were just humpies, really. The Pinnacle people were on the lookout for girls—not little girls, but young women whose breasts were starting to grow. That's the kind they wanted to steal. They would take them back to their camp in the south.

Sometimes they would come as far as the Jeannie River. They would steal the women and take them back to their own area. Or else they might go farther west and north, stealing girls from Bathhurst Head, or from the other side of Princess Charlotte Bay. They got a big lot of women from up that way and brought them home again.

After a while it got to be a huge camp of people. Many young men were living there, and it was just as well. Those girls would begin to get hungry, so the men would have to go out hunting to feed them all.

They got enough girls there to keep them going. Then they said, "Eh? Let's go north. Let's go and visit our 'older brothers' and bring a few young men back from there." So they set out north, toward the coast.

Now you know those men from the north side of Barrow Point, the coastal side, were a bit older, more mature. They were mighty tough talkers, too. When the younger men came up from the south, their "older brothers" on the coast were taking care of a group of youths who had been sent there for initiation. The "younger brothers" wanted to see how the initiated boys were coming along.

When the Pinnacle men got to the coast on the north, they said to the elders, "Give us the youths. We're going to take them back to the south. They have become men, now."

You see, they had an oversupply of girls down in the south by this time.

The people there in the north, the "older brothers," hardened their hearts. At first, they remained silent and wouldn't answer their "younger brothers."

"No," they said at last. "We aren't going to send the boys south. We have made our youths **thabul**, 'sacred'. They have been through **nganyja** 'initiation'. If you people want to disobey the law, go ahead. You may get speared, but go on and be disobedient if you want."

"Give us the youths."

"No. We don't agree with you people. We've heard about your plans, but we can't go along with them."

"Come on, let the boys come south with us. They'll get wives."

But they weren't going to get wives, you know. They were just going to copulate with those girls one after the other.

The "younger brothers" began to look closely at the boys' heads. When they saw one or two grey hairs, they would say, "All right, you'll do." They looked through the whole lot, picking only the biggest boys. Finally they had about a dozen or so.

They insisted on taking those youths back south.

They went around to the place where all the girls were staying. Each boy picked out the girl he wanted and took her.

All those boys from the coast brought their new wives back north. But the rest of the people stayed down around Pinnacle. They used to go out hunting every day, looking around for game.

One day something happened. Early in the morning the young men left the camp to hunt. The other people stayed behind, a good few. The sun rose higher. It might have been about 10 o'clock in the morning. Suddenly the earth simply opened up. It swallowed the whole lot of them. They fell right into the earth.

There was just that one old lady who survived. She wasn't swallowed up. Only her leg was caught in the earth. Her foot was covered by the great hole, and her leg was broken. She was trapped there.

By and by someone returned to the camp from hunting. He found the old lady with her leg stuck in the earth.

"Why, where are all the people?" he asked.

"All the people went down into the earth. They're inside. A great **yiirmbal**[5] swallowed them up."

They managed to lift the old lady out of the hole she was trapped in. They took her north then to Barrow Point.

After a while her broken leg healed. That's when Toby's grandfather married her. She had a good few grandchildren, too. I saw that old woman when I was a boy. I used to call her **gami,** too, 'grandmother'. She was lame from her broken leg. Oh, she was a terribly old lady, too. I think she was from the tribal area of Wuuri. Down there in Pinnacle, they had women from all over, from the Jeannie River right west as far as Princess Charlotte Bay.

Me, I've never seen that country. I've only seen the mountain from afar. I think you go through a place they call Cockatoo Yard, and from there west, to the corner of the mountain, and from there south. Some people still know the place, though, because Banjo used to take them around there.[6] He told them, "Don't go over there! You might go down!"

The **yiirmbal** swallowed all the people for being lawless and disobedient. It punished them before they did any greater damage, before they destroyed Aboriginal people. You see, that Pinnacle mob had great power, and all the tribes along the coast were afraid of them. "Don't get mixed up with those **Yiithuu**[7] people!" they would say.

Part Two

BARROW POINT

Barrow Point at the Turn of the Century

THE INVASION OF THE COOKTOWN HINTERLANDS

By 1900, the gold that had brought European invaders into far North Queensland twenty-five years earlier was largely played out.[1] In place of the miners, pastoralists had installed themselves in the richest country and at sources of fresh water, casually (and often illegally) incorporating into their workforces the remnants of Aboriginal populations whose lands they had appropriated. Fishermen began to visit the coasts, in search of inexpensive Aboriginal labor and other diversions. Disruption of precontact patterns of subsistence, introduced disease, routinized murder, contact with at least the fringes of the European economy coupled with a growing dependence on its commodities, and a general dislocation that made ordinary patterns of social life impossible for Aborigines soon reduced their numbers and distributed them in new ways across the landscape.

At the turn of the century there seem to have been two identifiable Aboriginal populations in the area centering on Barrow Point and Cape Melville. Archival accounts of the people from around Barrow Point are scanty, but they allow a patchy set of inferences about life in the area after European invasion.[2] Walter Roth, the first northern protector of Aborigines, made several visits to Barrow Point in the late 1890s, taking anthropomorphic measurements of two men whose names he gave as Oonquilba and Onawin.[3] Roth counted twenty men and ten women at Barrow Point in December 1898, though he commented that the normal population was certainly higher, "the main mob having left for C. Melville."[4]

Local tradition suggests that people came to concentrate in just a few camps, including one at Ninian Bay, as a result of police "dispersion" of coastal groups following the Lizard Island affair in 1881. A European woman, Mary Watson, put to sea and died stranded on a coral island after Aborigines—probably Guugu Yimithirr speakers from around Cape Flattery—stormed her house and speared her Chinese cook.[5] The events scandalized the European population of the north and prompted punitive police attacks on coastal Aborigines south of Barrow Point.

In the early years of the European invasion of the north the government had several devices for the "pacification" of its Aboriginal inhabitants. Through the institution of the protectors of Aborigines—usually, at the local level, police officers or magistrates—the government tried to enforce a series of laws regulating the legal employment of Aboriginal labor. By nominating certain designated Aboriginal elders "kings" of their respective "tribes" (themselves in part bureaucratic inventions), the protectors in turn sought to install their own proxy agents in positions of authority in what was perceived to be a diffuse native sociopolitical structure. Most important, the government made extensive use of "native troopers," men recruited from already "pacified" Aboriginal groups. Usually under the nominal command of a European officer, these Aboriginal policemen were outfitted with uniforms, weapons, and sometimes horses, as well as with considerable license to perform mayhem in the name of civilizing heathen tribes. Although at first native troopers were brought to the north from southern parts of Queensland, as areas gradually came under European control, their Aboriginal inhabitants often found that the policemen raiding their camps and stealing women and children were their kinsmen from neighboring territories, and sometimes even closer relatives from their own tribes who had left to seek employment on stations or in towns.

The events at Lizard Island were probably too far away to have had a direct effect on Aborigines at Barrow Point. But stories record other massacres. For example, in the clan area of the **Muunhthi-warra**,[6] from the Jack River, south of Tanglefoot, police troopers are said to have made regular raids, shooting people indiscriminately. On one occasion a large group of survivors was reported to have fled to Cape Melville, where they hid in a cave. In another story, survivors of a police rampage on a salt pan inland from the mouth of Wakooka Creek came upon one of the native troopers abusing a local woman and killed him on the spot.

By 1902,[7] Roth was tracing the activities of an Aboriginal miscreant from Barrow Point, one Charlie Bushman, who had committed "two or three murders of other than members of his own tribe—as well as threats to Europeans." Roth commented that "his removal has not yet been effected," using a standard euphemism, "removal," for the practice of forcibly deporting Aborigines to penal settlements far from their home areas.

By the end of the first decade of this century, the initial violent confrontation between black and white in the area had settled into a pattern of relationships more routine, if for Aborigines equally devastating. Individual Aborigines seemed to move widely through the area, occasionally finding themselves in difficulties with the authorities. Sgt. Bodman, of the Cooktown police, reported a trip in December 1910 to a coastal Aboriginal camp at Red Point, an area some "60 miles north of Cooktown," whose people were closely related to those from Barrow Point. The policeman had a warrant for the arrest of an Aboriginal man called Chucky who was wanted for horse theft.

> There were about sixty boys and gins in the camp, and the boys were all armed with spears. When we arrived at the camp Chucky was not there and three of the boys came at us with spears and threatened us not to take any boys from camp. They were a dangerous crowd . . . On enquiries we learned that Chucky had left a few days previous and had gone up to Barrow Point.[8]

Bodman abandoned the search at that point.

Chucky was apprehended in April 1911 as he got off a boat in Cooktown.[9] Protector Bodman recommended his "removal" to Barambah, on the following grounds:

> This Aboriginal is a very bad boy and has several times been in prison for stealing . . . Government notes were issued for his arrest [for stealing a horse after his release from jail in Townsville] . . . some days later police found Chucky at Cooktown, but they were unable to prove the charge and he was discharged . . . I as Protector of Aborigines am holding Chucky until . . . [ordered to deport him] which I would strongly recommend as this boy has given the police a great deal of trouble, and I have received several complaints from . . . miners and others of robbing their camps in this district. He is a good worker and would be better away from this district under supervision.[10]

Chucky was ultimately sent to Brisbane with a number of other Aborigines who had been recently removed from Laura.[11]

CONTACT FROM THE SEA

Contact proliferated between Aborigines and commercial fishermen whose boats regularly visited coastal camps, as well as between nomadic Aborigines and Europeans whose settlements and mining operations extended into the hinterlands. As the Aboriginal reaction to the police visit to Red Point suggests, these relations were not always amicable. The Cooktown police reported in 1910 that several Aboriginal men had accused a Japanese boat captain of having killed one of his Aboriginal crew members.[12] The correspondence in the case reveals that the boat captain had several times been denounced to police up and down the coast as "a bad man." One Aboriginal told police at Cardwell that the captain "had killed one boy like himself" by "biting him and knocking him over the side."[13] Cooktown police were at the time holding in jail a group of eleven Aborigines who had signed on to the ship in question but who had since run away. The original permit to the Japanese captain named twelve "local boys" ranging in age from 16 to 28. Seven of the twelve, including the missing man, were shown as natives of "Barrow Point."[14] (See Pl. 3.)

Roger Hart remembers hearing as a child from a crew of Barrow Point boatmen that their Japanese captain had flown into a rage against one of their companions, picked up a rifle, and shot him through the heart. The crew rose up against the captain and tied him to the mast, taking him to the nearest port to denounce him to the police.

Young men spent months and even years working on fishing trawlers and luggers along the Queensland coast. Reconstructing family histories from Barrow Point turns up many cases of men, like Roger Hart's maternal uncle or older brother, who signed on to boats and were never heard from again. The office of the chief protector of Aborigines tried to regulate the fishing industry by requiring that boat captains officially contract to employ Aboriginal labor and that they pay salaries directly to the local protector for "safekeeping." The government also tried to prohibit the established practice by which a captain would pick up men from one part of the coast and later simply put them ashore wherever it was most convenient, sometimes in a completely different part of Australia or even farther afield. Roger Hart says that many people from Barrow Point ended up marrying at Lockhart, Bamaga, or on the Gulf of Carpinteria and never returned to their homeland. Others never married at all and died, he imagines, in such places as Cherbourg to the south, Thursday Island to the north, or, for all he knows, even in Japan.

Missionary Schwarz at Cape Bedford, who had by the early 1920s begun to take a protective interest in the Aboriginal population to his north, was a particularly eloquent critic of the whole bêche-de-mer trade and its noxious effects on Aboriginal social life. Writing to Chief Protector of Aborigines Bleakley in his yearly report for 1926, he observed of the Cape Melville and Barrow Point camps:

At present nearly all the able-bodied men out of these two northern tribes are away on fishing boats for about nine months of the year, come home at the end of their term with a hard earned but very slender supply of provisions, a new rig-out of clothes, a few useless articles of personal adornment, etc., all of which is either discarded or used up in a ridiculous short time, that one would think these boys would come to the conclusion that it would be better to stay at home and help their wives and families (the latter very scarce now-a-days) to make a better living. However the thought never seems to strike them and when the recruiting boats come back after two or three months, a few drinks of something more to their easily acquired taste than "sugar-bag" soon induces them [to sign on again].[15]

Against the suggestion that employing Aborigines in such productive work enhances their "civilization," Schwarz wrote,

Up along the coast where these boys have been recruited from, we find a "camp" of Aboriginals, a miserable sorry lot, not to be compared with their relations in the same locality 40 years ago, which were fine healthy people. There are some old people, not many, there are a lot of women, many suffering from filthy diseases, some children—not many either—some of them half castes . . . This . . . I think could rightly be called "Starvation, misery and syphilization."[16]

Still, for many people to sign on to a boat meant to escape from the heavy restrictions placed on young men by watchful elders, including very limited possibilities for correct marriage. Japanese boats would anchor at Cape Melville, and young men would travel there in search of work, spending months at sea and only from time to time bringing provisions from Cooktown to their parents who had remained in camp. Boat skippers, like Captain Monaghan in the *Spray,* would make a series of stops, dropping off men and supplies, as the Christmas season (and accompanying monsoons) approached. He would call in at Barrow Point, then at Cape Melville, and continue northward, where he would ultimately drop off the "Island fellows"[17] in his crew.

Fishing boats rarely stopped at Ninian Bay for long, although they frequently collected fresh water at various places up the coast, especially at Cape Melville itself. Roger remembers that people in the camps were always on the lookout for the boats and that they would set large signal fires when they saw a boat approaching. Other crew members would rarely accompany the Barrow Point men to shore—"I think they [were] frightened of bama"—except when there was some sort of dance organized.

Boat work was both physically exhausting and dangerous. Aboriginal crewmen diving for trochus shell or collecting bêche-de-mer worked with no equipment other than simple diving goggles and their lungs, and the fishing boats frequently left them for hours on barely exposed reefs. Roger Hart's Barrow Point kinsman Yagay used to describe how one of his fellow divers was simply snapped up by a shark—its jaws clapping shut with a characteristic "tuk!"—leaving behind no trace except a spreading stain of blood.

The Japanese boat captains left singular impressions on the Aboriginal population, and many Hopevale people believe that their deportation southward during World War II was due as much to their long association with Japanese on boats as to Missionary Schwarz's German nationality. Barrow Point men worked on boats for one Black Otto, master of the boat *Sunshine*, another captain called Moo Kai, and also for a Captain Sakata. Barney Warner, an old timer from Barrow Point who spent much of his life at sea, used to tell Cape Bedford boatmen about his adventures with the latter, whom he considered a "real gentleman." Sakata's reply to the Cooktown harbormaster who wanted to borrow the Japanese master's dinghy in order to make a daybreak trip to the beacon opposite the Cooktown wharf—"Early morning go!"—remains a classic example of "Japanee English" for Aboriginal storytellers.

The boat captains left a rather different impression on those concerned with Aboriginal welfare. The same Captain Monaghan who called frequently at Barrow Point was reputed to pay his white crew members £3 per week. By contrast, Missionary Schwarz reported in 1925 to Protector Bleakley that the Aboriginal boatmen were paid a truly pathetic wage. He describes a conversation, evidently with Captain Sakata.

> If these boys were recruited without the introduction of strong drink, treated fairly and paid on a scale somewhat in accordance with the amount of money they earn for their masters, little could be said against their employment on boats. But how do their wages compare with the earnings of such boats? The master of a Japanese boat called here about a month ago. I have known this man for a good few years. He seems to me to be a man far above the average Japanese masters of boats one meets up here. In the course of conversation he volunteered the information, he had—during this season—shipped already 43 tons of Trochus Shell and that he would easily get another 10 tons. The price of

shell he informed me was £90. It is not hard to figure out what, approximately, Owner and Master of this boat will be able to divide amongst themselves at the end of the season and what the crew of that boat (by the way in this case boys from Barrow Point and Cape Melville) would receive as their share of this wealth they procured by their labour. By these figures the gross proceeds from the season's sale of Trochus shell would be nearly £5000.

Schwarz continues,

This captain informed me that their wages were £1/8 a month. I don't know if this is true, it seems too ridiculous to be so, for the value of the shell they often gather in ONE day, exceeds the amount of wages paid to a whole crew of Aboriginals for a whole season. It can hardly be fair that these simple Aboriginals should be signed on to work on these fishing boats for a nominal wage, piling up fortunes for Japanese and wealthy ship owners, whilst their own families are forced to starve or become a burden to your department or to the various missions.[18]

Schwarz suggested £5 as a fair monthly wage that the industry could bear.[19]

Aborigines around Barrow Point and Cape Melville also had regular contact with other boats that visited their coast, many of which stopped to take on fresh water from known springs in the area. Supply ships heading north to Cape York and New Guinea also passed inside the reef, often in sight of coastal-dwelling people. King Harry of Cape Melville knew many of those who sailed up and down the coast. He had several stepchildren through his many wives whose biological fathers were non-Aboriginal seamen and others whose father was the Danish lighthouse keeper at Pipon Island.[20] However, not all of his interactions with passing boats were amicable, as the following story from Roger Hart illustrates.

KING HARRY IS THROWN INTO THE SEA

This is a story I heard when I was little, but I didn't know it very clearly. Then Banjo and Toby told me about it again. It's about King Harry, old man Bob's father.[21]

There was a big steamer called the *Kalatina*. I used to see that steamer going past on its way to Thursday Island.

Figure 6. King Harry thrown overboard

One day a big boat came into view from the east, around the point at Cape Melville. It was that same steamer *Kalatina.*

Old man King Harry was staying there then, with a big lot of people from Flinders Island. They saw the steamer passing, and they jumped into their dugout canoes to go north to try to meet it, maybe to beg a little bit of food.

They managed to catch up with the ship while it was in the passage between Stanley Island and Flinders Island itself. King Harry used to do that all the time, see? He was always coming around that boat in his canoe, asking them to give him some food.

Those white fellows were probably getting a bit tired of it. They found him something of a nuisance.

This time, the men on the steamer saw the canoes coming. They pulled up.

"Let's wait for them," they said.

They threw down a rope ladder, and those bama climbed on board. Even King Harry climbed up, wearing his plate on his chest.[22]

The crew members said, "All right, we'll give you some food." But instead they picked King Harry up off the deck. They shook him like a stick and heaved him overboard. He fell straight down into the water.

Well, that old king climbed back into his canoe and paddled away. After that he didn't come begging food any more.

They were all white men on that boat—some of the same crew members as used to sail on the *Melbidir*[23] during the war. I think they were sick of him, and when they got wild they threw him into the water, poor thing.

EUROPEAN SETTLEMENT AROUND BARROW POINT

People in the Barrow Point camps were seasonally nomadic. They traveled to exploit traditional sources of food, to maintain social relations within a severely reduced population, and in response to the encroachments of European settlement. They visited inland tribal sites near Wakooka during the wet season and in the dry season migrated between Barrow Point, Cape Melville, and beyond, along the coast or to coastal islands. Though all the sites on these migratory routes had Aboriginal "owners," many places were largely depopulated by the early decades of this century.

The European move into the hinterlands had disastrous consequences for Aborigines who had managed to survive the violence of the gold miners in the latter part of the previous century. As gold mining waned, authorities turned their interest to more settled and durable exploitation of "vacant Crown land," which officials considered to be "a real no man's land." Europeans gradually settled the territory north of Cooktown, pushing Aborigines still living in the bush into ever smaller refuges and, ultimately, to the fringes of European settlements.

Though most of the area north of Cooktown had been declared open for occupation in the late 1880s, settlers only began to apply for occupation licenses around the time of the First World War, when special benefits were offered to returning soldiers. Two large occupation licenses were squarely in the middle of what Roger Hart describes as his tribal territory.

ABBEY PEAK

Abbey Peak, on the shores of Ninian Bay, included the area called **lip-wulin,** Roger Hart's birthplace.[24] The area around Barrow Point was already in unofficial use by pastoralists before the First World War.[25] In 1916, a Mr. James Bennett, a former sapper with the Australian Army, had applied for an area of 50 square miles that appeared to be "lying idle" despite there being adjoining properties under 30-year lease to a certain Maurice Hart and to two brothers named O'Beirne.[26] It was recommended that, because Bennet was a returned soldier, his aspirations should be accommodated if possible, and in August 1916, he was granted a 25-square-mile occupation lease, "which includes Parrow [sic] Point Creek," adjoining a similar-sized area granted to his partner, Thomas Edmund Thomas of Cooktown.[27]

Sapper Bennett does not seem to have spent much time actually living on his newly acquired property, since he reenlisted within the year and leased his property to one of the O'Beirne brothers.[28] Bennett's fate is not revealed in Lands Department records.

By 1918 several pastoralists were in a struggle to acquire the Barrow Point holdings.[29] The government decided to consolidate several occupation licenses into a single run, a preferential pastoral license to be called Abbey Peak.[30]

The property was finally transferred on 18 June 1920 to Allan Critchley Instone of Cooktown for the sum of £227.[31] Instone's property on the shores of Ninian Bay formed the central magnet that attracted the Barrow Point Aboriginal settlements when Roger Hart was a little boy. Instone stayed at Barrow Point until 1926, when he sold his lease to the larger neighboring Starcke Station.

Instone apparently did not have a family when he lived at Barrow Point, although several Aboriginal girls kept house for him. He also officially "signed on" or contracted with the local protector of Aborigines legally to employ a few Barrow Point men as stockmen, gardeners, and boatboys. Cape Bedford's Rev. Schwarz, in a letter to the chief protector of Aborigines in which he discussed plans to try to move the entire Barrow Point population south onto the mission reserve, mentioned two such cases.

> Jackie Red Point was here for a considerable time until, by your special permission, he was signed on by [Cooktown police constable and] Protector [of Aborigines] Kenny to Mr. Instone. With King Nicholas (another of Mr. Instone's boat boys) all our boys seem to be well acquainted, although I myself do not remember seeing him here [at Cape Bedford] unless it was under another name.[32]

Jackie Red Point later returned to Cape Bedford and worked on mission boats. King Nicholas, the government-appointed "king" of the Barrow

Figure 7. Instone's house

Point camp, resisted the missionary's plans to move the Barrow Point people from their own land to Cape Bedford and was ultimately deported to the penal colony at Palm Island.

King Nicholas, Nelson, Billy Salt, Toby Flinders—all people that Roger Hart remembers from his childhood—worked on Instone's boat or helped clear his yards, plant melons, and look after the farm. Jackie Red Point tended the garden or fished with a net in the bay, the children following behind hitting the water with sticks to chase the fish into the net and to pick up whatever came their way. They might also beg a few potatoes from Jackie or his wife Sara. Other men maintained the property—fencing, digging, mustering, that is, rounding up cattle. Instone also kept a large vegetable garden, tended by a Malay gardener whom the Aborigines knew as Sam Malaya.[33]

Instone was generally very strict with the Aboriginal children and did not like them to play around his yards and gardens, even less around his high house. He kept what Roger recalls as a savage dog to chase the children away. Still, the little boys occasionally raided the garden when they could sneak in without being seen.

The settler's house, gardens, and stockyards sat on several small hills just to the west of a large rocky outcropping that jutted out from the southern shore of Ninian Bay. Amidst the mangroves lining the beach, Instone's workers had cleared a landing place for his boat, the *Iona*, which an Aboriginal crew sailed to Cooktown in fair weather, to bring supplies. Although commercial fishing boats moved freely along the coast and frequently picked up young Aboriginal crewmen, Instone refused to allow such boats in his own harbor at Ninian Bay, perhaps to protect his exclusive access to local Aboriginal labor.

Instone's official responsibility to the Aborigines living on his station under the Protection Acts was unclear. Roger Hart thinks that he was "something like a superintendent," supplying official government Aboriginal rations—blankets, steel tools, fish hooks and line, flour, tobacco, and the like—to the nearby camps. Barrow Point people who later came to the Cape Bedford Reserve reported that Instone had misappropriated wages channeled through him for delivery to men who had been discharged from fishing boats. Instead of simply paying the monies out, he demanded work, or as Roger Hart put it, "double time . . . he used to make them work first." According to local lore, two Barrow Point men, Tracker Billy McGreen, Sr., and Jackie Red Point, sailed to Cooktown in the ketch *Soapbox* to report Instone for malfeasance—"he was making bama work for their own money."

WAKOOKA

Wakooka Station to the south was the other large pastoral holding in the Barrow Point people's traditional territory. Maurice Hart, whom Roger Hart conventionally mentions as his non-Aboriginal genitor, began raising cattle in the area north of Starcke sometime before 1916. Having survived a fire on his previous holding, Hart began a campaign to acquire lands in the Wakooka area.[34] He feuded with his neighbors at Mt. Hope over grazing and droving rights.[35]

In November 1916, giving his residence as Ninian Bay, Hart applied for the lease of Occupation License 397, known as Wakooka.[36] He immediately began to build improvements, run cattle, and raise a family on the property. Hart remained at Wakooka until 1932, when his property, like Instone's at Abbey Peak, was absorbed into the vast Starcke holdings.[37]

In the mid 1920s Missionary Schwarz was trying to persuade the government to move the remnants of northern tribes, including the people at Barrow Point, to the Cape Bedford Reserve, where he was the superintendent. In a letter to the chief protector of Aborigines he listed possible obstacles to his plan to bring the Barrow Point people south.[38] One of

these was the presence of cattle stations. Schwarz wrote of two properties between Cape Melville and Barrow Point that made free, and illegal,
use of the local Aboriginal labor force.

> Although, as a rule Aborigines are considered a nuisance any-
> where near a cattle station—I do not think that any of these cattle-
> men would like to have the Aborigines removed from up there
> and assistance in the matter could therefore hardly be expected.[39]

Maurice Hart may have been the sort of Cape York cattleman Schwarz
had in mind. Although Hart employed Aboriginal workers to clean his
yards and to muster his stock, he restricted the movement of Aboriginal
bands across his land. If Hart encountered people hunting for honey on
his property, for example, he was likely to whip them before running
them off.[40]

Other Europeans frequented the Barrow Point area as stockmen, yard-
builders, or harvesters of sandalwood.[41] Stockmen gathered at campsites
around Barrow Point for mustering, and Roger and the other children
knew them to be potential sources for bread, damper, or tea. One person
Roger particularly remembers was old Billy Burns, a famed yardbuilder
throughout the region. He had a severe hunchback, and in order to lay
out his swag he would first make a space for the hump by digging a hole
in the sand.

In the second decade of the century, when Roger Hart was born, the
properties of European settlers like Instone and Hart had attracted semipermanent Aboriginal camps, oriented both inland to the settlers, who
provided meager domestic and stock work, and also outward to the sea
where most young men made their livings, usually exchanging hard labor on Japanese luggers for flour, tobacco, and a minimal wage. Settlers'
and fishermen's interests crucially involved Aboriginal labor, but they ignored or actively obstructed claims on the local environment from Aboriginal camp life.

THE CAMPS AT BARROW POINT

Exactly how the Barrow Point people understood their "ownership" of
the land where they lived is difficult to reconstruct fully from current
memories. Before the European invasion of their country, Aborigines in
this area were organized into small groups, nowadays often called clans.
The territory was dotted with named places, some of great ritual or economic significance, and people knew to which groups each place be-

longed. Similarly, individual Aborigines were associated with named "runs" or areas, within which specific sites lay. Normally one gained one's language and territorial affiliation from one's father, although ties to the land and language of mothers and grandmothers were also significant. From your clan you also inherited an often discontinuous mosaic of "home" sites across the landscape, as well as a series of stories, totems, and kinsmen. Different clans could also be linked by shared claims to places and stories as well as by marriage ties that often endured over several generations. A person thus "belonged" to places, to languages, to stories, and to other people. Talk about places, words, and stories is the idiom in which both social distinctiveness ("this is my word; that is his") and social cohesion ("we are both one for that story") were phrased.

When Roger was growing up, clan affiliations, rather than personal names, were the polite way to refer to people. To identify someone seen from afar people might say, "Ah, **bama yalngaa-ngu**—it's the person from the [clan area called] **yalnga**." They would not simply call out the person's name.

The Aboriginal settlements at Barrow Point straddled Instone's Station and stretched out along the shores of Ninian Bay. The largest camp was called Iipwulin,[42] on the beach just to the east of the rocky outcropping that separated it from Instone's Station. The camp extended for several miles farther east, as far as the mangroves that grow along the northern edge of Barrow Point itself. It was watered by seasonal creeks and by a large permanent lagoon inland to the south, also a favorite hunting place for fish and game. Iipwulin was Roger Hart's birthplace. It served as the main campsite in the whole Barrow Point area, the central home of the "older brother" half of the Gambiilmugu people. From this camp people would travel to the coast or south and east to other campsites and tribal areas.[43]

Instone's Station was a source of supplies and work for Aborigines at Barrow Point. Roger Hart recalls that the men "would go over to the west [from Iipwulin] for tobacco. A few bama used to work as stockmen. Those who worked for Instone would bring tobacco for the others. But not too much, just a bit."

Another large Aboriginal camp was located inland from Instone's compound, on the high, flat ground to the south, where another freshwater creek could be found. This camp was named *liwalin*. There was also a small camp on the beach at the western end of the mangroves in Instone's harbor where families of Aborigines who worked on Instone's Station stayed.

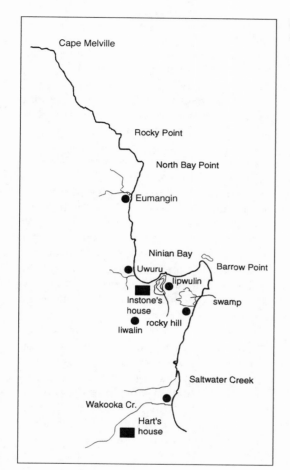

Map 2. Aboriginal camps around Barrow Point

Farther west, in the southwest corner of Ninian Bay, was another fair-sized camp, centered around the freshwater creek, *Uwuru*.[44] In the summertime the people would shift camp to the mouth of this creek, which emptied into Ninian Bay and provided easy access to a series of reefs and to campsites higher up the creek where other sorts of bush foods could be harvested. Roger remembers that people from Cape Melville, Bathurst Head, and others he associates with the area called **Walmbaarrga** on Princess Charlotte Bay camped here frequently when visiting Barrow

Point. During the dry season this corner of the bay was a good place to hunt dugong, and Roger recalls Uwuru as a well-fed camp. "Bama used to harpoon turtles [there]. On the low tide you could see the reef, poking up from the corner of the bay right north to *Imeenhthin*."[45]

A more frequent campsite was slightly farther up the coast, about halfway to Eumangin Creek, where freshwater flowed from a spring right on the beach. During mustering season, many adult men with their families would move to the creek at Uwuru to take part in the cattle work, which Instone evidently sometimes performed jointly with his neighbor Maurice Hart from Wakooka. The stockmen were paid with tobacco, flour, and tea leaf, which they shared with the others.

The creek at Eumangin marked the northern edge of the territory of Roger Hart's clan, the people of Gambiilmugu. There were small groups of Aborigines living right up the coast. The territory of the people known as **Thagaalmugu-warra** began at Eumangin, according to Roger, and extended north to North Bay Point, then west to Cape Melville, and beyond to Flinders Island.[46] Although he considers the camp at Iipwulin to have been his home, as a boy Roger Hart visited areas as distant as Cape Melville and Bathhurst Head in one direction and Cape Bowen in the other, all before he was six or seven years old.

In the territory of the "younger brother" half of the Barrow Point people there were also several camps. By the mid 1910s, most people from this region no longer maintained semipermanent independent camps but instead lived near European settlers' properties. The Aborigines who lived and worked at Wakooka Station came from many different groups in addition to the Gambiilmugu tribe. The main camp in the area was located on the beach near the mouth of Wakooka Creek, a way station between Barrow Point and Cape Bowen to the south.[47]

Bush Tucker

Living on the shores of Ninian Bay, the Barrow Point people depended on the sea. They fished and caught shellfish on reefs exposed at low tide. They pulled mud crabs, bottom-feeding fish, and shell bait from the mud flats around the mangroves. They harpooned more substantial marine game—turtle and dugong—from dugout canoes.

There were seasonally plentiful fruits growing along the beach, both introduced plants like coconut and native foods like **ngundarr,** 'wongai plum', a datelike fruit that grows in great abundance along the coast from Cape Bowen to Cape Melville, ripening from a bright inedible red to a sweet inky black as the rainy season gives way to spring and summer.

Nonetheless, Roger Hart remembers the Barrow Point camp as a hungry place, for children at least. First of all, many foods were prohibited to children, declared off limits or **thabul** (*awiyi*) for them by the older people.

"We were not to drink any honey with wax inside. We could only have it really clean. They never used to give us scrub turkey eggs; that was taboo food.

"'Don't eat that scrub turkey egg!' they would say, 'lest Thunder strike you!'

"We couldn't eat emu. If they killed and cooked a crocodile, no child was to eat it, because afterwards a crocodile might turn around and eat a child.

"There were lots of other things we couldn't eat, but I've forgotten many of them. I never used to eat a lot in those days. My belly was narrow, then."

When they traveled in the bush, Roger's mother would mix something up in ashes and give it to him to drink, to diminish his appetite. A similar treatment was meted out to children who cried too much for food.

Honey was a central part of the diet, and its importance is still evident today although few people have the patience or skill to track native bees to their nests as they fly through the air. Roger points out, "You've got to have a good eye to see it. Most of us just walk around without noticing anything." In the camps, people would soak a sponge made out of dry grass in the liquid honey to extract it from the nest. The favorite way to consume the honey was then to mix it in water. A billycan full of **mula,** drunk in the morning, provided energy for a full day's trek.

On our walks through the bush, Tulo and Roger repeatedly pointed out old scars on trees where bees' nests had been chopped, or new nests waiting for more energetic souls to open. On a trip to Cape Melville, when most of our store-bought sugar was ruined by a leaking gasoline container, several elderly men preferred to forego fishing and crabbing to spend the day tracking down and robbing a bucketful of **mula** to sweeten the tea.

At Barrow Point, honey near the beach was quickly exhausted in the fine weather months of the spring when people concentrated on hunting for fish, turtle, and dugong. The bees, likewise, were not collecting nectar and storing honey in the winter dry season. It might be February before the rains would drive people inland, to Wakooka and beyond. From February to June honey would be plentiful. People who had moved inland in this season would also hunt echidna and other small game.

As elsewhere on Cape York Peninsula, individuals were associated with particular bee species—an affiliation that you also inherited from your father. People were therefore partial to certain kinds of honey. The two varieties of native bee that distinguish the two basic "kinds of people," or moieties,[1] throughout the Guugu Yimithirr area, **walarr** and **thuuru,** were also to be found at Barrow Point. The first variety, called *Ulmuru* in Barrow Point language, builds up a long tunnel-like entrance to the nest. The second, called by the generic *uulgaal,* is the tiny black "bally bee."

Green ants were used for medicine to treat everything from flu symptoms to diarrhea. They could also be chewed on long treks between fresh water sources, when their refreshing sourness would moisten the mouth and replenish one's saliva.

Fresh meat was roasted or boiled without salt. Sea turtles and shellfish such as crabs or lobsters were usually cooked in seawater. Men speared red kangaroos, gray wallaroos, as well as smaller wallabies. They also hunted lizards and goannas.

"They were eating such things, and they weren't starving."

Nowadays wild pigs abound throughout his homeland, but Roger Hart remembers that spearing pigs in the early days, before the territory was abandoned to such animals, was extremely rare.

The search for seasonal foods took the Barrow Point people as far as Princess Charlotte Bay, to the south past Cape Bowen, and inland beyond Wakooka. They used to dig for yellow yams and make starchy breads out of white yams. They also gathered the tubers of wild lilies, *unthiin,*[2] in the inland swamps and lagoons. The old ladies would travel great distances in search of these plants when they were in season. Roger remembers a favorite place for gathering lilies on a lagoon upriver from the mouth of the Mack River, south of Cape Melville.

"Now only pigs eat them. But in those days there were no pigs. The old ladies would get the roots of the lilies, and also the seed pods, once the flowers had fallen off. They would cook big heaps of them in earth ovens. Once the pods were soft they would take out all the seeds, and then scrape the pulp off, make something like bread out of it. That was good **mayi.**"

The final process involved baking the pulp of the roots once they emerged from the earth oven to make a kind of bread or damper. Roger remembers that *ayi unhthiin* was "good, but tasted a bit like water inside. It was dry, though, something like cooked potato."

At Barrow Point in addition to various yam species, people also used to eat the fruit of white mangroves, called **udan**.[3]

Other bush foods required more preparation. Throughout this part of Queensland, Aborigines gathered the nut of the zamia palm, which had to be pounded and leached of toxins before it could be eaten. The same sort of preparation was required for **yulnga** or "matchbox" nuts.[4]

One of Roger's childhood playmates was too impatient to wait.

NICHOLAS AND THE ZAMIA NUTS

We were staying up near the creek at Uwuru. All the old ladies were sitting around in a circle, preparing the nut of the zamia palm, **uthiwi**. They had put the nuts into the ashes to roast, and they were just taking them out of the fire. They would pound on the shell of the nut, take out the edible part inside, and throw it onto a heap. The **mayi** was already soft.

Nicholas[5] was watching them, and he must have thought, "Well, nobody is looking at me now." He grabbed some of that food and ran off with it. He sat down to eat it. He got very sick after that, because even though they had softened it in the ashes, it was still raw.

After they open the nut, they pound it flat on a rock. Then they put it in a dilly bag and tie it in a stream or under a waterfall, where the water is running swiftly. They might leave it for weeks, or even months. When you take it out, it's bland, no taste. That's the way that **mayi** is. You have to put honey on it.

Dugong and turtle were the most prized game of all. Neither was easily found off the beach where Roger's people had their main camp. Therefore men embarked on harpooning expeditions north to Cape Melville, east beyond the tip of Barrow Point, or south toward Cape Bowen.

"This used to be a great place for dugong—might still be a good few here, if we went out in a dinghy.

"People used to go out hunting from Iipwulin. Some would go by boat, and others would walk. The oldest people, who couldn't walk, would also jump on the boats. They would go right around the point, and head south down the beach. The other men would cut across inland, and come out onto the beach to the east. They would meet up then, having agreed on a place in advance.

"If they caught a dugong, they would make camp, cut up the meat. They wouldn't shift camp again until the dugong was finished.

"I still remember that Long Billy went out hunting one time with old man **Ngamu Wuthurru**.[6] Ngamu Wuthurru was a loner, and he didn't hunt much with the other men. But that time he went with old Billy, looking for turtle. It was morning, and we were camped up at Cape Melville. We were about to shift camp from there. I still remember the place.

"Well, that morning they caught no turtles, but they harpooned a baby dugong. They brought it up on the beach and cut it up. Then we had to stay in camp there to cook the dugong in an earth oven. It was a good feed."

Despite the great variety of bush foods, the proximity of Instone's property exerted a profound influence on the Barrow Point people's diet. Men visited the station in search of tobacco, and women frequently were paid for domestic labor with wheat flour.

When old man Jackie Red Point hauled out Instone's fishing net, probably provided by the protector of Aborigines for the benefit of the Aboriginal people living in the camps, the children would follow him into the water in hopes of a few gift fish. Roger and his playmates would also pay covert visits to Instone's gardens. Sam Malaya tended the tomatoes, which Roger and the others occasionally tried to steal. His garden also had lettuce, cabbage, and sweet potatoes.

"We had to watch him all the time," Roger remembers. "We didn't want to come close to him. He knew we were stealing tomatoes, from the broken plants, but he wouldn't say anything to Instone about it. He didn't like us to come near the garden, so we were afraid of him, but other than that he was a good bloke. He didn't get angry."

The kids used to follow Sam Malaya around when he went hunting. He chewed plug tobacco, which they tried to cadge. He had a rifle, Roger remembers, and often went shooting birds, or the whistling duck species called **digalaba.**

He was also a source of fishhooks and other gear that camp people used. Roger remembers his mother fishing for jewfish with a line and fishing pole she had made from bits and pieces she had gotten from Sam Malaya.

The Barrow Point people used to travel to the west of Bathhurst Head for *ambaarr,* bamboo for fishing spears. They used the heart of black palm, *thuguy,* as well as *abulthabul,* 'grass tree' and a hardwood called **wurrbuy** for bullet spears, and they made harpoons for dugong from ironbark wood. They would also use stingaree barbs for fighting spears and purloin settlers' fencing wire to make the prongs on their fishing spears.

Yiithuu-warra

The early decades of this century saw massive restructuring of Aboriginal life in north Queensland, and virtually all aspects of social organization among Roger's people were in transition. The vagaries of abduction, adoption, serial marriage, and rape, as well as the violent dispossession of territory occasioned by the European invasion had seriously complicated the relationship between individuals, "tribes," and **bubu,** 'home country'.[1]

By the time Roger Hart was born, conditions of Aboriginal life had led to significant adjustments in the principle of inheriting from one's father, as well as to the social nature of clan affiliations. The devastating effects of dislocation and disease, coupled with exploitation of Aboriginal men and women by local settlers and fishermen, made it difficult for the Aboriginal population to reproduce at all, let alone to maintain the social and ceremonial practices that clan organization entailed. The European invasion brought about massive depopulation, a drastic reduction in traditional food and water resources for Aborigines, and the violence of forced relocations ("removals") and murder ("dispersions"). By the beginning of the century, the majority of surviving young Aboriginal men were involved in work that took them far from the camps. Many Aboriginal women were abducted from their own clan areas or pressed into various sorts of service by non-Aboriginal employers. An increasing number of children whose fathers were non-Aboriginal were born to Aboriginal mothers, complicating the question of "following your father's line." Should such children belong to the clans of their mothers' husbands? Should they be associated with their mothers, or even with their birthplaces? Or were they simply outcasts, nonpersons?

Sites associated with particular clans were often completely abandoned, and clans themselves began to disappear as their members died or became too few in number to sustain either ritual obligations or seasonal exploitation of their territories. Camps like those at Barrow Point came to be refuges for people from many different areas, transient stations in a continual series of migrations between European settlements—where tobacco, flour, blankets, and other provisions could be exchanged for occasional work—and more remote areas where traditional food collecting, socializing, and ritual could still be conducted.

Roger Hart assembled his knowledge of Aboriginal law and custom under these complex and unsettled circumstances. The clan affiliations he now attributes to individuals come not from where they lived but from what people said about their fathers, grandfathers, or in the case of part-European children like Roger himself, their stepfathers, their mothers' Aboriginal husbands. In Roger's childhood, people identified as belonging to the "younger brother" mob of the Gambiilmugu tribe lived side-by-side in the same camps as those from the "older brother" mob. Barrow Point people moved widely over the countryside, sharing campsites and social relations with people from widely scattered and often distant clans.

Although details of the kinship terminologies varied from language to language, Aboriginal people in this part of Queensland reckoned their kinsmen according to a largely shared system of categories. This system divided the social world into two halves, or moieties: those of one's father's line and those of one's mother's line. To a man, for example, this meant that one took one's own identity—language, clan affiliation, sacred animals, home territory, and stories, among other things—from one's father. One found one's spouse in one's mother's line, that is, from the other side. Indeed, an appropriate marriage partner was the child of a person categorized like a mother's brother—a distant uncle, for example, from the opposite moiety—and terminology identified such uncles and their wives as potential parents-in-law, people whose offspring would be the "right ones" for a person to marry. Such future inlaws received marked deference and respect. Siblings were ranked by birth order, and the oldest children in a generation were, in principle, "bosses" for their families, invested with a certain authority over more junior siblings, nephews, and the like.

Roger uses Guugu Yimithirr kinship terms to distinguish the two halves of the Barrow Point "nation"—**gaarga,** 'younger brother' and **yaba,** 'older brother'.

"My tribe belonged to the 'older brothers', to the west. My 'younger brothers' were people like Toby Gordon and old man Yagay, from the south. Those 'younger brothers' used to breed too much. They wanted to be the bosses. They were truly great hunters. *Uwu dhaga*— they had strong words. If people from the north spoke out against what they were doing, the younger brother tribe threatened to spear them."

Sometimes this "older brother"/"younger brother" terminology conflicted with what Roger thought were genealogical relationships, testifying to the confusion created by rapid social change. Here is how Roger responded to my question about his kinship relation with old man Yagay.

"At first he was my *uguya* [classificatory mother's brother]. But then they changed it and he became my **yaba**" [classificatory older brother].

Perhaps surprisingly, even in precontact times, kinship relations *could* change. After a death, for example, relationship terms were sometimes systematically altered, in order to help "forget about" or respect the memory of the deceased.

"But I am supposed to be Yagay's older brother, really, because we on the north were the 'older brothers.' Those people on the south were the 'younger brothers,' and they were supposed to follow that [for calculating kin relations], see?"

The interrelated clans from Barrow Point northward to Cape Melville and Flinders Island shared a social identity outside their own area. Just as the brash, disobedient, bellicose, and sinful "younger brothers' from Pinnacle had "hard words" and were feared up and down the coast, all the people from the Cape Melville and Barrow Point mobs, known collectively in Guugu Yimithirr as **Yiithuu-warra,** enjoyed a fearsome reputation.

"The people from around Cooktown, or the **Thiithaarr-warra** people from Cape Bedford, used to say, 'Watch out for those **Yiithuu-warra;** stay away from them!' They used to keep that in their minds, not to come too close to them. They were good hunters and good fighters, too."

Tulo Gordon, himself a Guugu Yimithirr man from **Nugal,** echoed these sentiments. "I still remember at the North Shore [of the Endeavour River, opposite Cooktown, where there was a large Aboriginal transient camp], that I heard the people talking about strangers coming at night. 'Beware of those **Yiithuu** people,' they said. 'They are dangerous, **warra thuul nubuun.'"**[2]

The Pinnacle mob was swallowed up for violating a strict Aboriginal code governing marriage and sexual relations. This "law" is the aspect of social life that resonates most strongly in Roger Hart's discourse about "old ways," even if "bama law" seems to have been more rhetoric than practice during his own lifetime, when almost everyone, whether by choice or necessity, married "crooked."

Early marriages were ideally contracted over long distances, frequently spanning different languages. Sometimes there were recurrent exchanges of women between clan groups. For example, Nicholas, the Barrow Point "king," was married to **gamba**[3] Rosie, a woman from the Lockhart River far to the north. Roger says: "The old people wouldn't let him to get married with their own relations, and so he went up there." When the Barrow Point people were afterward removed to Lockhart Mission in the late 1920s, they were brought into contact with distant people with whom they had already established links of marriage.[4]

Nonetheless, even the early history of the area is peppered with marriages unacceptable by strict Aboriginal standards. Severe depopulation coupled with disruption of previously normal social and ritual contacts between groups perhaps made it progressively more difficult to find genealogically appropriate partners to marry. Competition for marriageable women must have been intense.

A SPEAR FIGHT

My brother used to work on the boats. His boss was Mr. Monaghan, the skipper of the *Spray,* the same boat that the Cape Bedford Mission later purchased. A big lot of Barrow Point people used to work for him. Old man Charlie Monaghan used to work on that boat. He got his name from the white owner.

My brother used to sail far up to the north on those boats, as far as New Caledonia.

There was another man in the camp at Cape Melville named Yalunjin. In English they called him Jackie Barrow Point. He was my uncle. He was terribly jealous of my brother. The problem was a girl called Mary Ann, the stepdaughter of old man Imbanda. She was in love with my brother. That made Yalunjin jealous. He wanted her for himself—she was only a girl at that time.

Yalunjin asked the girl's stepfather if he could marry her. Imbanda refused. "You can't marry your own grannie," he told him. Mary Ann was like a grandmother to him, a **gami.**

Yalunjin got very angry because my brother was his rival. "You get ready there on the north," he said to my brother. He had his spears ready.

My brother jumped up on the north side. So did old man Imbanda, as a **mala-digarra,** my brother's champion or protector. He was there to block the spears as the other man threw them.

Yalunjin threw one spear after another at his rival, and old Imbanda knocked them aside. Imbanda was standing in front, and my brother behind.

When he blocked one of the last spears, he only managed to send its tail end askew. The spear flew up and hit him right in the eye. Old man Imbanda, there on the north, fell to the ground, speared in the eye.

Then Yalunjin threw one last spear. My brother fell to the ground, too, speared right through the side.

All the people cried out. Yalunjin, the guilty one, ran off toward the west, having speared his rival.

"Why have you speared my nephew, here to the east?" they called out after him. Old man **Wathi**—Billy Salt—wanted to spear him in return. He quickly ran off even farther to the west, to block Yalunjin's escape.

Yalunjin came running along the beach from the east. When he was very close, Wathi suddenly stood up. He called out to the fugitive, "Where are you running?"

Yalunjin couldn't run this way or that—he was too close. Wathi picked up his bullet spear and threw it. Yalunjin couldn't dodge it; he could only hold up his hands to block the throw, but the barbs of the spear tore deep into his arms. He fell to the ground.

They had to knock the stingaree barb off the end of the spear to pull the shaft back out. They carried the culprit back east to camp.

My mother took her digging stick. It was an iron bar, which she used for digging yams. She struck that man on the head, hitting him hard until the blood ran out. Again he fell to the ground. Then all the others took turns jabbing their spears into his leg and pulling them out again. We call it **wabu daamaayga**—pay-back spearing. That was his punishment for having speared my brother.

After my brother recovered from the spear wound, he went back out on the boats again. But he still had something inside him from the spear. He never really healed properly inside.

On the boat, he used to go diving for shells. Well, the cold got into that deep wound—perhaps it was pneumonia or something. He got really sick, and he died down there. Old Monaghan used to go south and sell the shells in Rockhampton, and he told me my brother died at Keppel Sands, near Rockhampton.

They couldn't bring my brother's bones back in a bark trough. "Never mind, leave him there," they said, when the news of his death reached Barrow Point.

After that they sent Yalunyjin away to Palm Island. He died down there under the name of Jackie Maytown.

Most of the people living permanently in the Barrow Point camps were elderly. The young men spent most of their time working on boats, leaving their wives behind. The wives, in turn, were easy prey for others to abduct.

"Bama used to come from farther west—from Port Stewart, Princess Charlotte Bay, or farther up Cape York Peninsula—and steal those women. Their husbands were out on the boats. The young men would come home and find their women gone. Then they would turn around and go back out on the boats again."

"Did they like working on the boats?"

"Oh, yes, they wanted to go out. I think they wanted to get away from those strict laws—like avoiding their sisters or their mothers-in-law. Or the rules about food. Some of the younger men got married in other places, like Lockhart, or even Kowanyama. They had their children there, and that's where their families grew up."

"When men abducted women, would they never ask permission first from the parents?"

"No, thawuunh, you know why? The old people used to follow the 'law.' If a man asked for a girl in the right relationship, like a cousin, and she was a full grown girl, the parents would willingly give her away.

"'Take her,' they would say, 'you're a good hunter.'

"That's if the girl was the daughter of an *imoyir*,[5] or the daughter of a proper father-in-law. But if she was from the same side as you, or like a **gaminhtharr**[6]—well, that's bad. They wouldn't let you marry that way. You had to follow the father, see?"

Young women were carefully supervised once they reached marriagable age. Old people kept girls "in one place; they never let them wander about." Girls went on short errands and were expected to return directly. If they went hunting or gathering, they remained in the company of mother, auntie, or grandmother. When they were of an age to get married, the parents would be sure to give them away to "the right bama," to an appropriately related man.

For Lutheran-educated Hopevale people like Roger Hart there are parallels between Aboriginal law and biblical precepts about proper marriage. Roger describes an Aboriginal levirate, in which a younger brother might take over the wife of a deceased elder brother.[7] The principle of classificatory cross-cousin marriage was guaranteed to be observed by such a match if the older brother himself had married properly. But in the violent first decades of the century, abductions and shortages of appropriate partners produced many marriages that ignored the strictures of such law.

Young women were liable to other predations, as the biographies and child-bearing histories of many individuals make plain. Women were **wali wali** 'all over the place,' living unsettled lives and sometimes traversing great distances as they moved from one husband to the next. Abduction of women was not limited to native troopers and European settlers. Roger Hart even has a little story to tell about how one woman escaped from her would-be husband.

ABDUCTION MAGIC

I don't know where she was stolen from—somewhere to the east of Barrow Point, I think. That girl didn't like her husband much. She was forced to come with him, you see. But they set out, and they walked and walked.

After a while it got to be late afternoon, maybe four o'clock. They wanted to make a fire. So the man got out his firesticks and tried to make a flame. He was facing to the west. The girl was sitting on the east side, but not facing east—at his back, you see? She was watching him.

Well, this fellow tried to get his fire started with the fire sticks. He twirled them round.

The girl cast a spell. She said to the fire, "**Suuuu!** Fire, don't come! **Suuu!** Flames, don't fall!"

Her husband kept on twirling and twirling his firesticks. He was so intent on making the fire that he forgot about that girl. He forgot about everything except his firesticks. His mind just more or less went to sleep.

Then the girl stood up. She started to walk away. She walked and walked and kept going. She left for good, never came back.

Meanwhile, that man was still twirling his firesticks. At last, the fire fell. He said, "Right! Bring me some tea-tree bark!" He looked around, but she wasn't there. She had gone back to her mother. He wasn't game to go back after her, since he had stolen that woman in the first place. If he had gone back, they would have speared him.

Many women from Cape Melville and Barrow Point were abducted by native troopers, but some crooked marriages seem to have been the result of less violent liaisons. One such "improper" union was contracted between an adult man from the Pinnacle mob and the same girl over whom Roger's brother had been speared. She was growing up at the Barrow Point camp with her stepparents, who came from the Mack River area near Cape Melville.

MARRYING WRONG

People used to come to our country from other areas farther west. Then they would mix up with our people. Old man Imbanda was a **Burrumun.ga** man, who became old Johnson's father-in-law. Johnson married Mary Ann. Imbanda was her father—well, really her stepfather. He was her **mugagay,** her uncle. She used to stay with Imbanda and his wife. I don't know who her real father was.

Now, old Johnson, they wouldn't let him get married to her, because he was a near relation. They were all near relations to us. Johnson and his brother were supposed to be like **mugur** [classificatory maternal uncle] to me, but later they changed it and told me they were like cousin-brothers. We all shared the same language. Toby Gordon called them "father"—they were like uncles to him.

Well, Johnson was always trying to get a wife.

That girl was staying permanently with her stepfather. We had moved to a camp at the Mack River. We were living in some little humpies there.

One night Johnson came over near our humpy. He said he was looking for a small billycan he had lost.

They said, "Nothing down here."

He was just putting it on, you see. He said, "Maybe it's over there?" He went over to the girl's humpy to look. Instead of searching for his billycan, he was trying to make love to her. It was night, and nobody saw what he was doing. That girl was only about sixteen years old at the time, staying with her stepfather. He just grabbed her and threw her down.

"I don't want you. Get out of here!" she said. She didn't like him, and she chased him off. He left her alone that night.

The next day he got his spear, and the disobedient fellow tried to spear old man Imbanda. Luckily the old man didn't get speared—Johnson missed him. Then they restrained him.

"Leave it alone! Don't spear him! Forget it!" they told him. He calmed down.

Not long after that they took me down to Cape Bedford. I never heard how he finally got married to that woman. When I left the camp, he was still a single fellow.

One day when I was working down in Mossman—just in recent years—I got to wondering: how did old Johnson finally manage to marry Mary Ann? I asked Toby Gordon. He told me the whole story.

They were staying to the west at Cape Melville, right on the beach not far from the point. There's a fresh water spring there, and they used to camp near it. After a while they decided to shift camp over to the east side of the point. There used to be an old path there, and it's not far to walk around to the east.

They started to shift camp. All the adult men were walking along. They had spread out to look for game.

The ladies, too, were carrying their stuff around to the east side of the Cape. They walked and walked. Before they had reached the beach, that girl Mary Ann—she was still unmarried at the time—stepped on a sharp stick. It lodged in her foot. She sat down and began to weep. She couldn't pull the stick out, and the other women started singing out for help.

Now old Johnson wasn't too far away from them. He heard them calling out, and he thought, "Maybe someone is trying to abduct our women."

So he called back, "Oooy!"

"Come here! Come here!"

He went north and found them. "What's wrong?"

"She has a stick lodged in her foot."

Johnson had a look. He pulled the stick out. He bound her legs, and then he just lifted her up. The old lady—her auntie—couldn't say anything about it. She couldn't stop him.

They continued east. He was carrying her on his shoulders. He said to her, "Look. Now you aren't going to leave me. Now you must stay with me." He was trying to cast a sort of spell on her.

When they got to the east side of the cape, he made himself his own house, separate from the rest of the camp. Old Imbanda and his wife couldn't say anything. They just left the matter that way. And from that time on, he kept that woman until he himself died, down in Yarrabah.

Other marriages contravened normal standards of propriety not because of incorrect kin relations, but because the forced relocation of Aboriginal people by government and mission authorities brought together strangers whose kinship relationship could not be easily reckoned. This happened to Barney Warner, a Barrow Point man who had gone as an adult to live at the Cape Bedford Mission. He had only one child, the product of a union with a widow whose tribal land was well to the south near Proserpine.

THE THIEF'S WIDOW

There was a man at Cape Bedford called **Marrbugan**, 'Cave'. Once he stole some tinned meat, which he had found on a white man's boat that used to be tied up at the old mission wharf. He was hungry, and he ate the meat.

Missionary Schwarz came to hear about the theft. He said, "Who ate that meat?"

Poor Marrbugan confessed. "I ate it," he admitted.

They wouldn't keep him on the mission after that. He had to be sent away for stealing from that white man. Schwarz said to Marrbugan and his wife: "Go! Leave!"

About that time Barney Warner came up from Cooktown. He was working on boats all the time, and he passed through the mission camps on his way home.

Marrbugan asked him, "Where are you headed?"

"I'm going west to Barrow Point."

"I'd like to go with you," said Marrbugan. He was half sick, too. I think he had a guilty conscience, or maybe he was sick from eating that tinned meat.

Anyway, Missionary Schwarz approved the plan. He said to him, "Leave now. Go with Barney to his country."

So they set out. They headed north. The first night they camped at the McIvor River mouth. Marrbugan was feeling worse. Barney couldn't persuade him to stop there. "You stay here, and I'll go on by myself," he told him, but Marrbugan wanted to keep going.

They set out again and finally came to Cape Flattery. Marrbugan was really weak now. "Stay here," Barney told the sick man and his wife. "You're too sick to keep traveling." But he couldn't persuade them.

They shifted once more, traveling west now. They came to a place just to the east of Point Lookout. The beach is called **marramarranganh**. They camped there.

Marrbugan was very sick and also very hungry. Barney said to the woman: "You stay here and look after him. We need some food." He headed out fishing.

While Barney was fishing, poor old Marrbugan died. His wife went to call Barney. "Come," she said, "he has died."

Barney returned to camp and dug a grave for the dead man. They buried him right there. Barney wouldn't just leave him though. They stayed and waited by the grave for a long time. They camped there for several weeks. Finally, when they had mourned him long enough they had to decide what to do.

Marrbugan's wife was one of the people from the south, from the Marie Yamba Mission near Proserpine.[8] Her name was Daisy.

Barney didn't want to take that woman with him to Barrow Point. He was afraid of what the other people would say. Why was he bringing a strange woman home with him? They would get angry. He couldn't run off with her himself.

"I think I'd better take her back," he decided. Off they went again to Cape Bedford.

Missionary Schwarz met them. "Barney. So you've come back again?"

"Yes, I have brought this woman back. Her husband died after all."

Schwarz must have thought they had been living together for a long time already. "Why didn't you just take her to your country in the west?"

"No, I brought her back."

Even the woman's kinsmen at the mission urged him to take her away with him. They were all George Bowen's[9] people, from Proserpine. "Take her." They freely wanted to give her to him.

But all the Barrow Point people told him he couldn't marry her. "Leave her," they said.

He began to feel shame for having stayed with her. "Well, never mind," he thought, "I'll leave her."

After a while he set out again, alone, back to Barrow Point. He stayed there in the camps with us then.

That woman had a little girl, and later she married another man. George Marie Yamba his name was, from her own country down Bowen way. That little girl, Barney's daughter, was called Connie.

Connie went to school with the other girls at Cape Bedford until the missionary sent a big mob of them away to live at McIvor. That is where she died.

~~~~~~~~~~~~~~~~~~~~

The Porcupine

Here's a story about porcupine.[1] I call it *arriyil,* and in Guugu Yimithirr they call it **balin.ga**. This story belongs to the beach south of Barrow Point. Bama used to hunt for porcupines near a big swamp just inland from there. I don't know if all those porcupines are still there. Maybe they've died out by now. (See Pl. 4.)

Some porcupines live in the soft ground near the swamps, but not in the water. People used to set bush fires near the swamps. They would walk over the burned country hunting for food. They could see where the porcupine had dug its cave. It would show up like a lump in the ground. Then they would dig out the animal and kill it for its meat.

Long ago porcupine used to be a human being, a woman. Porcupine-

Figure 8. Balin.ga hunting

girl was terribly disobedient. She wouldn't listen to anybody. We say *uyiin-mul,* 'no ears'. She used to go off by herself, walking all around, hunting.

Now this girl had a baby. She had to look after her child. Who knows if it was a boy child or a girl child?

When the baby grew, porcupine thought, "Well, this baby is a little bit bigger now. I can leave it with other people and let them take care of it. That way I can go off hunting on my own."

After that, she would go off every day hunting. She would leave her baby with someone else, and they would have to look after it for her.

Once, after the porcupine-woman had left it for a good while, the baby got hungry. The baby was crying. The people went out looking for the mother. They sang out to her, "Where are you? Your baby's hungry!"

She answered them from the south. "Here I am."

But when they went down to the place where she had answered, she wasn't there.

Figure 9. Balin.ga speared

They called out for her again. "Where are you?"

Again she answered, "I'm over here, to the east!"

They went looking to the east, but she wasn't there.

Now they called out to the north.

"Here I am."

"Come back. Your baby is crying for you."

When they went north to look, there wasn't a sign of her.

Finally they went to the west and called out for her. "Where are you?"

"Here I am."

They kept on like that following the sound of her voice, but they could never find her. The people began to get wild with her. They all went back to camp and picked up their spears. Once again they began to search for her.

She kept doing the same thing. She would call out from all sides, and the people would go around following the sound of her voice.

"I am over here."

But now they were getting closer to where she was calling out.

"Aha! Here she is!"

They took their spears, and they speared her properly. They speared her and speared her. They left her totally covered with spears. Those same spears turned into her quills today.[2]

Now when you see porcupine walking around covered with spines, those are really bama's spears.

~~~~~~~~~~~~~

Nganyja

Aboriginal law defined proper behavior around powerful "story places." Large stones mark the earth oven at Jones's Gap where the Magpie brothers butchered and cooked the Devil Dingo. Roger Hart says that people would not pass too close to the spot. When they were nearby, they would remain silent, speaking if at all in hushed tones, anxious lest they attract the attention of the giant dog.

The boulders on the east side of Barrow Point were also avoided, probably because they concealed ancient graves. People walking that way would pass in silence. The custom was to throw leaves onto the path. Before starting up the mountain, people would break a few branches and carry them along, laying them down one by one as they passed silently over the crest of the hill.

On the range of mountains just inland from Cape Bowen was another sacred place, a bald spot surrounded by a small round scrub. As a child Roger Hart was taught that when a person from his tribe died, his or her spirit would travel first to that spot, atop the mountain at Cape Bowen, where it would rest for a time. Afterwards the spirit was said to fly north. "It didn't go up to heaven but to New Guinea."

A **yiirmbal,** or guardian spirit creature, was said to inhabit **Wurrguul-nyjin,** Noble Island, east of Cape Bowen.[1] This was a place that the old people told Roger one could not visit. Barrow Point canoes always stayed well to the south of the island when traveling along that coast.

BURIAL

Complex practices and ritual prohibitions surrounded the treatment of the dead. Roger Hart has particularly strong memories of this aspect of the Barrow Point life from his childhood. A newly deceased person would be buried under ground. After about a week the rest of the group would dig the body up again and take it out of the grave. They would take off all the skin just as, in Roger Hart's comparison, one skins a scalded pig. They would also pull out all the hair, separating the hair from different areas of the body. This they would make into amulets, to pass on to the deceased's relatives.[2] The body prepared in this way was called **munun urdiiga** '[with] skin opened/removed.'[3] When they had finished cleaning the corpse, they would bury it again.

Once the body was fully decomposed, the dead person's relatives would collect the bones, especially those of the chest, the legs, and the head, leaving the other remains in the grave. They placed the selected bones in a bark trough, which they carried for several months as they shifted from camp to camp. Only after about six months of such care would they finally finish mourning the deceased and take the bones to a mountain cave to be hidden away permanently. The burial site was thereby rendered "sacred" or "taboo."

ETIQUETTE

Aboriginal law, even in the somewhat desperate social conditions of Barrow Point in the first part of this century, extended to realms of conduct more mundane than marriage rules and taboo places. Proper behavior was partly a matter of ways of talking: polite and impolite, respectful and insulting, angry and conciliatory. There were also rules about silence. Roger Hart's stories about life in the Barrow Point camps give glimpses of propriety and impropriety, about how people were supposed to comport themselves as well as how they actually did.

Alongside stories of spearings and physical violence, Roger remembers how old people dealt with verbal aggression. When the party of adults who had taken Roger to Cape Bedford Mission returned to their homeland without the little boy, one man in the camp became enraged over their decision to leave the boy behind.[4] "Why leave a child with white people?" he shouted, picking up his spears.

Rather than respond, the rest of the adults simply sat in silence, saying nothing. Had they spoken, Roger thinks, they would have provoked the angry man to action, and he surely would have speared someone.

"That was the rule. If someone shouted at you, wanted you to fight and argue, you didn't give him an answer back. You stayed silent. Whoever spoke up would be speared straight away. Better to let the angry one talk and calm down."

Story telling in the camps was a formal affair, often with a single orator, whom Roger characterizes as "something like a preacher." While the rest sat in the shade, one man would stand up and declaim. He would recount old spear fights, grudge or pay-back killings. He might pick up his own spear and wommera, acting out the events, showing how one protagonist hurled his spear, how another was hit or fell to the ground.

STORIES AND MISCHIEF

"One day Toby and I were digging in the ground behind the meeting place. One man was walking back and forth telling his story. He stepped backward without looking, and his heel caught on the edge of our hole. Down he tumbled.

"All the people jumped up then, wild with us, and they chased us down the beach."

Aboriginal Australia is celebrated for elaborate speech styles, including special vocabularies that were appropriate around people—especially certain in-laws—one had to treat with special respect.[5] Nothing remains of any such avoidance vocabulary from the Barrow Point language, but Roger Hart describes the special etiquette that surrounded interaction with men or women who stood in a potential mother-in-law or father-in-law relationship.

"They never used to talk to in-laws. If I had to do an errand like take something to my brother-in-law or father-in-law, I couldn't take whatever it was—food or something—straight over to the person and just give it to him. I would have to go carefully, bent over, carrying it with both hands, and set it down near him. He would pick it up. Then I would back away, still bent over. That could be for someone like a sister's husband, a mother-in-law, or a sister-in-law.

"Suppose I were going to give him some tea. I would have to hold the billycan up with both hands and hand it over very carefully."

In the camps, even children were taught to identify and show deference to potential in-laws, the relatives of the people who could properly become their husbands or wives.

"Even with a namesake, *wurri-yi*,[6] a person who shared my name, I had to do the same thing. He might ask me for tobacco. Well, I would hold it out to him with both hands and drop it into his hands without touching him. Sometimes you would take food to someone like that, but he would be facing away from you, facing north, say. You would set it down some distance away, to the south of him. When you went away, he could turn around from the north and pick it up.

"You had to respect such people. Even little children if they were naked couldn't approach their taboo relatives; they had to cover themselves with their hands or put something around their waists."

Male initiation, which still survived in some form into the 1920s, was closely connected with story places. Initiation brought together all parts of Aboriginal law, from knowledge of territory and tradition, to social norms and marriage rules. Most vivid in Roger Hart's memory is the initiation linked to **Mungurru** 'Carpet Snake', which he saw at Cape Melville.

NGANYJA

The mountain at Cape Melville where the bones of Mungurru are scattered was worshipped by bama. That's where all the young men were brought to be initiated, to be made **thabul** or *awiyi* 'sacred'. It was something like a festival.

Many of the young men had returned from the boats, which stopped work during the Christmas monsoon season. All the camps gathered together. The old people decided that it was a good time to do the ceremonies and to initiate the youths.

I was in the camp then, just a little boy.

The elders went around the camp picking out the uninitiated men and boys. They couldn't refuse.

"No, no, I don't want to be initiated."

"Never mind, you come anyway," the elders would say.

They took married men who hadn't been through the ceremony yet. They also took young boys. Only when a boy's grandmother would come and put a little breast milk on his head, then they wouldn't touch him—he was too small then. They did put that milk on my head, so I wasn't taken, but maybe they took Banjo. I'm not sure. Toby and I were a bit smaller. I think their father had just died a short time before that— sometime in the early 1920s. I think perhaps Johnny Flinders[7] and his older brother Diver were in that initiation, too.

They took all the boys, and they watched them closely. They were not allowed to eat any rubbish. If they drank honey, it had to be completely clean, strained of any bits of wax or other parts of the nest. They couldn't eat any eggs. When they were allowed to eat they could only take a little bit. The old people watched over them.

The initiates were not allowed to walk about. They couldn't visit their wives, if they were married.

We stayed in that camp for a long time, perhaps a month, and they watched over those boys the whole time. Then we shifted away from that place, heading south to Blackwater, near the turn-off that leads out to Eumangin on the beach. We set up camp there, north of the place they now call Billy's yard or Billy's paddock. That is a couple of miles from Cape Melville. Plenty of good water there.

They took all the new initiates there, too, although the rest of us were camped some distance away, apart from them. We weren't supposed to meet those young men, to look them in the face, or even to come close to them. They were **thabul,** you see. *Awurr awutha awiyi aamila* 'don't go to sacred ground'.

There were four or five old men there watching over the young men. One of those old men was **Ngamu Wuthurru,** and another was my father *Wanyjarringga,* but there were other elders, too, some from farther west, from Flinders Island or Princess Charlotte Bay. They built a special house near a small hill, digging a kind of pit in the ground all around. They kept the young men inside there. They used to go out to hunt and bring back meat. They would spear it, but they couldn't eat it.

The young men were not supposed to meet or talk to anyone: not their wives, not their children, not their relations. They were to stay well away from the rest of the camp for several months, even if the whole group shifted several times in the meantime. The ceremony might start in, say, January, and it wouldn't finish until March or April.

Well, I still remember one night. We were all lying down. It must have been about nine o'clock at night. The young men had their camp off to the east side, whereas our main camp was on the west side. We were asleep. My **mugagay** [senior uncle] Barney Warner was there, too. Maybe he was guarding the young men.

Suddenly I heard a loud noise. It was like an explosion, in the camp-fire over in their camp. It was just like dynamite or a cannon. Boom! People started to run in all directions.

As soon as they heard the explosion, the old men knew that something was wrong. "Don't run," they said. They spread out and started checking all the young men. Who was it?

One fellow was missing, you see. He had sneaked away to visit his wife.

They went straight to where that woman was. When they found the missing man, let me tell you—they nearly speared him on the spot. If there had been a more ill-tempered leader among the elders, they would have put a spear straight into him for breaking the law. This time, though, they let it pass.

Later I asked Barney about it. He told me it was the yiirmbal of that place that caused the explosion. He knew who the man was who had sneaked away, too. It was Nelson, the brother of Wathi—the same Nelson who died later at the mouth of the McIvor River.[8] He had gone off to sleep with his wife, you know, and they nearly killed him for his misbehavior.

"Don't do that next time," they warned him. "Leave such things aside. That's bad. The spirit of this place caught you," they said.

They knew the giant Carpet Snake had caused the explosion. Its spirit saw him sneak away and knew he was doing the wrong thing. The people had great faith in that mountain.

They never used to have such initiations at Barrow Point. Instead they would wait until people from all the camps gathered together at Cape Melville. That was the right place for it, because of the Carpet Snake mountain there. But they wouldn't have the ceremony every year, only every ten or eleven years. They would wait until a number of boys were big enough to be made **thabul.**

After the explosion, they decided to shift camp again. They told the rest of us to go to Eumangin. They would come along afterwards. So we moved out to the coast and waited for them.

I don't know what they were making those young men do. I suppose they were teaching them how to behave: not to do this, not to do that, teaching them the law. They kept them away from women, taught them to marry only the right way.

After some time, one of the old men came with a message. "They'll be arriving here tomorrow," he said. This business of making them sacred— I am not sure if it was the same as **nganyja**[9]—was coming to an end. So we waited. Round about two o'clock another message came: they were on their way; they were just to the west.

Around four o'clock, we could hear their shouts as they approached. They were carrying a long piece of tea-tree bark, and they danced along shouting and crying out. They would stop and then start up again, shouting and dancing. We watched them as they approached the beach, coming down from the west.

The women were all happy. "Our husbands are coming back," they thought, "The hunters are returning!"

The piece of tea-tree bark that they carried was very long, tied together out of many smaller bits. It was painted white and yellow to represent the Carpet Snake. They had decorated it themselves, using different clays to make the colors. Another part was red. They were trying to copy the markings of Mungurru.

They kept coming to the east. They left that long tea-tree snake behind, then. They took up their spears and continued to approach, bran-

Figure 10. Men dancing at initiation

dishing them. They had grass spears, with tips of wax. When they reached the beach to the east, they split up into two groups, the **thuuru** men on one side and the **walarr** men on the other.[10] Then they had a kind of mock war. They speared and speared each other with their wax-tipped spears until finally they had had enough.

That was the end. They were finished now. They had been made sacred. They knew the law about proper behavior and marriage. They could all go home. Some waited for the boats to come and pick them up, to take them back out diving for trochus shell. Others headed back to Instone's place or to the other camps.

Of course, some of those boys never got married at all. They went out on the boats. They got sent away, who knows where. They might have ended up down in Cherbourg or somewhere else in the south. A lot of those boat crew were Japanese, living up at Thursday Island, and maybe some of the boat crew got taken away to Japan and died there. Other boys would come back to marry and would find that people from the west had come down and stolen away their sweethearts.

That's all the story I know.

~~~~~~~~~~~~~~

Witches

Witchcraft and the fear of revenge by witchcraft were pervasive in north Queensland Aboriginal society in the early part of the century. Adults who came and went from the Cooktown area often took refuge in the "heathen" camps of non-Christian adults on the Cape Bedford mission reserve because they feared witches. "Well, a few of them old people were knocking around inside the mission boundary here. They used to go **dambun** [i.e., witch] one another," is how Roger Hart put it.

Revenge killings by witchcraft were often suspected many years after the events that gave rise to a grudge, and even in subsequent generations. Because native troopers took part in the abduction and murder of other Aborigines, they or their descendants were especially vulnerable to revenge. Several men in the Barrow Point camps worked as trackers for one Sgt. McGreen at the Laura police station, and they were implicated in the removal of people to penal settlements such as Palm Island. Later, according to Roger Hart, other people "knew they had been trackers and had sent many of their relatives away. Well, they couldn't catch that bloke [i.e., the tracker himself], so they turn around [and do something] to his children."

Roger Hart heard from old Mickey Bluetongue[1] one version of the events surrounding the death of old man Billy McGreen,[2] a native trooper originally from one of the Barrow Point clans. The events took place at Elderslie, a property on the McIvor River where a semipermanent Aboriginal camp lasted until the 1930s. McGreen, whose clan area was **Manyamarr,** south of Cape Bowen, had been involved in the arrest and deportation of many Aboriginal men and women. For example, in the late 1920s he was reported to have come across Charlie Burns[3] while the latter was chopping honey at Glenrock, another property on the McIvor River. Long Billy offered him tobacco. When Burns approached, McGreen slipped handcuffs on the other man and delivered him to the police for "removal" to Palm Island for an offense that people now remember as cattle theft.[4]

Some years later, a group of people came up to the McIvor from another large Aboriginal camp at Flaggy on the Endeavour River with the express purpose of performing witchcraft on old Billy McGreen. They made a large fire and heated an iron bar in it. This bar was then magically used to cause McGreen's death.[5] "But when they do that thing, when they witch that bloke, you don't see anything on the person's body. It leaves no visible mark."

People from one area were often suspicious of people from others. They would be constantly on the lookout lest some strange enemy manage to slip them a dangerous substance or catch them with a spell. In the Guugu Yimithirr area, people from Barrow Point and elsewhere in the west were feared as potential witches. When they came to visit, the Barrow Point people camped separately from the others and kept separate food supplies and campfires. The late Peter Gibson, from Hopevale, recalled that as a young man he used to sneak across the mission boundary in order to visit the old people at the McIvor River, who would give him tobacco. On one visit he was invited by the Barrow Point people to have a drink of wild honey in a **bila,** or leaf cup. Afraid to drink their offering, Gibson followed the example of old man Fog: he poked a hole in the **bila** and pretended to finish the honey while secretly letting it all run out.

In the Barrow Point group itself there were several people known to be dangerous. The legendary Ngamu Wuthurru (Old Man of the Night) was already grizzled and ancient, with white hair and a full beard, before Roger Hart was taken to Cape Bedford.

All the people at Barrow Point used to get a bit nervy for him, because he had the habit of witching people. Barney Warner told me a story about him. It was after I had left the camp. A little girl had died at Iipwulin, and they had buried her. One day, some months after that, all the men were sitting around telling stories. Ngamu Wuthurru spoke up. The little girl was already in her grave.

He said, "I have killed many men. I have witched them. I started right down in the east. *Ugu imbay-ayu.* I killed this one. I killed one at **Thi-ithaarr** (Cape Bedford). Then I moved west. I killed another one at **Yuuru** (Cape Flattery). Then I killed another at **Thanhil** (Point Lookout). Then I moved along, farther and farther west. I killed another at **Galthanmugu** (Red Point), another at Wuuri (Cape Bowen). I have [magic] bones for killing people," he told them.

Well, they heard him bragging about witching people all the way from Cooktown to Barrow Point. Then they thought, "So, probably this old man was the one who killed that little girl."

They grabbed him. They took him south to the lagoon. Some started chopping wood. Others went hunting. One man had a flat iron bar, and he smashed Ngamu Wuthurru with it. The old man fell down.

Just at that moment there was a very loud noise. All the people were frightened, so they left the old man there, right by the lagoon. Perhaps the spirit of that place caused an explosion, because they had tried to kill the old man. When they heard the noise, they all went running back to their camp, leaving Ngamu Wuthurru for dead.

They waited for a good long time, and then they ventured back to the lagoon to look for him. They found the place empty.

"Where has he gone?" they thought.

They started searching for him, all around there to the south. Finally their search took them back to the beach. The other people from the camp, who had been hunting, had heard the noise. "What was the explosion?" they asked.

"Well, we killed the old man there to the south, by the lagoon. Who knows what the noise was?"

They kept looking around. They were sure Ngamu Wuthurru must be dead, you see, because that metal bar had cut him deeply in the forehead. They blamed him for the death of the little girl.

But they hadn't killed him after all. By and by my father just happened upon that old witch, sitting down by himself, still alive.

"They tried to murder me," he said.

My father warned him. "You just go on and keep killing people! You'll see what happens to you then," he said.

But Ngamu Wuthurru didn't stop witching people. Many years later he was camped at **Muguulbigu,** north of where Hopevale is today. He went out hunting with old Norman Arrimi—Roy Dick's father.

They found some honey, and they came down to the creek at Billy Boil to mix it with water. The old man started to brag again. "I killed this fellow, and I killed that fellow, and then again I killed this other fellow."

His companion also got to thinking. "Aha, perhaps he's the one who killed my wife."

Arrimi grabbed his tommyhawk and planted it right in that old man's chest. He, too, left him for dead.

Then he went back to his camp. The other people asked him, "Where's that old man?"

"I don't know," he replied. "Who knows where he is?"

But the very next day, late in the afternoon, that old man appeared in camp again. "They tried to kill me," he said.

He must have had nine lives like a pussycat, I think.

In later years, when he was an extremely old man, Ngamu Wuthurru's exploits as a witch were still known to people living on the Cape Bedford mission. It was said that he could appear on a boat anchored off the

coast, causing crew members to choke in their sleep.[6] He was also reputed to have had a wrestling match with King Jacko, of the Cape Bedford Reserve, after the latter had caught him trying to sneak up on the
Bridge Creek camp, where many non-Christian adults lived.[7]

~~~~~~~~~~~~~~~~~~

The Problem of 'Half-Caste' Children

When Roger Hart was a child, travel was the norm for Aboriginal people.
The coastal camps had become refuges for people who claimed widely
scattered areas as their own. Roger remembers that speakers of half a
dozen different languages lived off and on in Barrow Point camps. Many
of these people came from the north, but even Guugu Yimithirr speakers from far to the south, from Cooktown and the McIvor River, camped
at Iipwulin. Roger's kinsmen from inland around Laura would walk
across the Jack River, through Jones's Gap, and out to Wakooka and Barrow Point, visiting for weeks or even months before returning the way
they had come.

Aborigines were driven to travel partly by a desire for European
goods, such as tobacco, flour, metal tools, and blankets, which they
could earn in exchange for work. They also responded to the rhythm of
the seasons. In the winter months, when the weather was fine, people
would live on the coast, fishing and hunting. When the rainy season
was upon them, from January to June, they would head inland, chopping honey, hunting bandicoots, perhaps picking up a few dingo pups,
and settling in areas around Wakooka, Tanglefoot, and the Pinnacle
Range. As the weather permitted, they would return to their coastal
camps, coming again into contact with settlers like Instone or Hart and
the ubiquitous Japanese fishing boats.

In the first two decades of this century the missions and the government, under the auspices of the protectors of Aborigines and their en-
forcement arm, the native police, took an ever widening interest in regulating—and ultimately eliminating—Aboriginal camp life. By the time
Roger was a child, the people at Barrow Point actively avoided areas
where they ran the risk either of violence or of being "removed" to penal settlements in the south. When King Nicholas, the government-
appointed spokesman for the Barrow Point camps, would return from

work at Instone's place with news of impending police visits, in Roger's words "bama [would] just roll up [their swags] and get away." Native trooper Chookie McGreen, Roger's maternal kinsman, worked as a tracker for the Laura police station. Although he was careful to warn his relatives of impending raids, so that the Barrow Point children would not be removed from their parents, several children from Cape Melville were nonetheless taken away in the 1910s.

Ironically, life was freer and more secure for Aboriginal men and women who worked for European settlers than for those who remained in bush camps. Nonetheless, living in proximity to white people was fraught with other dangers. People who set up camp with their families on European properties exposed themselves to the whims of their landlords. The Wallace brothers, long-time property owners at the McIvor, were notorious for flogging Aborigines, both men and women, who were caught hunting honey or game and "unsettling" the cattle. Although their children were less likely than those living "wild" in the bush to be sent away to reformatories, Aboriginal parents living under the "protection" of European landlords were liable to have their children abused in other ways.

The clearest evidence of the interactions between Aborigines and the foreign invaders of their territory is indirect: the proliferation of part Aboriginal children, called in the parlance of the time "half-castes."[1] Government policy had long considered the very existence of such children not only a problem but an embarassment. As early as 1896, the northern protector of Aborigines, Archibald Meston, in a report on Aboriginal conditions in Queensland, viewed the circumstances with alarm. He wrote that "freedom for the [Aboriginal] women to come and go when and where they please will ensure a permanent increase of half-caste population."[2]

Northern Protector of Aborigines Roth's 1899 report described what he regarded as a common practice, infanticide of light-skinned children born to Aboriginal mothers. He outlined plans to improve the situation, essentially by abducting children—especially part Aboriginal and female children—and placing them in institutions.

> It is . . . quite within the realms of possibility that when once the blacks can be made to understand the intentions of the Government in making provisions for these waifs, this form of infanticide will cease. The little girls have especially claimed my active and earnest solicitude, and arrangements continue to be made for their removal to different Mission Stations. My recommenda-

tions . . . are not necessarily made on account of present ill-
treatment, etc., but only for the future welfare, care and happiness of the children themselves. It is far better to know that all
such are ultimately legally married and protected by the missionaries, and through them by the State, than to realise that as soon
as they get old enough to be tampered with by unscrupulous
whites—the present normal condition of things—they are sent
back into their camps as bad girls and left there to ultimate disease and ruin. My efforts to ameliorate the condition of the little
true-blooded girls lie in a similar direction.[3]

In his 1901 report, Roth bluntly assessed the future of part Aboriginal
children.

Half caste children should enlist our sympathies perhaps even to
a greater extent than the full-blood ones. If left to themselves the
majority of the girl half castes ultimately become prostitutes, and
the boys cattle and horse thieves.[4]

In some parts of Queensland part-Aboriginal children were especially
sought after as domestic servants, prompting Roth to further observa-
tions.

As no inconsiderable animus appears to have been unwarrantably
raised among certain sections of the public over my action in ad-
vising the transfer of half-caste and true-blooded children from
the hands of private employers to the various Mission Stations
and Reformatories, it may be as well to state here that all action
. . . has invariably been with a view to carrying out . . . the spirit
of the law . . . My chief aim is to ensure the future welfare and
happiness of the children themselves . . . As things are at present,
the majority of these female children are engaged mostly as
nurse-girls, kept in a false position by being brought up as "one
of the family"—a fact which will probably account for their receiving no regular wages—and when they get into trouble are
no longer wanted, but packed off to shift for themselves as best
they can.[5]

Exactly such a case almost a decade later can be inferred from correspondence, dated 20 April 1910, between the chief protector of Aborigines in Brisbane and the Cooktown protector of Aborigines, Sgt. Bod-

man. Bodman requested a removal order for a half-caste woman who was in the employ of a Mrs. Gorton, on the McIvor River.

> She has a half-caste girl since she was 4 years of age . . . given to her by Dr Roth. This girl is now seventeen years of age . . . She is now in the family way and expects to be confined very shortly. This half-caste will not say who the father is. Mrs Gorton is very anxious that this half caste should be sent to Yarrabah [an Anglican mission station outside of Cairns] as soon as possible.[6]

"WAIFS AND STRAYS"

At the turn of the century, Roth had envisioned that missions and reformatories should be special refuges that would offer practical training to Aboriginal children, especially those of mixed ancestry.

> Many employers have screened themselves behind the 4th section of the Act, which does not deem to be 'aboriginals' those half-castes who . . . were not living or associating with aborigines as children . . . I was obliged to have recourse to the Reformatories Act; without the latter I could have claimed no rights whatsoever for these little waifs and strays . . . The State takes upon itself the responsibility—a serious one, to my mind—of taking such children from their aboriginal environments, but at the same time hands them over to the various Mission Stations which are now under direct Government supervision and control.[7]

The Cape Bedford Mission, where Roger Hart was destined to land, was one of the mission stations Roth had begun to use to implement his plans. Missionary Schwarz had for many years refused to accept the "waifs and strays" that the protectors of Aborigines wanted to send his way, hoping instead to insulate the small population of newly Lutheran Aborigines from evil outside influences, both black and white.

Circumstances conspired to force him to change his policy. First, the sister Lutheran mission on the Bloomfield River, south of Cooktown, ran into serious difficulties, including the birth of a light-skinned child whose mother was a Christianized mission inmate and whose self-confessed father was a European mission worker.[8] Ultimately both mother and child were banished to Cape Bedford, obliging Rev. Schwarz to accept at least one locally produced part-European child onto the mission.

Second, the failure of the Lutheran Marie Yamba Mission near Proserpine just at the turn of the century meant that a large group of Aborigines from the Bowen area was also sent to Cape Bedford. Some of these people were part-European, and one of them grew up to be an important leader at Cape Bedford who later established a large and influential family.[9]

Several other light-skinned children whose treatment in the bush brought them to the attention of the local Cooktown authorities also found their way to the Cape Bedford Mission, sometimes as a result of direct petition from their Aboriginal parents who preferred to deposit them with Missionary Schwarz than to leave them on the "outside."[10] Archival sources document the case of Dora, the woman who was later to become Roger Hart's mother-in-law.

DORA, DAUGHTER OF MATYI THE RAINMAKER

Rev. G. H. Schwarz, the missionary at Cape Bedford, maintained cordial relations with the first northern protector of Aborigines, Dr. Walter E. Roth.[11] In February 1902, Schwarz wrote to Roth shortly after the protector had visited Cape Bedford. In his letter Schwarz mentions that he hopes to get a few new children for the Hope Valley school from surrounding tribes, especially the group of Aborigines living on the McIvor River. He goes on:

> That half caste among them, a girl about ten years of age, of whom I was speaking to you is still in the camp. Her relations do not want to leave her here, but it is a pity to see her grow up in the camp. Could you not have her removed to Yarrabah?[12] It would be good for her if she could be taken away soon. Her mother's husband is Matyi, the rainmaker among the McIvor blacks.[13]

This casual mention comes in the first letter of an extensive file among the records of the northern protector of Aborigines. The file relates to the official disposition of the girl Dora, who eventually was taken to the Cape Bedford Mission, went to school there, married, and raised four children, including one daughter who later became Roger Hart's wife.

Within a week of receiving Schwarz's letter the northern protector of Aborigines had written to the undersecretary for Home Affairs asking for "authority to have this child brought before the Cooktown bench as a neglected child and sent to the Yarrabah reformatory."[14] Shortly thereafter, Roth instructed the Cooktown police to arrange for Dora's removal, suggesting that Rev. Schwarz could give them more information about the girl's whereabouts. There followed several months of wrangling while Constable Kenny of Cooktown tried to take the girl from a settler named Charles Wallace, who held her at Glenrock, his property on the McIvor River.

The first attempt to remove the little girl was on 23 June 1902. Constable Kenny reported calling at Glenrock where he had heard that the girl "has been employed occasionally." His description in dry police prose continues:

> The constable informed Wallace that he was instructed to take the half caste and send her to the reformatory at Yarrabah. Mr. Wallace at once sent her inside and shut the doors as she was on the verandah at the time. He then informed the constable that she could only be taken by force as he would not consent to give her up, as she was given them by her parents and he intended to fight it out. The constable then took no further steps but informed Mr Wallace that he would notify his superior officers with whom he Mr Wallace would have to deal in future.[15]

In a subsequent note, Kenny explained that Wallace had applied for an official permit to employ the little girl the preceding February, but that shortly thereafter the girl had run away from Glenrock and no permit had been issued.[16]

For his part, Charles Wallace wrote directly to the home secretary asking to be allowed to keep the girl.

> I am writing to you in reference to a half caste gin. Constable Kenny came out to my place and wanted to take her away. I objected to him doing so until he shewed me some authority for doing so. I know myself that it is the law that they shall all be taken from the blacks, but the facts of the case are this: that the father and mother of this gin brought her in to my place and begged of my wife to take her and keep her. I may also tell you I have a half caste boy from the same tribe and have had him ever since he was a baby, and he is about 10 years old. The mother has just about died, and makes me promise I would look after the boy. How that promise has been carried out can largely be ascertained if you wish to make any enquiries. I am sending him in a p[rimary] school here with my own two children. . . . The gin herself does not want to leave.[17]

Although Wallace was notorious then (as today in people's memories) for mistreating the Aborigines who lived on or near his property, he portrayed his relationship with them in a positive light.

Dr. Roth[18] can also if he wishes inform you of the treatment my wife would be likely to give any child, although he and myself had a misunderstanding over blacks, I am quite certain he is too much of a gentleman to stoop to saying anything false on that account. I can't understand why this particular gin has been singled out to you when there are many others employed by my neighbours about the same age, and who haven't been taken . . . You must have been led to believe she was still with the tribe. She is perfectly contented and happy. I think you will see she does not wish to be forced away against her own parents' wishes . . . She and my children have become very much attached to each other and I don't like to part with them.[19]

Because of the settler's protests and complaints it was not until August of the same year that official moves were again taken to have the girl Dora removed to Yarrabah. The protector of Aborigines was by this time considering legal action against Wallace, basing his position on a further detailed report furnished by Constable Kenny:

The constable reports the half caste above alluded to has been known to him for the past four years and during that time she has been in the blacks' camp until recently. Her mother belongs to the tribe known as the Binjouwara[20] and about fifteen months ago a young black from a neighbouring tribe was desirous of annexing her according to their custom. This the parent objected to and the tribe to which the black belonged being the stronger of the two the parents became alarmed that their girl would be taken by force. As a result she was taken and placed for protection in Mr. Gorton's care where she remained a short time until the feud had been settled, when she again returned to her tribe, at this time camped at McIvor River near Mr Wallace's, and at whose place the Constable next saw her. Mr Wallace informed him, the Constable, that the parents have given the half caste to him and he applied in the usual way for a permit. The blacks however told the constable that Mr Wallace had given the parents a bag of flour for the half caste. The constable at that time was on his way to the Starcke goldfield, and on his return he called at Mrs Wallace and [she] informed him that the half-caste Dora had ran [sic] away, and asked the constable to bring her back and caution the blacks not to keep her. This the constable refused and informed Mrs Wallace that it was no use forcing half-caste into agreement if she was not willing to stop with her. This took place at the end of February of this year 1902. Some time afterwards the constable learned that Mr Wallace had brought the half caste back and was subsequently informed by a European that she had again ran away, which she did several times, and each time Mr Wallace brought her back. On the 23rd of June 1902 the constable called at Mr Wallace's and at the same time read a communication to him which he the constable had received through his inspector, instructing him that the minister had authorized the removal of the half caste to the Yarrabah Mission Station. Wallace refused to give her up, telling the constable that she would have to be taken by force, the authority was not sufficient, and in any case he intended to fight it out and see whether the half-caste could be taken from him or not. Shortly after Wallace again applied for a permit to employ the half caste Dora which was objected to by the police and refused by the protector. The only thing known about Mr Wallace in his dealing with the blacks is a complaint by the blacks in May '99 when they informed the constable that Mr Wallace had used the stock whip upon them, and threatened to shoot them if they did not keep away from his cattle, many of which were running on the Aboriginal Reserve at the time.[21] The constable told the boys to inform Dr Roth. As regards Mr Wallace himself, he is an old resident of this district, and so far has no police record against him. Although his actions at times are not above suspicion. As regards to the home, she would be far better off at Yarrabah, where she would be removed from the immediate vicinity of her tribe and the influence which the tribe and parents would exercise over her, in spite of all Mr Wallace's care and vigilance, and furthermore she has shewn by repeatedly absconding that she is not by any means content to remain in the employ of Mr Wallace.[22]

Roth, commenting on Kenny's report, writes that "on my way out to Cape Bedford I came across Dora's father, Matyi 'the rainmaker' who told me also that Wallace had bought the girl for a bag of flour some sugar and tobacco, and that he had seen her on a chain."[23]

In September 1902 the Home Office again issued orders that Dora be taken from Glenrock and removed to Yarrabah. Wallace continued to protest that he was being unfairly singled out since "there are other half castes about here."[24]

In October 1902, Constable Kenny reported that Dora had again run away from Glenrock. Her tribe had taken her to Cape Bedford and asked Rev. Schwarz to keep her.[25] There followed a further wrangle in which Wallace accused the police constable of having threatened Matyi with deportation unless he handed his stepdaughter Dora over to the authorities.[26] Kenny answered Wallace's charges in a subsequent report.

> The last time the Constable saw Matyi, father of the half-caste Dora prior to her [removal . . .] to the Mission station by the blacks, the constable was accompanied by Dr Roth and the Rev Schwarz. Matyi then complained to those gentlemen that his child had been ill-treated by Mr Wallace. This statement Dora herself amply bore out when recently interviewed by the Constable at the Cape Bedford Mission School. The blacks themselves without any threat or inducement from the Constable took the half caste Dora to the Mission Station and entreated the Rev Schwarz to take the child and keep her. This the Rev Schwarz told the blacks he could not do. The blacks however went away and left the child at the station. Rev Schwarz then sent word informing the Constable of the fact. The Constable then wired Dr Roth for advice. That gentleman gave his sanction for Dora to remain at Cape Bedford.[27]

Despite Wallace's later complaint that Dora was put to work "doing housework at the Cape Bedford Mission station if what the blacks tell me is true,"[28] the little girl was allowed to stay at Cape Bedford. Some years later she married one of the mixed-descent young men who had come from the failed Marie Yamba Mission, a man from the Bowen area. Dora's children, in turn, all married people with non-Aboriginal ancestry. Her daughter Maudie married Roger Hart shortly before the Second World War.

By the end of the first decade of the century, its difficult financial situation obliged the Cape Bedford mission to accept several more waves of removals, including many children with mixed parentage, in order to guarantee continued government support. After several years at the mission, a group of "removed" children was baptized at Cape Bedford at Easter 1916, prompting Dr. Theile, the president of the Lutheran Church of Australia at the time, to offer the following thoughts about the "so-called 'neglected children'" who had come to Cape Bedford from all over Queensland.

> Most spoke good English when they came, which made schooling easier for them. Nonetheless some came directly from an Aboriginal camp and spoke not a word of English, but only their own tongues. For them the first few weeks on the station were difficult; for example three girls came from the west coast;[29] they knew not a word of English; they were not at all clean, and they had sore eyes and therefore hung dirty handkerchiefs over their heads, so as to look as becoming as they could. They soon learned that they were among friends and eventually joined in the play of the other children. It made one think of the 137th Psalm. It wasn't long before homesickness and homeland were forgotten and they were as happy and cheerful as the other children. What surprised me most was the speed with which they learned English. They were not full-Aborigines: one had a Japanese father, others had South Sea-Islanders as fathers. In fact, of the seventeen girls [baptized on this occasion], eleven were half-castes. But now they have all found their true home. Whatever their descent they have found their Saviour.[30]

Many of the children sent to Cape Bedford in the first decade of the century came from distant areas of Queensland, ranging from the northern tip of Cape York Peninsula to places as far south as Stonehenge.[31] At Cape Bedford they joined a community mostly derived from survivors of local Aboriginal groups from Cooktown, Cape Bedford, and the McIvor River. By the 1910s, however, children from the Cooktown hinterlands began to be sent to missions and settlements at an ever increasing pace, starting with children of mixed ancestry and gradually extending to any children caught in the bush.

Children from Roger Hart's people farther to the north were not spared. Four girls whose biological fathers were non-Aboriginal were removed from Cape Melville to Yarrabah in 1916, and another boy, their brother the late Bob Flinders, was taken from Cape Melville to Laura in 1918 and sent on to Cape Bedford the following year.[32] Roger Hart had faint memories of a visit to Laura Station with his mother in 1919, watching as Bob was taken away to Cooktown on the train.

~~~~~~~~~~~~~~~~~~

From Barrow Point to Cape Bedford

Roger Hart escaped abduction by native troopers. It was his own relatives who in the end gave him up to the care of the missionaries. (See Pl. 5.)

Roger's mother was called Alice in English. Her Aboriginal name, as recalled by the old people of Cape Bedford, was *Tharrwiilnda.* Her tribal country was Muunhthi, an area around the source of the Jack River. Her life was typical of many young women of her time: moving from place to place, abducted by a succession of men, both Aboriginal and non-Aboriginal.

Roger's mother was still a young, unmarried woman when she first came to the Wakooka area in the company of her brothers,[1] who worked for Maurice Hart at Wakooka Station. A large group of Aboriginal people from the region would camp near Wakooka at that time. People were on the move, arriving at the coastal camps and nearby properties from all directions, then moving on. As Roger put it, "young-fellow-**galaaygu**"— 'young people were like that'—in those days.

When Roger was born around 1916, his mother's husband was Charlie Lefthander, a claimant of the Gambiilmugu-warra mob from Barrow Point. The family moved between the old man's home base at Ninian Bay and other camps in the region. It is from his Aboriginal father that Roger derives his Barrow Point tribal affiliation.

As a boy Roger also had sporadic contact with his mother's relatives. He remembers, for example, a long canoe trip with his mother's father, along with another old man called German Harry, or **Wujilwujil,**[2] who took the boy all the way to Flinders Island and then down to Lakefield, where German Harry had a second wife.

When Roger was just a child, his mother was abducted by old man Wathi, Billy Salt, from the clan known as Wuuri-warra. A group of people from Barrow Point, including his mother, had gone to Laura "to get a bit of a smoke." Roger, who was a lad of no more than six, had stayed behind at Iipwulin, as had his father, "taking care of me, I think." His mother had intended to visit kinsmen in Laura. She never returned. Roger later learned that Billy Salt had stolen her away from Laura and taken her south, as far as Innisfail, and later back to Mossman.

"THE LAST TIME I SEEN THEM, AND NO MORE"

After his mother left Barrow Point, Roger's Aboriginal father began to find the presence in the camp of a small, motherless, light-skinned child to be more and more of a problem.[3] Native troopers had blanket authority to raid camps where part-European children were to be found and to take these children away by force. It was known that several light-skinned children had been picked up from Cape Melville and taken away to mission stations farther south. Some of the Barrow Point people were already planning a visit down the coast to the Lutheran mission at Cape Bedford, just north of Cooktown, in search of government rations. A decision was made to take the little boy along and leave him there. It was around 1923.

Roger's account of the trek south is a jumble of images, with many gaps and chronological twists. It is a dramatic and heart-wrenching tale, one well known to the people of the Cape Bedford community. A large group including Roger's Aboriginal father and several of the boy's playmates set out toward the south.

"We kept coming down the coast from the west. We didn't walk straight through. We would camp for a few days, might be two nights, and then off again; then another two nights a little farther on, and off again. Sometimes we'd jump into our dugouts, when it was rough country. When there was good beach, we would walk instead."

Roger had no idea why his tribe was taking him away. Even now his understanding of their motives is filled with ambivalence. "You see they wanted to get rid of me," he says, thinking of the native police who preyed on camps where part-European children were known to reside.

"I didn't know they were taking me to Cape Bedford you see. I heard that old fellow [his Aboriginal father] saying to me, '**Nhanu walaarrbi wuthinhu nagaar,**' I'm going to give you to the Beard there to the east.[4] Well, I couldn't understand what he was meaning."

On this trip, Roger Hart ventured farther from home than he had ever been before. They reached Cape Bowen, where he had camped once in a cave, but rather than turning back they continued down the coast.

"We stayed at Cape Bowen, camping for a few days. Then one morning we set out further east . . . We left the coast and traveled inland, I don't know how many days and nights, until we reached the Jeannie River, not far from the lagoon where Wurrey caught all the fish in his net. We went downriver in our canoes and kept on traveling down the coast.

"That is when they told me they were going to leave me with the white man, the **walarr** 'beard'. That's what they called the missionary at

Figure 11. Setting out with Roger

Cape Bedford, although I didn't understand them at that time. The kids started teasing me about it, and then the adults, too. They were all making fun of me. I thought they were joking. But I didn't cry about it until later, not until they finally left me at the mission."

The Barrow Point group passed through several large Aboriginal camps, first at Starcke, then on the McIvor River, where established groups of Aborigines lived near white settlers' properties. Roger met some of the children he was later to know at the mission.

"We stayed in the camp at Glenrock, on the McIvor. A big mob of Barrow Point people stayed there, but there were a lot of strangers, too. I was playing around with the kids. I remember Tom Charlie[5] and some others. But I was older than they were, see? They were a bit smaller."

At the same camp were several old men of the Cooktown tribes who mediated relations with the German missionary, Rev. Schwarz—known as **Muuni** 'black' in Guugu Yimithirr. These elders urged the Barrow Point people to deliver Roger to this man, known for his flowing white beard.

Ultimately Roger went to Cape Bedford with his father and one of the local elders, old man **Gun.gunbi.**

"When I saw Mr. **Muuni,** I was frightened of his beard, see?" Roger refused to move into the boys' dormitory, as the missionary instructed.

"I wouldn't go."

Figure 12. Roger tied up by his father

Instead, after staying at the mission only two days, Roger accompanied the adults back to the camps. The Barrow Point people remained for several months in the mixed, shifting communities of Aborigines who alternately squatted on the fringes of white settlement and led a more traditional life in bush areas around the McIvor River.

"We used to stay at the property called Flagstaff, on the north side of the McIvor River. I used to go over to the south side to **Buga Thabaga**. That's where **Dabunhthin**[6] lived. I would visit the camp there."

Missionary Schwarz did not forget about the little light-skinned boy, however, and he soon sent orders that Roger be returned to Cape Bedford to attend school.

"After a time, word came again. Schwarz asked, 'Where's that little boy gone?'

"'Oh, he's west at Glenrock.'

"'Bring him back, then.'

"It was old man Arthur, Willie Mt. Webb's father.[7] He came up to the McIvor with orders from Schwarz.

"'Hey, that little boy is wanted to the east. Better take him back.'"

Accordingly, Roger's father and some of his tribesmen went back to the mission station at Cape Bedford and handed the boy over to Mr.

Muuni. The missionary tried again to persuade the child to stay in the dormitory, where there were other part-European children his age.

"Schwarz said, 'All right, take him to the dormitory.' Leo Rosendale and Bob Flinders[8] came to take me, but I didn't want to go with them. I was frightened, and they didn't know my language. I didn't know English."

Schwarz dispatched the terrified little boy, with his father, to the wooden hospital building, at the edge of the mission settlement, where there was a large plantation of sisal hemp bushes. This time his father made sure Roger would not try to follow him back to the camps.

"We went south to the old hospital. My old man said, 'Come here.' He went off to the west and started breaking some sisal hemp shoots. Well, I didn't know what he was breaking them for. He took the shoots back east and sat down on the verandah. Then he started teasing the fibers, breaking the sisal hemp into strips. I was just sitting down there. I didn't know what was going on. He was making a rope.

"Suddenly he grabbed me. He tied my legs, and he tied my arms. He lifted me up. He put me inside the old hospital building, and he locked the door."

With Roger safely locked in the wooden hospital building, his Aboriginal father and the other Barrow Point men left Cape Bedford. The little boy, abandoned by his tribe and family in a Lutheran mission hundreds of kilometers from his home, with no near kinsmen and no one with whom to speak his language, was not to see his birthplace or return to the camps of his childhood for more than sixty years.

A Sunset Glow

Forced deportation of people from their Aboriginal homelands, children of mixed-ancestry, violent encounters between Aboriginal owners of the land and European and Asian invaders—all suggest the tumultuous and fragmented state of Aboriginal life during Roger Hart's childhood. Europeans in this period uniformly believed that the native people were destined for extinction, and in fact the same view had already been expressed decades before. Johannes Flierl, the Bavarian missionary who had founded the Cape Bedford Mission in 1886, wrote in his 1898 report on the progress of the tiny community:

> In our work in Elim and Hope Valley we ministered to the few people who represent the remnants of tribes which are dying . . . All the mission can really achieve for them is a kind of Christian burial service, a kind of promising sunset glow, which cannot be followed by any bright dawn in this life here on earth . . . Mission work is hard and not very rewarding, but it is sufficient to know, that we have at least some success in lighting the way to extinction with the guiding torch of God's Glad Tidings.[1]

Nearly thirty years later, a few years after Roger Hart's Barrow Point childhood had been supplanted by a Lutheran education at Cape Bedford, the social Darwinist confidence of the first years of contact between Aborigines and a European population convinced of its natural superiority had been somewhat tempered by a clearer, if still fatalistic view of the circumstances local Aborigines faced. Mission Director Theile described the camps nearby the mission in 1926 in the following terms:

> When 40 years ago the work amongst the natives of the Cooktown district was begun the Lutheran Mission had around it a large population of fullblood Aboriginals. Today the situation is totally different. Rev Schwarz says where today there are 10 natives there were 100 forty years ago. I.e., for the 200 under influence of the mission today there were then 2000, and the 200 of today are about two thirds full bloods and one third half castes. The Aboriginals as a people, as a nation, are dying out . . . there are still a few small camps of blacks to be found . . . but their ancient customs are gone, their old-time worship has vanished, and whatever moral force was contained therein has also gone. Hangers-on they are to the various cattle stations and small towns, campbummers, pitiable creatures . . . The white race has not dealt fairly with them, and as it has usurped the land which was the birthright of the Aboriginal, it has robbed them of self-respect, of manliness and of moral standing.
>
> They have no fixed place of abode; as nomads they roam about the bush, or they live semi-permanently near a township or a cattle station, sometimes working, sometimes hunting. Station owners and residents of townships and small towns rather

like such a camp of natives near by, it affords them opportunities of obtaining cheap labor—and the numbers of half-white children are proof of other uses these poor people are put to. The King of the McIvor blacks had two wives, he had no children of his own; his wives had three half-caste sons who are now under the care of Hope Valley Mission. The king, his wives, his tribe, all are dead. King Jacko[2] a few years ago decided to settle on the Mission Reserve, he brought along about forty to sixty people. They had six halfcaste children among them. On the Mission there are half-Europeans, half-Japanese, half-Malayan![3]

The Cape Bedford Mission Station became a last refuge for many Aboriginal groups. The Cooktown language, Guugu Yimithirr, was by default the *lingua franca* of the community, spoken by traditional owners, Aborigines from elsewhere, and missionary alike.[4] Guugu Yimithirr to a large extent supplanted other Aboriginal languages spoken farther away, such as Roger Hart's native Barrow Point language. Although small groups of Aborigines continued to live in independent camps both on and off mission territory until the Second World War, only the Lutheran enclave at Cape Bedford permitted continuity of social life for most Aborigines in the Cooktown hinterlands.

The Scrub Python at Cape Melville

This is a story about *Thuurrgha*, the Scrub Python. Guugu Yimithirr people call him **Mungurru**. His story starts at **Manyamarr**. This Scrub Python used to have his camp there, on the top of the mountain range just above Cape Bowen.[1] There is a mountain there that looks red in the afternoon sun. As a boy, I once camped in a cave on that mountain called *wundal uyiirr*—a place filled with rats. Near there was Scrub Python's camp.

Scrub Python would lie about in the day. At night he would crawl down from the mountain and hunt for food. In the morning when he woke up he would climb back up the mountain. There he would stretch out again in the sun.

Figure 13. Mungurru traveling

By and by, along came **Gujal**, the Eaglehawk. He started to annoy python by pecking at him. Poor python's skin began to get sore from all Eaglehawk's pecking. He began to ache all over.

Finally Scrub Python made up his mind to move. He descended from the mountain top. He crawled right under the earth, to escape his tormentor. He headed north, moving underground. He kept going north, kept going and going.

At last he poked his head up to look around. There's a little black mountain there, all alone, north of Wakooka, near the Mack River. That's where his head came out.

Well, he ducked down under ground again and kept going. He poked his head up again a little farther north. By now, his body was sick all over. When he came up out of the ground at Cape Melville, he could go no farther. His head was pointing north, out to sea, and his body was stretched out behind. By now he was dead tired and sick. There he died, with his head lying in the water to the north.

Up came flocks of little birds. There was Scrub Python, stretched out, dead. The birds began to eat his flesh. They pecked and pecked at his body. They stripped his bones clean. (See Pl. 6.)

Those bones little by little turned to stone. The sun burned them, turned them hard. There they remain to this day. People say that's the **guurrbi,** the sacred place of the Scrub Python. It belongs to Barrow Point people, to Cape Melville people, and to Bathhurst Head people. The final resting place of that python became the initiation ground for all those tribes.[2]

Part Three

DIASPORA

The Barrow Point People Visit the South

During the 1920s the Barrow Point people made two trips south to the Cooktown area, staying for extended periods at the McIvor River and at the Cape Bedford reserve. The first trip, in about 1923, was to leave Roger Hart at the Cape Bedford Mission. Roger's countrymen also wanted to visit relatives, both distant and close, living in the south. Unbeknownst to the Barrow Point people themselves, there were behind-the-scenes machinations between the government and the missionary at Cape Bedford that would soon bring the Barrow Point people south again.

THE PROBLEM OF THE NORTHERN TRIBES

Missionary Schwarz had been attempting for many years to persuade the government to allocate more coastal land to the Cape Bedford Mission north of its original boundaries. His concern was the economic survival of the mission, which had repeatedly failed to produce enough income and food to maintain its small but growing permanent population. Another of Schwarz's arguments to the government for extending the mission was to accommodate remnant tribes to the north and west.

As early as 1919, Schwarz had threatened to resign if the government failed to gazette more coastal lands in the area of Murdoch Point to serve as exclusive fishing grounds for mission boats.[1] Schwarz ultimately stayed on at Cape Bedford, although the government took no action on his request. By 1923—the year that Roger Hart was brought to the mission by his Barrow Point relatives—Schwarz had reiterated his desire to extend mission holdings. In a letter to the chief protector of Aborigines dated 17 December 1923, Schwarz

> applied for fishing rights along the foreshore up to Murdoch Point, with the idea of setting up a station on the mouth of the Starke River, with some land for cultivation. The idea . . . [was] that Aborigines from further north might be interested in settling there under the auspices of the Mission.[2]

The mission had already established a small farming outstation at Wayarego on the McIvor River. More farming and fishing sites at Starcke would dramatically increase the mission's ability to employ the labor of Aboriginal adults to produce food and income for the community as a whole. New land would also provide a suitably separated location for the tribes from the north that Schwarz hoped to bring under mission control.[3]

By this time, several Barrow Point adults had settled near Cape Bedford. In addition to old man Wathi (Billy Salt or *Alman.ge:r*), who had earlier run away from Barrow Point with Roger Hart's mother and had arrived in the Cooktown area, Jackie Red Point, Instone's former boatman, was periodically working around Cooktown. Also in the area were **Wanhthawanhtha** (known in English as Tommy Cook), Barney Warner, and another man called **Jujurr,**[4] who stayed at Bridge Creek on the mission reserve or in other seasonal camps on the McIvor and Endeavour rivers. All three had been young men at Barrow Point when Roger Hart was a child.

A FRIGHT

Mission people were supposed to avoid contact with those from outside the mission, both Europeans and Aborigines. Sometimes young men from Cape Bedford took advantage of the isolation of mission outstations to sneak across the mission boundary. One day two boys, Peter Gibson and Hans Cobus, set out to visit their relatives on the McIvor River. They were heading for the station at Elderslie. What they were after was tobacco.

Suddenly they got a fright. Someone sang out to them, from right up close.

"Hey, where are you two going?"

It was old man Jackie Red Point. He had been sitting by a big mango tree when he saw them coming. He ducked down to hide in the tall grass until he could make out who they were. When they came close he called out to them. They hadn't seen him, but they knew him when he showed himself. They were afraid he might report them for crossing the mission boundary.

Old man Jackie was on his way back from a trip to Barrow Point. He settled down around the mission after that. But he never said anything about those two boys to the missionary.

Another Barrow Point man who stayed at Cape Bedford was the former tracker and jailkeeper, Billy **Galbay,** or Long Billy McGreen, who set up his own camps near Bridge Creek and at **Ngandalin** on the north side of the McIvor River. Later Long Billy established a small camp at a mission site called Elim, and his wife Lizzie brought her kinswoman, Roger Hart's mother, to live there for a time. Billy McGreen was also known as Billy

Wardsman, since he had worked for the Cooktown police as a caretaker at the venereal disease camp and lockup at Cooktown.[5] The chief protector's suggestion to Rev. Schwarz that the former native trooper be sent to Barrow Point to help lure his countrymen down to Cape Bedford was the beginning of the end for Roger Hart's people.[6]

Toward the middle of 1925 the office of the chief protector of Aborigines began to investigate complaints against Europeans in the Cooktown hinterlands accused of abusing their positions as distributors of government relief for Aborigines. One of these was the telegraph lineman at the Musgrave Station, who was "no doubt the worst of a bad lot because not alone will he bully and sweat [the local Aborigines] but he will also satisfy his lustful passions on them where possible."[7]

The other complaint was against Alan Instone, the leaseholder at Barrow Point. The Laura protector had written:

> There is an aboriginal in Palm Island . . . who informed me that Mr Instone told him to work for a man named Wallace in the Laura district for a few shillings a week, out of which he he the boy stated he used to purchase tobacco from Mr Instone.[8]

The issue was whether Instone, whose settlement was a kind of unofficial supply depot for Barrow Point, was exchanging the free government relief, mostly blankets and tobacco intended for indigent Aborigines, for unpaid labor. The question was also raised whether Instone was supplying his neighbors with Aborigines for illegal employment.

> The practice of creating protectors such as Instone at Barrow Point . . . has a bad effect on aboriginals and makes the local protector's duties more difficult. As you are aware the natives, not unlike ourselves, are possessed of a certain amount of gratitude, and those that give them anything, especially tobacco or blankets, are looked upon by them as bigfellow boss. The latter in order to be good with his neighbour instructs the natives to work for them, and pays them for the services with tobacco etc. supplied for use of destitute aboriginals.[9]

Chief Protector Bleakley sought advice from Sgt. Guilfoyle, the Cooktown protector, clarifying the official situation as follows:

> Mr Allen Instone holds no appointment as a protector but by arrangement with one of your predecessors acted as a distributor

of blankets and such relief, the reason given being that dumping large supplies of blankets, calico, tobacco etc., on the beach for the native campers only resulted in waste.[10]

At the same time, the chief protector did not want tribal Aborigines brought closer to settled areas.

> While recognizing the likelihood of unofficial distributors of re- lief abusing the trust it would not be wise to do anything to en- courage the natives to hang around the towns. If in your view the depot at Mr Instone's place at Ninian Bay is not satisfactory, could not the Barrow Point people come to McIvor River outsta- tion of Cape Bedford [mission] for their blankets etc.?[11]

Protector Bleakley also initiated inquiries at Palm Island into Instone's alleged misdeeds, asking the superintendent there to interview Instone's accuser, both about the illegal employment practices and about In- stone's other activities.[12]

Sgt. Guilfoyle sent the following somewhat cryptic report on his in- vestigations.

> The man Instone has a motor launch and he resides at Barrow Point. I understand he keeps a small herd of stock there but he does not make a living out of the stock. He probably has plenty money or other ways of making money, as some of the move- ments of the motor launches between Cooktown, Cairns and Thursday Island are suspicious and when people who are not members of the police force or superintendents of missions or aboriginal settlements are made protectors of aboriginals, and supplied with blankets, tobacco, tomahawks etc. for distributing to aboriginals, the aboriginals are encouraged to hang around these person's homes and are worked without being paid any- thing for their labour, as some people in remote parts seldom sign on an aboriginal and they often use [Aborigines] to cut un- dergrowth along telegraph lines and remove flood rubbish in the wet season, and persons who sign on aboriginals complain of other people who do not.[13]

Immediately after receiving this report, Chief Protector Bleakley pro- posed to Rev. Schwarz at Cape Bedford that future "indigent relief" for the Barrow Point Aborigines be channeled through the mission and distributed at the Cape Bedford outstation on the McIvor River.[14] He confided in Schwarz his opinion that Instone was up to no good.

> The belief is that these men use the goods as trade for native labour for their own benefit, improperly presume on the appearance of official authority which such distribution gives them, by using the natives to oblige friends . . . there is apparently suspicion as to what use Mr Instone puts his launch to, probably opium traffic.[15]

He also asked Schwarz for his suggestions about what could be done to put the Barrow Point people and their northern neighbors under stricter supervision, cataloging the vices—opium, prostitution, and venereal disease—to which they were exposed in their homeland.

When Instone was informed that henceforth the yearly issue of blankets and food relief for the Barrow Point people would not be sent to him but was instead to be distributed by the Cape Bedford Mission,[16] he wrote to the chief protector defending his treatment of the "70 odd" Cape Melville and Barrow Point natives to whom he had been distributing government rations. He had also been "attending those were sick and giving them medicine provided by myself . . . I may say here I have strictly adhered to the honorable understanding of such distribution, and on no occasion asked the boys to do anything for me in return."[17]

At the same time, Instone made it clear that if he was to be denied the opportunity to distribute government supplies to the Aborigines on his property, he would rather be rid of them.

> McIvor is about 100 miles from Cape Melville so that the aboriginals of this country will have to walk 200 miles for their blankets etc. Most of the old people [for] whom I take it the blankets are particularly intended being quite uncapable of making this journey. I have taken a considerable amount of interest in these tribes and have done what I could to help them, and with your permission will continue to do so. But if McIvor or Cape Bedford Mission is to be the center for distribution in future I would suggest that the Cape Melville and Barrow Point aboriginals be removed and settled onto one or the other of these places where possibly in time they would become self supporting.[18]

Rev. Schwarz and the chief protector had already begun to try to work out a plan for removing the Barrow Point and Cape Melville people from their unsupervised lives in the north and onto the mission. Replying to Bleakley's earlier question how such a removal might be effected, Schwarz described how he understood the Barrow Point people to live.[19]

He first noted that there should be no difficulties about their traveling down the coast to the mission.

> I understand that the Aboriginals in question are all 'salt-water-blacks', and that therefore they have canoes and know how to use them. If they WISHED to come whatever is there to prevent them to come by easy stages along the coast, up and down which they, no doubt, have traveled many times before?[20]

He was positive about prospects for bringing them to Cape Bedford, since good relations had already been established between the Barrow Point people and others at the mission. If the Barrow Point people wanted (or could be made to want) to come they would have lots of friends and relations at Cape Bedford.

> Many of them have paid us occasional visits, stayed for a while and went back again. There are, for instance, two half cast boys in school here, one from Cape Melville,[21] the other from Barrow Point[22] who were visited only the other day by their brothers.[23] There is one Barrow Point family[24] at Bridge Creek (King Jacko is well known to all of them having been for many years on a cattle station up there[25]), another couple[26] was at the McIvor until the other day . . . Long Billy— the wardsman in Cooktown's old gaol, mentioned in your letter—asked my permission some time ago to settle down in Elim and has been very busy putting up a substantial house, proving thereby that he does not intend to go back to Barrow Point in a hurry. This will show you that the Barrow Point people are not altogether strangers at Cape Bedford. Long Billy has been here before working in Elim, in fact one of his boys[27] you saw in Cooktown was born in Elim. At present there is another woman—a relation of his wife,[28] I think—with that family. This woman[29] came from Barrow Point too, the half cast school-boy mentioned above is her son and she has another little half cast boy[30] . . . with her now. So should the people from up there make up their mind to come over this way they would find quite a number of acquaintances and relations here to meet them.[31]

Schwarz was careful to let the chief protector know what an impossible economic burden it would be for the mission to encourage the people to take up residence at Cape Bedford without giving them the means to make a living. He emphasized that the "greatest difficulty" would be "what provisions could be made" for their survival if they were to undertake a "migration."

> As far as native food-supplies are concerned I have no doubt, that they are better off where they are now, for from an Aboriginal's point of view this reserve, or at least nine tenths of it, represents the poorest hunting ground imaginable and from an agricultural point of view it is very little better.[32]

Ever ready to launch new schemes to improve the precarious finances of the settlement at Cape Bedford, Schwarz thus set the stage for asking the government to provide the mission with a fishing boat on which the Barrow Point and Cape Melville people, many of whom had considerable experience working on Japanese luggers, might be recruited to work. He linked the plan with the desire to get these people permanently away from their customary haunts where they were, he thought, doomed to continual exploitation, not to mention reinfection with venereal disease. He also renewed his request for widening the mission boundaries to include areas farther to the north where he proposed to settle his new charges.

> Curing them [of venereal disease] in Cooktown and sending them back to the same life seems to be of little use. To be able to look after these people has been and still is one of the reasons why I would like to establish an outstation at Point Lookout or Cape Flattery.[33]

Schwarz wrote to the mission director, Dr. Theile, to describe these negotiations with the chief protector. So long as no financial burden on the mission board was incurred, he wrote,

> I AM in favour of this immigration-scheme, because these people 'are our neighbours and need our help.' Further, they together with the Bridge Creek people (altogether some 150 souls) would possibly allow the Board of Foreign Missions to consider it worth while to send a young energetic Missionary for Wayarego, where they all could be drawn together.[34]

The mission administrators saw an opportunity to acquire more government support as well as control over a larger population of Aborigines. On the other hand, they were concerned that they might be burdened with the care of significantly larger numbers of Aboriginal adults with neither resources nor manpower to deal with them. Thus, they proceeded cautiously, applying for the new fishing boat without explicitly committing themselves to taking on the Barrow Point and Cape Melville people. They located a European ship captain who could supervise a mission fishing operation. Theile wrote to the chief protector requesting money in advance to buy a fishing boat as follows:

> Once we can firmly establish the fishing industry on our Reserve I feel confident that the Cape Melville and the Barrow Point natives could be drawn onto the Reserve and their help in the industry itself would be of no little value, seeing they are coastal natives with much experience with regard to fishing.[35]

The mission's suggestions met with initial approval from Chief Protector Bleakley, who thought the government might be able to aid in the purchase of a fishing boat as it had already done for groups of Thursday Islanders. He had a further suggestion for Schwarz:

> It could also be directed that the men who signed on the outside fishing fleets have the major portion of their wages paid to their tribal accounts at the Protector's office and only drawn upon as ordered by you, instead of . . . being spent on trade articles and sent back with them when they are returned to their camps.[36]

The missionaries agreed to convert Cape Bedford into the ration depot for the northern coast only after being assured that this meant a new allocation for potentially increased costs. After a visit to Cape Bedford in July 1926, Theile reported to his mission board that government aid had been increased to £700 per annum, which included

> an extra sum for the purpose of providing food for aboriginals along the coast to the north, and who come to Cape Bedford for food and clothing. It grants an annual supply of blankets to all natives, and as our boys and girls take care of theirs, and do not all need new ones every year, they are supplied with some other goods in place.[37]

Schwarz next dispatched Barney Warner, Jackie Red Point, and Long Billy McGreen back to Barrow Point to try to persuade the people there to come down to Cape Bedford to live permanently on new reserve lands. These three men were unable to convince their countrymen that life on the mission was preferable to staying at Barrow Point, whatever the predations of settler and fisherman. They therefore merely left word with King Nicholas that he should bring his people down to Cape Bedford for their yearly rations. Under explicit instructions from the missionary, Barney also managed to pick up Roger Hart's half-brother Jimmy—probably from **Guraaban,** where Roger's mother was then camped with the little half-caste boy—and to carry him back to the mission school.[38]

The Second Trip South

The Barrow Point people returned to Cape Bedford as a group in early 1926.[1] The official reason for the visit was to pick up blankets and other rations under the new distribution arrangements. They also came to reclaim the bones of their countryman Nelson, who had died and been temporarily interred at the mouth of the McIvor River. But Roger's people were unwittingly being moved by forces that were to prove too strong for them. (See Pl. 7.)

Rev. Schwarz submitted to the chief protector of Aborigines the following list of the entire remaining population of Barrow Point.

Arrived at C[ape] B[edford] 5/2/26 for Relief-Provisions:
King Nicholas, Rosie (his wife), Leah, their daughter (left at Barrow Point in Mr Instone's care)
Charlie (ex-trooper),[2] Florrie (his wife), little boy (their child)
Jumbo,[3] Linda (his wife)
Charlie old man (his wife at present at North Shore with Wardsman's family, 1 HC child)[4]
Dick Hall, Minnie (his wife)
Billy,[5] Nellie (Barrow Point people at present in camp at Wallace's McIvor)
Wardsman Billy, Lizzie, 3 children

Old people said to be still at Barrow Point not inclined (?) to come here:

Nicholas,[6] Johnny,[7] Billy, Tommy, Harry, Tommy, Maggie, Lantern,[8] Kitty, Lena, Bridged

---

Boatboys remaining Barrow Point, ready to go on fishing boats: Albert,[9] Toby,[10] Tommy, George, Billy, Barney

This list does not include any of those in Mr Instone's permanent employ, otherwise it appears to be a complete list of all Barrow Point people.[11]

Schwarz's remarks about the Barrow Point people who appeared at Cape Bedford on this occasion are worth quoting in full.

King Nicholas of Barrow Point arrived here some time ago with some of his followers for the Barrow Point relief goods. Not counting Billy Wardsman, the 2 women and 4 children he has with him, there were only 13 of them, 7 boys who had only been returned by a Jap boat a short time ago did not come down as they were waiting to be taken on board again by a boat, so their king informed me.

There also are 6 or 7 old people somewhere about Barrow Point besides those in permanent employ of Mr Instone. Of those who were here some say that they are working for Mr Instone but are not under agreement only working on permit. They seemed however satisfied about the arrangement and informed me that they always got plenty tobacco and clothes too. The latter no doubt are facts and I should think that there should be plenty tobacco available at Barrow Point for some time to come if their annual supply is to be like the amount given to them last year.

The natives from Cape Melville have not yet come. King Nicholas and ex trooper Charlie one of Instone's stockmen informed me that they were afraid to come at present. Accidentally or otherwise they had set fire to a portion of Mr Instone's run and were threatened with all sorts of punishments worst of all being sent to Cape Bedford where all such punishments were to be measured out to them. However King Nicholas promised to come down here with those people as soon as Mr Instone will let them pass through his run.

I tried to give these people who came for relief goods to understand that it was not your idea that there should be sent a deputation down here occasionally to get fresh supplies, but that those needing relief rations should come and settle down somewhere within an easy reach of Cape Bedford so that they could get their rations regularly whilst those in employ of any of the little squatters along the coast up there signed on or on permit should get their clothes and tobacco from their employers. They seemed to quite understand this too.

It was rather amusing to note how well they knew what to say and what not to say. They seemed to take it for granted that I would ask them certain questions and as I did not do it they gave the information or answers without the questions being put to them, so that they will be able on their return to report they have said what they were supposed to say.

I said in a former letter that I did not expect any assistance whatever from Mr Instone or his neighbours concerning the migration of the aboriginals in their neighbourhood. I am quite sure of that now. However the supply of tobacco etc. will give out someday at Barrow Point and if the aboriginals know that such supplies are available for them at Cape Bedford they will come. Any other way of forcing them I would not be in favor of.[12]

On this visit to Cape Bedford the Barrow Point people, along with some of their relatives who were already living in the vicinity of the mission, set up a long-term camp in sand dunes west of the central mission station, not far from the existing "heathen" camps on mission territory, where Aboriginal adults were allowed to live in return for work. There they remained until around Christmas of that year when they left abruptly.

THE DEATH OF YAALUGURR

A large group of people from Barrow Point had come down to Cape Bedford to pick up some blankets and other government-supplied rations from the missionary. They were camped in the sandhills to the west of the mission station. They didn't stay on the south side of the cape, because there was another large camp of people there. These were the Bridge Creek people,[13] who lived within the mission boundary most of the time. These two groups didn't want to mix up with one another, and they kept their camps well apart.

Old lady Yaalugurr was a widow. Her husband, Barney,[14] had died some time before. He was from **Yuuru,** right at Cape Flattery, so that he and old Charlie **Digarra** were relations of the Barrow Point people—my "uncles." Barney's wife was kin by marriage to all the people from farther west, Barrow Point and Cape Melville. She had gone to stay at the Barrow Point camp for a while.

One day she said, "I think I'll go and visit William."[15] William lived in the other camp with the Bridge Creek mob.

"No," they said to her. "Don't go, stay here. We have plenty of food here. Stay with us."

"No. I'm going."

"Well, all right. Go on, then."

It was late in the afternoon, but they couldn't stop her from leaving. She went to the other camp.

Then something happened. The people she went to visit were making tea, and they must have mixed something up with it. It was nighttime. They gave it to her. It might have been old man Bullfrog—perhaps she had sworn at him or something.

She died that very night. It was Christmas time. Who knows why they did it? Perhaps they were paying her back for something that happened years before.

The people there in the west, all that Barrow Point lot, started crying when they heard the news. "That old lady who left us earlier—she has died." They all wept for her.

Then they said, "*Wa!* They might blame us for this. We had better run away." They decided they would have to leave the place. They were getting frightened of the other tribe. They blamed the Bridge Creek people for that death, you see, and they were too suspicious to remain there, far from their own country.

"*Ama uwu yindu, adanhu.* These people have different language. We'd better leave."

They went east to the mission, and they asked the missionary for their blankets and clothes. Then they left Cape Bedford and never came back again.

Schwarz tried to convince King Nicholas to keep his people on the mission territory rather than to return to their own land where they were, in Schwarz's view, prey to evil influences from both land and sea. Apparently agreeing, the Barrow Point people headed north to the McIvor River, still within the mission boundary. Once they reached the McIvor they collected the bones of Nelson, who had been temporarily interred after his death at the mouth of the river.

Plate 1. Fog and the giant dingo's head

Plate 2. The people of Pinnacle swallowed by the earth

Plate 3. On the beach at Ninian Bay, lugger in the bay

Plate 4. The porcupine

Plate 5. Native trooper warning camp people of an impending raid

Plate 6. Birds eating the flesh of the scrub python

Plate 7. The Barrow Point people at Cape Bedford

Plate 8. King Nicholas bitten by snake

Plate 9. The camps at Barrow Point burning

Plate 10. Ngamu Wuthurru alone

Plate 11. Bush fire at Iipwulin

Plate 12. Two brothers hunting

Plate 13. Delousing

Plate 14. The Magpie brothers fishing for turtle

Plate 15. Fog visits his daughters

Plate 16. In a cave at Cape Bowen

THE DEATH OF NELSON

Nelson was the brother of Wathi, old man Billy Salt, who ran off with my mother. Nelson was still living at Barrow Point, but he got sick. So Mr. Instone called Barney Warner and told him to take the sick man to the hospital. Barney took both him and his wife east to Cooktown and left him with the doctors.

Well, I guess he didn't know how to talk English, old Nelson. He stayed at the hospital only a little while. His wife was looking after him in town. But he made up his mind to run away from that place. So he left the hospital and headed north, finally getting back to the McIvor River.

When he left Cooktown he wasn't cured. He was still sick. He camped at the river mouth for a few weeks. Then he died.

Barney Warner was back west at Barrow Point by this time. He had just left Nelson off in Cooktown and then gone home with the boat. After a while, the news came that the man had died.

Well, about six months after they heard about it, they decided to set out again, to get more blankets and other rations from the missionary at Cape Bedford. Nelson's widow mixed up with them again, when they got to the McIvor. Before they went back to Barrow Point, they dug up the dead man's bones and carried them back west. He was a person from the Wuuri area, so they must have put his bones in a cave somewhere on that tribal land, perhaps high up on a hill.

~~~~~~~~~~~~~~~~

Point Lookout

In early 1927 authorities were scandalized by the abuse of Aboriginal women at various fishing camps along the northern coast. Sgt. Guilfoyle had detected a new series of outrages.

> The beche-de-mer and shell fishing boats under Japanese masters are still troublesome on the Bloomfield River, also at Cape Melville and Barrow Point, I understand that these masters encourage their crews to go inland to handy camps and make the king or boss of the camp supply women to the Japanese . . . I un-

111

derstand [a certain fishing company] have a caretaker . . . residing at Flinders Island near Port Stewart and they keep the wives of all their aboriginal crews on the island. I am not aware if this Company has Flinders Island leased or how they hold it but am of the opinion that the female aboriginals detained on this island should be visited now and again by some responsible person not under the control of any of the beche-de-mer or pearl shell fishing companies.[1]

Sgt. Guilfoyle now bought a small sailboat. Former Native Trooper Billy McGreen, with Jackie Red Point as his mate, was to use the boat on police errands that arose from the protector's preoccupations. He described the case of a young girl whom he had dispatched Long Billy to rescue.

In January last it was reported to me . . . that an Aboriginal named Jackson stole a young female aboriginal and took her from her father, an old boy named Harry Cootes, to Noble Island where he would then trade her with the Japanese boat crews. In consequence of this complaint I arranged with Long Billy ex native Wardsman at old jail here to take Jack's sailing boat, also Jack,[2] and another boy named George to accompany him and proceed to Noble or Flinders Island and arrest the boy Jackson also bring the little gin back to Cooktown with them and I would then return her to her parents per Billy overland.[3]

The girl eventually turned up at Barrow Point. Instone reported a visit from Billy McGreen in February 1927.

Long Billy came up to see me today regarding the aboriginal child Gladys who was taken away from her family at the McIvor by a boy named Jackson, brought to Barrow Point. He then handed her over to her uncle, a boy named Tommy who is working here for Mr R. Gordon.[4] Tommy will be going to the McIvor in the course of the next few weeks and will take her back with him to her parents . . . She is at present at the house here being well looked after.[5]

In 1927, Missionary Schwarz had acquired his own fishing boat. He had established a bêche-de-mer curing operation at Elim, under the supervision of a Jamaican expert. He had also induced a number of adults, including several Barrow Point people, to begin dugong hunting at a new outstation, called **Wawu Ngalan,** at Point Lookout near the northernmost boundary of the mission reserve.

Though skeptical, the missionary was relying on King Nicholas to keep the Barrow Point people at the new camp. Schwarz repeatedly sent "Long" Billy, along with his offsider Jackie Red Point, to scour the coastal camps at Cape Bowen, Barrow Point, Cape Melville, and Flinders Island. They were to try to convince any people they found to return with them to Point Lookout. Inducing the Barrow Point and Cape Melville people to exchange camp life and work on the boats for dugong hunting on the mission was not easy.

> Billy (Wardsman) and Jackie Redpoint who were sent up north to collect these people scattered along the coast and at the mercy of Japs and others went to Flinders Island too and tried to get the abos from there too to come with them to the camp now formed at Pt Lookout.[6]

A month later Schwarz had more information about the people at Flinders Island.

> They appear to be chiefly women and apparently some influence stronger than Billy's prevented them from being successful there. Billy says that they told him that they would all come down when their boys would be paid off at Christmastime.[7]

Nonetheless, in May 1927, Schwarz was able to report that there were more than forty people living at Point Lookout, eating well from their dugong operation. He was still hopeful for more, especially able-bodied working men.[8]

By the end of that month Schwarz was still more optimistic about his new colony of Barrow Point dugong fishermen.

> Billy, King Nicholas, and King Charlie from Cape Melville seem to work together now. Billy and Nicholas were here the other day . . . They informed me that all Barrow Point and Starcke natives were in their camp at Point Lookout, and Billy said that he had sent a boy, Dick Hall, across to the McIvor to get the few Starcke or Barrow Point people who were camped there. He thought that they would be at the Pt. Lookout camp before he would get back up there.[9]

Sgt. Guilfoyle thought that the process of bringing the remnants of the northern Aboriginal camps to the mission would be made easier if Long Billy were given some sort of official status, as he apparently found himself in conflict with the current kings.

> I . . . also informed Billy that it was reported that King Nicholas and King Harry were not behaving as kings should do, that they were encouraging their tribes to hang about the coast for the purpose of trading aboriginal women with Japanese and other boat crews. I instructed him to inform all the aboriginals that he was made king of the tribes along the coast and that he was boss of all the tribes and he was to bring them back with him to Cooktown in his boat if they did not go inland, that King Nicholas and King Harry would be sent away if they did not obey Billy's instruction, informing the aboriginals that Cooktown and Laura police would have to go out if Billy came back and reported that the Aboriginals still remained along the coast . . . I have promised that I would write to the chief protector when Billy and Jack were on their departure and apply for Billy to be appointed king of some tribe, either Cape Melville or Barrow Point. If he Billy was able to use influence over the tribes and make them do what he told them to do. I would now respectfully suggest that Billy should be appointed as a king over one of the tribes along the coast, he would be of great assistance both in reporting how the aboriginals were behaving themselves also reporting venereal disease cases and conveying patients to Cooktown in his boat with his mate Jack for medical treatment.[10]

Chief Protector Bleakley duly appointed Long Billy "native policeman of the Point Lookout station" in order to give him "authority to control the natives of the coastal camps in the vicinity."[11]

Plans were also laid to mount a surprise raid on the camps at Noble Island and Flinders Island, to catch the fishermen there in violation of the employment laws that further prohibited "harbouring" Aboriginal women for immoral purposes. Guilfoyle thought that "Long" Billy's new status would help, and that

> the police should make one trip to Flinders Island and return all the aboriginal females who are detained there onto the mainland. These people would then always obey Billy when he found them away from their proper place and instructed them to return.[12]

Rev. Schwarz at Cape Bedford was more dubious about the efficacy of the government's proposal.

> The appointment of Billy as "Native policeman" for Pt. Lookout and its surroundings will prove of some value provided the present kings in that vicinity are deprived of their authority and their plates, the signs of such authority, otherwise Billy will be unable to do anything with these people.[13]

Escape from Wawu Ngalan

Despite all the official maneuvering, the plan to resettle the Barrow Point people fell suddenly to pieces. One night in August 1927, having rigged their dugout canoes with sails made from new government-issue blankets, King Nicholas and nearly the entire Barrow Point mob escaped back to their homeland.

The people used to stop at Wawu Ngalan, in the year 1927. They lived there for a while. But then they got tired of staying there. I don't know what happened, but they made up their minds.

"I think we'd better get away from here."

Toby and Banjo Gordon were living with them at that time. Toby was still a kid in those days. Old man Long Billy McGreen had been saying he wanted to get those two boys and put them in school at Cape Bedford. Well, their relatives didn't like that idea. They made up their minds.

"Come on, let's go back west [to Barrow Point]."

Their parents, you see—it wasn't that they were tired of the place there at Point Lookout. But there was some trouble about those children. I think King Nicholas's daughter Leah was among them, too. Maybe also Nicholas Wallace and some other boys.

Well, they didn't leave during the day. They waited for the sun to set in the west. There was no moonlight that night. They didn't want to be seen, because the missionary might have sent his boat *Spray* after them. It used to anchor up there.

So they quietly rigged up their blanket sails, late at night around ten o'clock when all the boat crew was asleep. They set sail then, out to the north and then making west back toward their homeland. I heard that by daybreak they had already sailed as far as the Starcke River. They camped there, but just for one day, and then they set out again, perhaps sailing as far as Cape Bowen. They would have stopped for just one or two nights there and then off again, right back to Instone's old place at Barrow Point. I don't know if Instone was still there at that time, in 1927.

That's the story that Toby Gordon himself told me. Once they got back home, all the old men set out to work again. Some went to Hart's place for stock work, those who knew how to ride horses. They camped around Barrow Point again. Later the stockmen from Starcke picked Toby and his brother Banjo up, and they went to work themselves.

Schwarz's report of these events was characteristically terse.

> Billy the new policeman arrived here two or three days ago to get his uniforms which your department provided for him. He informs me that King Nicholas had taken most of the people Billy had gathered at Pt Lookout away to Barrow Point again. There, according to Billy, the police from Laura met them and supplied them with blankets, tomahawks, etc. and told them to remain about there. That of course is Billy's version. If correct I cannot say. The Barrow Point people however had received their supplies of blankets a short while previous to this here at Cape Bedford. This I know.[1]

Roger Hart believes that after the comparative freedom of the northern coasts, the migratory Aborigines from Barrow Point found it hard to accept the controlling hand of Missionary Schwarz. They were also uncomfortable so far from their own country, too close to potentially hostile and dangerous strangers.

The Missioner's Revenge

Schwarz's enthusiasm about bringing tribal remnants from the north to the Cape Bedford reserve now turned to scorn against the kings of these tribes, to outrage at the thought that they would continue to live a marginalized and immoral existence, prey to unscrupulous settlers and fishermen, and to disappointment that he would get from the government neither additional funds nor his fishing boat to support the new congregation. In January 1927, Schwarz had submitted his annual report for 1926 to Chief Protector Bleakley. Remarking that the Barrow Point people "do come for their rations and tobacco" but could not be induced to stay under his supervision, he had bitter words about King Nicholas.

> King Nicholas has his way of making a living—supplying boat crews with women—a much more convenient one than settling down and doing some work. I have suggested to the Protector in Cooktown that it would be to the advantage of taking his plate from him [and] tak[ing] him to a place where he would have to earn his living.[1]

Of King Harry from Cape Melville Schwarz's opinion was no better.

> King Harry appears to be the same type of man as King Nicholas and I really believe that they only have been raised to the exalted position they are holding on account of proving pliable tools in the hands of unscrupulous employers of aboriginal men and women. If these two kings were deprived of their authority and removed and two more suitable men put in their places [their tribal people] might be persuaded to come and live on this reserve, otherwise I am afraid that they will never do so unless some force is used and that I would not recommend to be applied . . . Supplying them with food and tobacco is something but it would be far better for them to be removed from where they are now and where all control and supervision is impossible.[2]

Now that he felt personally betrayed by these men, Schwarz was even more withering.

> I also know both Nicholas and Charlie[3] the kings of Barrow Point and Melville respectively and if you look at some of my corre-

spondence concerning these people you will note that several
times I expressed the opinion that nothing could be done with
these two tribes as long as these two rogues were left in authority
over them . . . These two kings will never give up their dealings
with Japs and others along the coast and Billy's influence even as
"policeman" will be insufficient to counteract the bad influence
of these two kings in question, supported as they are by the few
little squatters and representatives of owners of fishing boats
along this coast.[4]

Schwarz's displeasure could have drastic and permanent consequences for Aborigines. Fifteen years earlier Schwarz had lodged an un-
specific complaint against King Johnny, **Ngamu Binga,** from the McIvor
River. This king was afterward sent from Cape Bedford to Cooktown and
deported to Cherbourg by Sgt. Bodman, then the Cooktown protector.[5]
    Once again, Schwarz's complaint about Nicholas and Harry prompted
action. Chief Protector Bleakley had already suggested to Guilfoyle that
the Barrow Point and Cape Melville kings ought to be removed.[6] Now
hearing that the protector at Laura, D. W. McConnell, had aided
Nicholas after his flight from the mission, he fired off a stern reprimand.

For some time the Superintendent of Cape Bedford Mission with
the cooperation of the protector in Cooktown has been endeav-
ouring to induce the natives of the coastal camps at Cape
Melville and Barrow Point to emigrate to the mission reserve and
quite a number of them have taken up camp at Pt. Lookout on
the mission territory where they were being looked after by an
aboriginal named Billy, at one time wardsman of the VD compound at the old Cooktown jail who had recently been appointed a policeman for this purpose. These camps have for the
last year or two received their annual blanket and clothing supplies through the mission as an inducement to migrate as wanted
and had always previously received such supplies through the
Cooktown protector. Billy has now returned to the head mission
station and reported that the old king Nicholas had taken these
people away again to Barrow Point where they were met by the
Laura police, supplied with blankets and tomahawks etc., and
told to remain about there. These people had only shortly before
received their supplies at Cape Bedford and the old King Nicholas
and Charlie were well aware of it. I should be glad to know if this
is correct and if so the reasons for the action as if so it had seri-

ously undone the work of the mission and this department during the last three or four years in its efforts to draw these tribes
away from the surroundings where they have for years been
abused and exploited by the Japanese pearling vessels and others
the evil effects of which there has been ample proof in the numbers brought to Cooktown and treated in the jail hospital for
venereal disease. I should be glad of early report."[7]

In his own defense McConnell gave his perspective on the plan to
move the Barrow Point and Cape Melville tribes south to the Cape Bedford
Mission, which had never enjoyed much popularity with local settlers.

> The first intimation I had of the Cape Melville and Barrow Point
> Aboriginals being removed to Point Lookout was about six
> months ago when R. Gordon, present owner of Abbey Peak Bar-
> row Point, whilst at Laura asked me for what reason were the
> blacks being removed from their native homes, Barrow Point and
> Cape Melville, to Point Lookout. I informed Mr. Gordon that I
> was not aware that any aboriginals were being removed from Bar-
> row Point or Cape Melville. Gordon then informed me that a few
> months previous an Aboriginal named Long Billy of Cooktown
> came to Cape Melville and Barrow Point and bullied most of the
> aboriginals from those places to accompany him to Point Look-
> out. King Nicholas and a small tribe of aboriginals from Barrow
> Point refused to accompany Billy and remained at Barrow Point.
> A tribe of aboriginals also remained at Cape Melville. Later a man
> named Mr Instone previous owner of Abbey Peak Barrow Point
> asked me questions similar to Gordon and stated that it was a
> crying shame that these aboriginals were driven from their native
> homes and their hunting grounds and not even brought to the
> mission station and fed but were left at Point Lookout to practi-
> cally starve.[8]

McConnell denied having intentionally obstructed the removal plan, of
which he claimed to have been left in ignorance.

> The matter of Billy reporting to the head mission station that
> King Nicholas of Barrow Point had taken these aboriginals to Bar-
> row Point where they were met by the Laura police and provided
> with blankets, tomahawks, and told to remain about there is a
> fabrication. On the evening of the 18/7/27 I arrived at Barrow

Point for purposes of executing a removal order on Aboriginal Dolly and her two children. I there saw King Nicholas, a middle aged aboriginal and who appears to be fairly intelligent. When questioned Nicholas informed me that there was only a small camp of Aboriginals at Barrow Point and stated that Long Billy had taken a tribe of Aboriginals from Cape Melville and Barrow Point to Pt. Lookout where they were then camped. Nicholas informed me that the Aboriginals then at Barrow Point had not received clothing or tobacco goods. I instructed Nicholas to bring all the aboriginals to my camp on the following morning where I supplied them with blankets and tobacco goods etc. . . . King Nicholas informed me that the small tribe of Aboriginals there were afraid that Long Billy would come up and want to take them to Pt Lookout and that the aboriginals did not want to go. I informed Nicholas that I had heard nothing about the aboriginals having to go to Pt Lookout and that if he wished he could remain and hunt about Barrow Point.[9]

Now Schwarz's recommendations about King Nicholas required immediate action. It fell to the Laura policeman to carry out the "removal" order. The story survives in the eyewitness account of old Yagay as he described the events, and as Roger Hart later reconstructed them.

THE REMOVAL OF KING NICHOLAS

After the Barrow Point people sailed away from Point Lookout with their blanket sails, somebody went east to Cape Bedford and told Missionary Schwarz about it.

"All those **Yiithuu** people have escaped again," they said.

"Those two kings told me lies," said Schwarz.

Then he turned around and sent a message to town, to the policeman.

"You should grab those kings and have them removed," he said.

That was Schwarz's idea—to have them sent away.

The policeman got the complaint from Schwarz, and he sent a message west to Instone.

"Tell King Nicholas to go down to Laura. Tell him to go for his supplies, blankets, and tommy hawks." He was telling lies himself.

From the camp at Barrow Point one could reach the Laura police station by traveling straight south. I think Instone knew what it was all about, but the policeman told him not to make Nicholas suspicious.

He just said, "Well, King Nicholas. I think you'd better go to Laura and get your stuff there. Go on south and pick up your clothes, your blankets, your trousers, your fishline, your axe heads."

King Nicholas believed what he was told.

He went back to the camp, and he told Yagay. "The policeman has sent for me down in Laura. I'm supposed to pick up supplies, blankets, and clothes. You come along to keep me company."

So they made a start the next day, heading down toward Wakooka Station, on the old road to the south. That was Nicholas and his wife Rosie with their daughter Leah, along with Yagay and his wife Obibini—she was my grannie.[10] They went right through Jones's Gap, on the east side of Wakooka, and then they headed farther south from there.

But there were bad signs. First Nicholas's wife Rosie took sick. Her breasts got swollen and sore with an infection. She got a kind of a lump. She had her little daughter, Leah, with her. So they had to camp out for several days until she started to feel better.

Yagay said to Nicholas, "Gaw, let's go back! This is bad."

"No," said Nicholas, "we'll keep going."

They treated Rosie's sore breast by washing it in hot water. Then they set out again.

They went farther and farther south. Then old King Nicholas himself stepped on a Death Adder. It bit him on the foot. (See Pl. 8.)

Yagay cut the bite and sucked out the poison. He knew how to treat snake bite. They made camp there and stayed for a short time.

Yagay was frightened by now. "Let's go back," he said again. Something was trying to stop them.

Nicholas wouldn't listen to him. "No, just let my foot get better. Then we'll keep going."

King Nicholas lay down, and he recovered from the snake bite after a few days. So they set out again. Farther south they went, and still farther south.

Then another Death Adder bit King Nicholas! It bit him on the other foot this time.

Again, old Yagay cut the wound and treated it. But he was really frightened now. He said, "Gaw! This is no good. We *must* go back."

"No," said Nicholas, "we can't go back. We have to go and meet that policeman."

Yagay was having premonitions: this trip was going badly, and it would turn out badly. Perhaps the policeman was planning to lock them up. It seemed like bad luck to him, you see. Something was wrong.

"Let's go back! Come on."

"No," said Nicholas. "Let's keep going." He wouldn't listen to Yagay.

Well, they camped out halfway, for a few more days, and then they set out again. I think they passed through Battle Camp. Then they went west, through the old Laura Station. Finally they came to Laura itself. They made their camp, and the next day they went to find the policeman.

"Hello, Nicholas, so you've finally come," said the policeman. "Oh well, you come along, follow me."

Then he turned to Yagay.

"Alright, Douglas," the policeman said, "You go out back there and chop some wood for me."

He took Nicholas back to the station house, and he put him into the lockup.

Yagay went out and chopped a big load of wood for the policeman. He chopped and chopped. He waited. He was beginning to get worried again.

Someone brought him dinner. He ate it and took his plate back and kept on waiting. He had already finished chopping all the firewood. He wasn't game to ask the policeman about Nicholas, see?

But finally he decided to confront the policeman. He went up to the house.

"Where is he?" he asked. "Where's Nicholas?"

"Well, Douglas," said the policeman. "You had better go on home now. Take his missus and his baby with you." He told him to clear out and to take King Nicholas's wife back north to Barrow Point.

"But where's Nicholas?"

"No, he's going to go down to Palm Island, now." The policeman just told him straight out. "You take his wife and go back. I'm sending him away."

Otherwise, Yagay would have hung around there waiting.

So Nicholas was locked up. Yagay and Rosie began to weep for him.

The policeman could have sent Rosie to Palm Island along with King Nicholas, but instead he made Yagay take her back to the camp at Barrow Point. Later when they shifted the whole Barrow Point mob up to Lockhart, she went along. She mixed up with her own people again back at Lockhart. That was her home country, anyway. She died at Lockhart.

Old King Nicholas never had any more children at Palm Island. He lived alone until he died.

King Harry's demise required no government intervention. He never made it back to his own country at Cape Melville after the escape from

Point Lookout. Instead he took sick and died either in the camp at Iip-wulin or at the creek Uwuru to the west of Instone's settlement. No tradition records whether simple disease or some slow-acting witchcraft from Cape Bedford prevented him from having a last view of his homeland. Later his relatives came down to Barrow Point to pick up his bones, which were said to have been buried on Flinders Island.

Exile

Once they returned to Barrow Point, Yagay and the rest of King Nicholas's people had little time to grieve over his removal. With the two kings out of the way, the government implemented a more drastic solution to the "problem" of the Barrow Point tribes.

First, with Schwarz's cooperation and chided by his disgust at what he perceived as government inaction, the protectors planned a series of further inspection raids up the northern coasts.[1] Throughout 1927 and 1928, however, one pretext or another forced cancellation of such trips. The weather was too rough; the necessary provisions could not be paid for; or Protector Guilfoyle thought that the targeted fishing boats would simply escape when they saw the police coming.[2]

For his part, Missionary Schwarz had now given up the idea of ever having the main body of Barrow Point people put officially under his care. By 1928 he had shifted the "heathen" adult populations on the mission reserve to an outstation on the McIvor River, where one small group of northern people lived in a camp headed by Long Billy McGreen.[3] Schwarz describes with no little irony the failed attempts to bring the rest of the northern tribes to the mission.

> We have not made any further attempts to get the rest of the Barrow Point people and those from Cape Melville and Flinders Island to settle down on this reserve, as it seems quite clear to us that they are meant to remain where they are for the convenience of owners and Japanese crews of fishing boats, and the three or four cattle stations along the coast.[4]

His prognosis for the Barrow Point people is bleak.

The hope of ever having anything done for them seems to have been shattered again and they are left to Japs and others to make use of them in any way they like.[5]

Roger Hart believes that Schwarz's anger over failing to incorporate the Cape Melville and Barrow Point people into an expanded mission prompted him to suggest further action. "He was a mighty vengeful man. He got wild with them and wrote the department a letter, and that was it."

Mr. Bleakley had visited Iipwulin at Ninian Bay sometime in the early 1920s. Bleakley had arrived with the old *Melbidir*—a ship familiar to North Queensland Aborigines in these days—with a crew of islanders on their way north. People had already spotted and identified the boat as it approached. "Boss, boss," they shouted. Anchoring just off the shore from Instone's place, the protector had disembarked to distribute blankets and clay pipes. Roger Hart, still a little boy, had observed him pegging out what he supposed was going to be a mission station, just to the east of Instone's settlement.

In 1928 the office of the chief protector of Aborigines arranged officially for all recruiting of Aboriginal boatmen "in the east coast between Lockhart River and Cape Bedford done in future only through the two missions,"[6] and Bleakley visited Barrow Point again. This time he had a very different purpose: he came to send the surviving Barrow Point people into exile.

Roger heard the story from Wathi, the man who had originally abducted his mother from Barrow Point. The government boat *Melbidir* again called in at Barrow Point. Troopers rounded up everyone they could find in the camps at Iipwulin—men, women, and children. All were trundled onto the ship. Once the camp was cleaned out, the humpies were burned. Then the *Melbidir* steamed up the coast, stopping to raze other camps all the way to Flinders Island. Finally the boat left everyone off at the old Waterhole Mission on the Lockhart River.[7] (See Pl. 9.)

ESCAPE FROM LOCKHART

The Barrow Point people found themselves in strange and dangerous circumstances at the Waterhole Mission. They disliked the unfamiliar conditions of their exile, and they feared witchcraft from their new neighbors. Roger Hart describes them as "really bad friends, the Barrow Point lot and the Lockhart mob." Relations between the groups when they were living at a distance were already hostile. With the Barrow Point people in their midst, the witches of Lockhart were reputed to be busy. People began to die. Toby Gordon's mother was one of the first.

Finally, a few men decided to escape. "They couldn't stop there for too long, otherwise they would have all been finished off." Albert Rootsey, Diiguul, Yagay, and Johnson, together with their families, fled on foot back to their own country. Banjo Gordon, who had made his own way to Lockhart to look for his mother, also ran away with them. Later Toby Gordon, who had married a Lockhart woman, began to fear the jealousy of his new in-laws. Feeling homesick himself, he took his wife and headed back south to Laura.

THE WHITE SETTLERS DEPART

Two and a half years after filing a report about his precarious economic state, in September 1926, Instone sold Abbey Peak to Messrs. Jimmy Stewart and Bob Gordon, who had been working the Starcke property since 1915 and were about the only successful graziers left in the area.[8] Maurice Hart, too, was considering selling out. In 1932 he transferred the lease on Wakooka to his former enemy, Stewart, who, together with the Thompson brothers, went on in the following half dozen years to consolidate holdings at Howick, Wakooka, and Barrow Point, as well as Starcke to the south and various properties on the McIvor River.[9] Thereafter, the Barrow Point lands became just one more tract in a pastoral empire that gradually swallowed up all the land from the Starcke River north to Cape Melville, traditional domain of Aborigines from dozens of clan groups, speaking half a dozen distinct languages. It was an area whose cattle could only be worked by teams of self-sufficient stockmen,[10] ordinarily recruited—sometimes by force—from the bands of Aborigines scattered throughout the territory.

Sutton (1993) reports that Toby Gordon was living with his family at Waliil, "just south of Barrow Point" in about 1929, when "he was taken to work for Bob Gordon and Billy Rootsey on Starcke Station." Toby told Roger that both he and his older brother Banjo went to work at Starcke when Toby was about nine years old.

Both boys had learned to ride and to muster cattle at Maurice Hart's property, in the years after Roger Hart was taken to Cape Bedford. They had returned with the tribe to their own country after escaping from the mission fishing operation at Point Lookout.

The older people used to hide the children whenever stockmen from the stations would come around an Aboriginal camp. They were always afraid that the stockmen would take older boys off to work, since they thought that riding horses was just plain dangerous work. When one of

Figure 14. Stockmen in the camps

the stockmen from Starcke, a white man named Billy Wallace, came for a visit while the people were camped on the beach south of Barrow Point, they told Toby and his brother to hide. But the brothers said to each other, "Why should we hide. We like riding horses!" When they showed themselves, they were straight away thrown on top of a pack horse and taken to Roy O'Shea, the overseer at Starcke, who put them to work.

The two boys were taken to the Manbara Station on the Starcke holdings, to start a new life as adolescent cattle workers. They thus missed the visit of the *Melbidir* and the subsequent razing of the Barrow Point camp at Ninian Bay. When he heard that his people had been taken from Barrow Point, Toby began to wonder what had happened to his mother. He ran away from his stock job and traveled on foot to Cape Melville where he jumped on a boat and went in search of his Barrow Point relatives at Lockhart. He found his mother still alive, and thereafter settled down to work[11] and to marry at Lockhart.

A similar story about children dragooned into stock work can be reconstructed from police removal records almost a decade later. Roger Hart, Tulo Gordon, and I visited the late Bendie Jack in Melbourne in 1984. Bendie had moved south as a successful boxer after World War II.

He told us about working as a stockman at Starcke when he was a very young boy. His parents—Guugu Yimithirr–speaking people[12]—were still living nomadically when the boy was picked up by stockmen and taken away to the cattle station. Bendie was ultimately "rescued" by police and brought to the Cape Bedford Mission, where his three older brothers had already been placed in school.[13]

Roger Hart at the Cape Bedford Mission

It was about 1923 when Roger Hart was left locked in the Cape Bedford hospital building, his arms and legs tied with sisal hemp. Tulo Gordon was a small child, not yet living in the mission dormitory but still with his parents, who cared for the mission's herd of goats. It was at the hospital that Tulo first encountered the little boy from Barrow Point: locked up and "singin' out and cryin' and kickin' the wall." Roger in turn tried to poke out Tulo's peering eye by jabbing a stick through the slat sides of his makeshift prison.

After staying for a while with Tulo and his family, Roger finally was moved to the dormitory and began school. He recalls a time of solitude and confusion. There was no one for him to speak his language with, and he was ignorant of the routines of mission life.

"They took me north to the dormitory. They had a cat there, you see. The boys used to talk to me, but I couldn't understand them. So I said, 'Oh, it's no use playing with them.' Well, I got the pussycat, and I used to play around with the pussycat. That was my friend, then."

The other boys dubbed him by the only word they had picked up from his language.

"They didn't know my language, but some of them used to sing out to me, '*Arrwala! Arrwala!*' That means 'Come!' They were naming me '*arrwala*,' too. That's the only language they knew.

"We used to go west to get damper for our meal. Mrs. Schwarz would give out the food. Each one got a single piece of damper. She would cut one damper into eight pieces. Well, I got my share and was walking along eating it. Some of those other boys were coming behind me. When they called out '*arrwala!*' I went back again—I thought they would give me another piece, you see."

Gradually Roger adapted to mission life, although he and his country-man and new schoolmate Bob Flinders often talked about running away.

I used to go around with Bob, you know, and he became a really good friend. He was a little bit bigger than me. We used to go out fishing, and he still knew a little bit of my language.

By and by I settled down on the mission. Sometimes I would get to thinking. I would ask him, "Thawuunh, let's you and me run away."

"Where to?"

"Back home. It's a very hungry country around here. Let's run away and get a good feed of dugong!"

"No," he would say. "Better stay here."

I used to pester him about it every night. I wanted to go. But he would say, "No, stay here." So I stopped asking him about it.

Then a few months afterwards, he started asking the same thing. "Come on! I think we'd better go, eh?"

"How are we going to go?"

"Never mind, we'll just run away."

"No, no, I'm settled down here now. I think we'd better stay." By this time, I was the one who didn't want to leave.

"Come on," he would say. "What about that dugong we were going to eat?"

"No, let's stay."

But if Banjo and Toby had come with me to the mission, we would have left straight away! Finish!

A couple of years later, when members of the Barrow Point tribe returned to Cape Bedford to receive their government rations and supplies from the missionary, Roger did not try to follow them when they left again.

"I didn't come near them because I was frightened. I knew them but I didn't want to mix up, you see. My mother was there, too, at that time. But those Barrow Point people—that was the last time I seen them, and no more."

Although Roger Hart knew that his mother was on mission territory, he was too fearful of the displeasure of Missionary Schwarz to visit her. He was only eight or nine years old at the time.

They told me my mother was staying in Elim. I was making up my mind to go down and see her, but the other boys told me, "Don't go! Watch out for Schwarz!" We were all frightened of him.

One evening we were coming back from work. Two women were

128

there waiting for the missionary. One was Lizzie McGreen, **Yuuniji**, the mother of young Billy McGreen. The other was my mother. We could hear them talking there to the south, waiting for the missionary.

She called out to me, "Come here!" There was a big lot of us boys walking along.

The others said to me, "Don't go over there! Schwarz will give you a good hiding."

"Why?"

"The Missionary will punish you. Don't go."

Well I was, you know, lagging behind. I wanted to go over and see my mother. She kept calling me. But the others said, "Come on!" So off I went. I didn't see her after all.

Afterwards, all those old people from Elim were shifted over to Alligator Creek.[1] Billy McGreen shifted there, too. Well, I made up my mind. "I'm going to go, too!" One Saturday morning I sneaked away, early in the morning. I met my mother then, at Alligator Creek.

At this time, Roger's mother was still caring for her newborn child, Jimmy Hart. The two brothers came together several years afterwards when Schwarz had the younger boy retrieved and brought to the mission. Later Roger's mother went to Cooktown, where she was employed for a period as a washerwoman by an Anglican clergyman, before returning to her own country in the north.

Roger Hart finished school at Cape Bedford, earning yet another nickname along the way.

MURDERER

Each group of schoolboys used to go out fishing together on the weekends. Sometimes we would go down to the beach or sometimes up to the wharf. Once we all went climbing up the hills on the north side of Cape Bedford, where we could climb down to the rocks by the water.

I was walking up toward the front, and there were several other boys behind me. Suddenly my foot slipped, and I kicked up a big rock from the path. It went hurtling down behind me and hit Jellico[2] on the side of the head just above his ear. He fell down, blood spurting from the cut. We had to carry him back to the dormitory.

They started calling me "Murderer" then, although I didn't learn until later what the word meant.

During the next few years, only isolated individuals from Barrow Point passed through Cape Bedford—men like Barney Warner, Long Billy

McGreen, and Jacky Red Point. Roger had now left tribal life in his homeland far behind. He had joined a small, select group of part Aboriginal children in the Cape Bedford community singled out for special treatment by the missionary. After leaving school, Roger Hart went to work on the mission boats, and he later moved to the new mission outstation at Spring Hill.

Roger Hart married Maudie (née Bowen, the daughter of Cape Bedford ship captain George Bowen) in a ceremony at Spring Hill performed by Missionary Schwarz on 2 June 1940. Roger remembers that he wore a green shirt and khaki trousers. It was already wartime.

Soon afterward he heard from Norman Arrimi, a notorious Aboriginal "outlaw" constantly on the run from government authorities, that his mother had come to Flaggy on the Endeavour River and that she had sent word for him to go see her. Previously she had been living near Lakefield in the north where she had had another child.[3] Roger was unable to visit her before the Cape Bedford people were shifted away to Woorabinda during the war. He never saw her again. She died three years before Roger and the rest of the Cape Bedford community returned to the Cooktown area.

~~~~~~~~~~~~~~~

Wartime

The Barrow Point people who fled from Lockhart and returned to their own country were the final remnants of the Gambiilmugu-warra people. A few of their compatriots had remained at Lockhart, and another few—like Long Billy Wardsman and Barney Warner—had stayed at Cape Bedford when the rest of the group had run away from Point Lookout.

When the escapees from Lockhart returned to Barrow Point, they found their own country empty—but not completely. One man had evaded deportation. He was Ngamu Wuthurru, the legendary bearded witch. While the others were in exile at Lockhart he had stayed in virtual isolation at Barrow Point.

TRACKING DOWN OLD MAN NIGHT

My old **ngathi**, Ngamu Wuthurru, had managed to sneak away when the rest of the Barrow Point people were picked up and taken to Lockhart. He never left Barrow Point. He had been living all by himself, for I don't know how many months. (See Pl. 10.)

When the rest of them ran away from Lockhart, they came back to Barrow Point and started looking for him. They wandered all around. They might find his old campfire, just the ashes. But he would have moved on. So they kept looking. Then they would find another old fire, more recent than the first. They were getting nearer and nearer, you see?

Then they found another of his camping places. "Ah, he made this fire just yesterday. And here are his footprints." They followed his tracks in the sand. Finally they saw him, lying down. It was the afternoon. "There he is, lying over there."

He saw them coming. He must have had some suspicions that they were tracking him. He just waited for them to approach.

"Ah, so it's you. You have come back, then."

"We've come back. The country is no good there to the west. Too many witches, killing our countrymen. We were frightened, so we ran away."

That's how they found him again.

By the 1930s, authorities were no longer speaking of Barrow Point or Cape Melville "tribes." The official Cape Bedford report to the protector of Aborigines for 1932 describes a desire to bring to the mission outstation isolated people from a wide area.

> Effort is being made to collect the remnant of the scattered camp people of Stewart River, Cape Melville and Barrow Point into the McIvor River because of their abused and desolate position.[1]

Little appeared to come of these efforts, and the "scattered camp people" continued to wander between beach camps, rural European properties, and mines, in search of a living.

The isolated contacts that Roger and other mission residents had with his people suggest that the Barrow Point survivors preferred to stick together as a group, although they clearly traveled far and wide and joined periodically with those from other groups who remained in the bush.

A BARROW POINT HUNTING PARTY

In 1937, Roger Hart was in the crew of the mission boat *Pearl Queen*, which sailed the waters north of Cape Bedford—fishing, collecting trochus shell, and hunting for dugong, which the mission was now converting into commercial oil.

They had set out north from Cape Bedford and camped for the night at Cape Flattery. The next morning they made for the rich dugong grounds at the mouth of the Starcke River. A few boys from the crew took a dinghy up the river.

Suddenly they caught sight of some women, running into the bush. They continued up river and tied their boat to a tree. They sat down to wait.

Soon, up from the south appeared old man Wathi, Billy Salt. He had been hiding in the bush, listening to them talk. They were speaking in Guugu Yimithirr.

Old Wathi sang out, "Gaw! Who is there?"

"It's us!" they replied.

The old man approached. "So, it's you all!" He knew them as mission boys.

He went back into the bush to the south then and called to his companions. "Why did you run away? These people are our countrymen."

The women came back. They had been afraid that the newcomers were men from Thursday Island.

The brothers Albert and Diiguul appeared in a dugout canoe, carrying two tortoises they had harpooned. They came up on the bank near the mission crew and began to butcher the meat.

All agreed to meet near the landing at the mouth of the river, where the mission boat was tied up. The rest of the boat crew was camped there, and the Barrow Point people came down river to see them. Old man Yagay appeared, in another canoe, joining the rest of the group. They camped together for a few days, sharing the turtle meat.

Finally, the Barrow Point people went up river again, intending to head for the mining camp at Manbara where some of their group—old man Johnson and his wife Mary Ann—had remained while the others were out hunting. They were camped at the place they now call New Hill yard. They left their spears behind for a later hunting trip, hiding them in the mangroves.

The mission boys waited for them to leave. Then they started to hunt for the spears. They stole all they could find before re-embarking for Cape Bedford.

Some fifteen years later, when Roger Hart again met Yagay after the war, the older man asked him: "Who stole all those spears?"

"I told him who it was. I didn't steal any spears myself—they had already given me plenty of good **wurrbuy** spears, with grass tree at one end and the heart of black palm at the other. You could use those spears for hunting wallaby and also for spearing people. The Barrow Point people had good fighting spears with barbs, too. They also made good wommeras, but two different kinds. Old Ngamu Wuthurru, from **Thagaalmungu-warra** used a thin little spear thrower. The Barrow Point wommeras were wide and flat, scraped smooth and light weight."

The few Barrow Point people who had avoided missions or penal settlements continued to live in very small groups and to eke out a living on or near their own homeland during the late 1930s. Only a few adults were left by this time, and virtually all the children had been taken either to work on stations or to be educated at missions. The Cape Bedford boat crews had other sporadic contacts with Barrow Point individuals, and occasionally one of the northern people would pass through the camps at Bridge Creek, McIvor, or Spring Hill where non-Christian adults were permitted to live within the boundaries of the Cape Bedford reserve.

In May 1942 the German missionary at Cape Bedford was arrested by the military authorities and placed in an internment camp as a potentially dangerous alien. Nearly the entire Aboriginal population of the mission was transported south, most to the Woorabinda settlement inland from Rockhampton, and some of the older people to Palm Island. Although the official pretext for their evacuation was fear of a Japanese invasion of the north, only Aborigines from the Cape Bedford mission community were deported. Aborigines in the Cooktown area living outside the sphere of influence of the Bavarian missionary were left to fend for themselves during the war.

Those Cape Bedford people who survived the cold climate and unfamiliar diseases of Woorabinda lived out the war in the south. When Roger Hart returned to the Cooktown area, in the early 1950s, he met again the very last of his countrymen and learned how they had spent the war years.

Old man Wathi had been living at the Bridge Creek camp, on the mission reserve, since about 1936. When the soldiers came to round up the mission people for the trip south, they arrived at the main settlement of Christian families at Spring Hill. But those nonmissionized adults living in more isolated bush camps on mission territory—as well as a few people who were out hunting when the soldiers arrived[2]—were not detected by the military police, and most of them remained in the north during the war. In the Cooktown area, one of the principal Aboriginal camps just before and during the war was at Flaggy, upstream on the Left Branch of the Endeavour River, and this is where Wathi and several Barrow Point companions took refuge.

The same small nucleus of people who had returned to Barrow Point from Lockhart—Albert, Diiguul, old man Yagay—remained isolated at **Guraaban,** Brown's Peak. They had established a more or less permanent camp in the area, which they left only for seasonal hunting.

When the war began, the Barrow Point people began to see warplanes flying overhead, on their way to New Guinea. The unusual activity frightened them. Even more frightening was their own dwindling number. Diiguul had already died, at Guraaban. As Yagay put it later to Roger Hart: "All the **bama** were dying. If the last one were to die, who would bury him? That's why we left the country **bama-mul** [without any owners]." Finally they too moved south to Flaggy to join other Aboriginal relatives. After the war, all the people living in such scattered fringe camps were gathered together in a new Aboriginal reserve in Cooktown. When the Cape Bedford people returned to the Cooktown area, that is where they found their surviving relatives. Roger Hart met Yagay again and began to relearn the stories of his own people.

"Oh, he was there hours and hours telling me the stories. I was really interested, too. He would speak to me in my own language, but I had forgotten some of it. He kept on talking to me, and gradually I got it back. Banjo knew those stories, too, but sometimes he would muddle them up. But old Yagay had them straight."

One by one the survivors from the original Barrow Point camps died, some—like Johnson and Yagay—living in destitution in the Cooktown reserve. Albert died at Boiling Springs, a property near the modern Hopevale, where he spent time during the war. Jackie Red Point died in Cooktown just before the war, leaving no descendants. Old Billy McGreen, by then a long-time resident at Cape Bedford, had already died in 1937, the reputed victim of witchcraft after a long life as a police tracker. Ngamu Wuthurru died at Barrow Point during the war and was buried in his own tribal land at *Thagaalmungu.* Roger's Aboriginal father had died some time before at Bathhurst Head.[3] He was thus one of the last people to die in that area before the remaining Barrow Point people fled south to Flaggy. Barney Warner, who had become part of the Cape Bedford community and been baptized a Lutheran at Woorabinda during the war, died at the newly reconstructed Hopevale Mission.

Roger Hart's childhood playmates also succumbed. Banjo died and was buried at Hopevale. King Nicholas's daughter Leah died in the Cairns hospital after a long illness in Cooktown.[4] Charlie Monaghan, who had visited the new Hopevale after the war, died on Palm Island in the 1950s. Toby Gordon died in Mossman in about 1979.

Roger Hart has made an effort to keep track of his countrymen and their descendants scattered all over Queensland, some at Lockhart, where they died or forgot about their homeland, others—like King Nicholas—banished to penal settlements in the south. "There must have been children but they don't know where they come from." Many people from Roger's tribal country were sent south and lost without a trace. During the war at Cherbourg he met a man called Arthur Sundown, who claimed his father had come from Barrow Point but who had lost the language. Others, raised to very different lives on reserves and missions, "took no interest" in their Barrow Point origins or traded them for new identities

"I think the only bama left, I think, is me."

Part Four

RETURN TO BARROW POINT

Iipwulin

The idea of returning to Barrow Point had begun to grow on us like an obsession. Our thoughts, both awake puzzling over Barrow Point words and in dreams doing the same thing, focused on Roger's homeland **guwa** 'to the west' where he hadn't set foot since he was a little boy. Bush fruits, profusions of oysters, dugong on the mudflats, wild yams— all called Roger home through his hungry childhood memories.

In the late 1970s old bush tracks were being reopened. Four-wheel-drive vehicles, bristling with fishing gear, pushed their way north from Cairns to Cooktown and beyond. A trip to Barrow Point began to seem possible. In the early spring of 1980 Roger, Tulo Gordon, and I, along with a group of Hopevale elders, took part in a two-car expedition to Cape Melville, reopening an overgrown track unused for twenty years, traversing abandoned cattle stations from the Starcke River in the south to the very tip of Cape Melville in the north. In the process we winched ourselves across the Jeannie River, forged a track to Cape Bowen, climbed Jones's Gap, descended to Wakooka Station, feasted on wild pig, and crossed sandhill and salt pan—freshly imprinted with the hoof marks of wild horses—to reach the beach at Cape Melville where the bones of the giant Scrub Python had been transformed into a huge mountain of black boulders. Our guide then was Pastor George Rosendale, a Lutheran minister at large and grandson of the woman from the Bloomfield River who had been sent with her mixed-descent child to the Cape Bedford community early in the century. In the 1950s Pastor George had been one of Hopevale's crack stockmen. He had been the bulldozer driver at Starcke who opened many of the original tracks we were trying now to follow. After a couple of weeks in the bush, running short of sugar, tobacco, and petrol, we returned to Hopevale without trying to make our way to Barrow Point.

Since then Roger, Tulo, and I had been plotting to try to reach Roger's birthplace. From former stockmen who had worked the area thirty years before we had gathered expert opinion about the best way to approach Barrow Point. An old stock road that some remembered was sure to be overgrown by now and cut by creeks. Several people offered to accompany us with a second vehicle, but ultimately all backed out, their cars broken down or with something better to do. We decided to strike out on our own, two sixty-year-olds and a tenderfoot Yank. We would head

Figure 15. Instone's house seen from Uwuru

again for the abandoned Wakooka Station and follow an old track down to the Rocky Waterhole on Wakooka Creek. From there we would make our way out to the coast, fighting through what was described as a formidable mangrove swamp, where stockmen remembered having once turned up a mass grave with many skulls, testifying to some early massacre.

If we got that far, we reasoned, we could walk the dozen or so miles up the beach to Barrow Point itself. Sixty years earlier Roger Hart had trekked along this same coastline as his tribe took him south to Cape Bedford. He had never been back.

After several weeks of planning, on 29 September 1982, Roger Hart, Tulo Gordon, and I set out from Hopevale, heading **guwa**—(north)west. We drove an old and battered Toyota Landcruiser, borrowed from the Australian Institute of Aboriginal Studies. We had packed supplies for the bush: sliced bread from Cooktown's German baker, butter and tinned meat, flour, sugar, tea leaf, baking powder, tobacco, powdered milk, several borrowed plastic containers filled with extra petrol, an old .22 caliber rifle with a handful of bullets, our swags into which we had each rolled a Chinese tin cup, a spoon and a plate, a couple of large milk tins converted into billycans, fishline and hooks, one rapidly defrosting package of frozen prawn bait, matches, and my small portable tape recorder with a supply of cassettes and batteries. I carried a topographic map showing Cape Melville and Barrow Point, folded up in my pack. We strapped to the top of the car the one long bamboo fishing spear, with four sharpened wire prongs, which we had managed to wheedle away from Tulo's grandchildren. Roger also tossed a wommera into the back.

We followed the dirt road north out of the mission, passing the McIvor River, then the Morgan River that ran beside the mission outstation at Mount Webb, then on to the massive Starcke holdings. Spring was young, and the road was not yet completely dry. Still, clouds of bull dust billowed up in our wake as we followed the track past 12-Mile. We were aiming to camp that night on the Starcke River itself, several miles up from its mouth, where the river bent sharply just beyond a pair of lagoons known as Bluewater, where we had camped two years previously. We arrived just before the light failed, choked with dust, and thinking about the fat half-meter blue mullet we had speared in the river on our last visit.

Quickly we built our camp, started a fire to boil the billy, laid out our swags, and rushed down to the bank above the swirling tidal flow of the Starcke River. Sitting well back from the water, so that no crocodile would take us by surprise, we fished for our supper, trusting to store-bought bait for the first night's meal.

Roger recalled his first visit to the Starcke River mouth as a child. He and his family were approaching the midpoint of the long trek from Barrow Point, heading toward Cape Bedford.

"All the bama had a camp here to the east, just north of the mouth of the river, on a little beach. There were people there from Barrow Point, and also from **Galthanmugu**.[1] We stopped there for a few days on our walk from the west."

"Was that where the other children started to tease you about the 'beard'?" I asked.

"No, that was farther east."

"At **Mangaar**,[2] then?" suggested Tulo.

"No, still farther east. We were playing with spears, made from broken stalks of **jigan** grass. We were spearing each other with them. Well, I must have speared one of the other boys a little too hard. He turned around and said, 'Poor fellow, they're going to leave you with the white man there to the south.'

"I didn't know what they meant. I thought they were joking. When they took me farther east to Cape Bedford, I found out what they had been talking about. I cried and cried."

"How many people came with you from Barrow Point?"

"Well, I reckon about thirty—perhaps a few more. A lot of people didn't come. King Nicholas stayed behind at Barrow Point with his family. Toby Flinders didn't come. But there were several children, young men, and women. Toby Gordon and I played together on the trip."

"Were you the only half-caste fellow?"

"Yeah. There weren't any others. They left me with the missionary, but they took all the other children back with them. Toby Gordon and his brother Banjo wanted to stay, you know, when they saw the other children at the mission. They said, 'Why do they only keep the kids with that kind of skin there? We want to stay, too.'"

"Did the two of them ever go to the mission?"

"No, thawuunh,[3] only when we came back from Woorabinda after the war. Well, they came then. Banjo died at the mission. His brother Toby stayed for a while, but he had married a woman from Lockhart, and when she wanted to go home, he went with her. Never came back to the mission."

"Those were your playmates when you were at Barrow Point?"

"Yes, we used to play all around. Banjo was a little bit bigger, then me, then Toby. Also Nicholas Wallace and Hector Wallace, they were both still just little fellows.[4] There were a few others, too. Who knows what happened to them? Even old man Harrigan[5] used to play around that camp—that's what Toby Gordon told me. This was after they had taken me away."

Later as we ate a meal of bread, fresh roasted fish, and sweet milky tea, Roger reminisced about the adults at Barrow Point during his childhood.

"Old man Barney Warner, *Wulnggurrin,* he was up and down from Barrow Point to Cooktown.[6] He was my uncle, *urrbithu athunbi,* already a full grown man at that time. When he was living in the camp at Instone's place he had a wife, Tommy Christie's mother **Magurru**. Then he went out working on the boats. Along came my 'nephew' old man Christie and stole Barney's wife away, even though her husband was still alive."

"Who were the other grown men?"

"Well, aside from Barney, there was old man Charlie Angry. They also called him Charlie Hungry. He later drowned at the wharf in Cairns when somebody hit him over the head with a bottle. He married Nambaji, after Mundy her first husband died. Then he drowned, and old man Jackie Red Point married her. I knew old Charlie while I was still in Barrow Point. But I met him again. He and Banjo Gordon were working on a boat called the *Noosa*. They used to take supplies up to the stockmen at Port Stewart.

"I was already working on the mission boat myself at that time, the *Ramona*. We were docked in Cooktown, and the *Noosa* came in.

"Someone said to me, 'Barrow Point people on that boat.'

"So I walked north to the wharf. I stood on the east side of the wharf. I saw Charlie Hungry coming from the west side. I recognized him clearly.

"'Hello, mate,' I said.

"He didn't know me. He kept walking east. I didn't tell him who I was. I just went to look inside the boat to the west.

"I saw Banjo stretched out beside the stove. He said, 'Come here, come here!' I went over and we started to talk. 'Did you meet Charlie Hungry?' he asked me.

"'Yes, I saw him there to the south.'

"Then he said my name. 'If you see Roger Hart, tell him that you met me. Tell Bob Flinders, too, and all my relations. Tell Roger Hart,' he said.

"There I was, Roger Hart, and I was supposed to tell myself!

"'Do you know me?' I asked him.

"'No, I don't know you.'

"'Man, I *am* Roger, I am **Urrwunhthin!**'

"'Oh, it's you!'

"So we hugged each other.

"That was about 1938, and it was the first time we had seen each other since I had said goodbye to him at the McIvor River, before they took me to school.

"Just like Nicholas Wallace.[7] I last played with him at the Jeannie River. We were jumping back and forth from tree to tree. Later, when he came to the Cape Bedford Mission I didn't know him. He had grown tall by then."

The next morning we set out again. More vehicles, probably belonging to Cairns fishermen, had obviously been along this road since our previous trip two years before. We no longer had to winch the car up the banks of the Jeannie River, nor did we have to fill in the track where swollen creeks had washed it out.

By mid afternoon we reached the abandoned Wakooka Station. We followed the Wakooka Creek toward the coast, camping by the Rocky Waterhole where we found traces of a recent fisherman's camp.

At the crack of dawn on 1 October 1982, we left our Land Cruiser on a sandhill overlooking a wide salt pan bordered by mangroves, near the mouth of Wakooka Creek. We repacked our swags for a long walk, carrying bread, flour, tea, sugar, and our fishing gear. Tulo—the best shot of the group—shouldered the rifle. Roger took the spear. I hauled along a couple of liters of fresh water, my tape recorder, and a supply of batteries.

After searching for several hours for a clear path through the mangroves, we finally made our way out to the beach, where we could see the hill atop Barrow Point rising some 13 kilometers to the north. Roger recalled only one large creek we would have to cross on our trek between here and there. We cooked and ate a scrub turkey that Tulo had bagged on the salt pan, and then we set out at a quick pace, a strong southeast wind stinging our right ears. We wanted to catch the low tide at the creek mouth.

The walk turned slow and steady, and the wind made conversation impossible. Roger walked through the small waves blowing across the beach, spear in hand, looking for something edible. Whether he was visited by thoughts of the past I do not know. Tulo, his humor darkened by thirst and shortness of breath, straggled somewhat, though he stooped to pick up a ball of ancient **gambarr**—pitch for making spears, testimony to an old bama camp somewhere nearby—in a sand dune as we passed north of Saltwater Creek. It joined the tobacco in his shirt pocket.

It was late afternoon when we reached the end of the beach and started to scrabble our way up the rocky hill that stood atop Barrow Point itself. Or at least the map said it was Barrow Point. By the time we had reached the summit and surveyed the prospects, watching the sun setting over distant mangroves, Roger Hart was confused and worried.

"This is not the place, thawuunh," he muttered, as I examined the map, and Tulo grunted in a kind of hungry disbelief. "I don't know this place."

By now we had finished our meager supply of water. No more tea. We were all exhausted from the long walk. Where were the old campsite, the freshwater spring, the **bulgun** or refuge from the wind we had been promised for laying out our swags?

Tulo and I sat in ill-tempered silence as Roger anxiously searched the horizon for some familiar landmark. Perhaps we needed to head farther up the coast? But maybe there was something familiar about the dark pattern of the mangroves to the west, now fading into the shadows of the evening.

"Come this way," Roger urged.

We pulled ourselves up and set off, at the fastest pace we could manage in the darkening twilight, stumbling down the rocky hill to the west, following what appeared to be an old bullock or pig track down onto a flat grassy plain, staying just inland from a thick mangrove swamp.

We trudged on in the dark, with Roger leading, picking his way barefooted through mud, then sand, heading with what seemed to be growing confidence always to the west. We met a small creek, narrow but very deep. Once we had managed to cross it, we found ourselves once again on a clear beach. There was only a little moon.

"I think this is it, **thuway,**"[8] Roger remarked optimistically to Tulo.

In any case, we could go no farther. Throats dry, with not a drop of fresh water, we stretched out our swags by a forlorn fire.

Roger urged me to ignore my thirst. "If you're hungry, thawuunh, eat. When I feel a little bit thirsty, I just chew on some bread."

He brightened. "Don't worry. We'll have a drink of water over there to the west, tomorrow. The creek in the corner of Ninian Bay runs down from above, and that water never goes dry. It's fresh water if you go up the creek a bit. It's only brackish down near the beach, where the crocodiles are."

Tulo and I were not to be consoled. "My back aches," Tulo complained. "My legs are tired. Tomorrow I think I'll go swim about half a mile!"

Only Roger was cheerful. "I'm feeling really good. I don't feel body sick, only a bit tired," he said.

A bird flew overhead and sang out in the darkness. "'My countryman has come,' he says." Roger was now feeling certain that we had reached his homeland.

We sat by the flickering fire, thinking of food. Tulo muttered that we were a mighty long way from anywhere. Back at Hopevale there had been talk of efforts to secure Aboriginal land rights in other parts of the country. But even if bama could reclaim an outstation this far into the wilderness, Tulo observed, and even if it were supplied by ships, people might only stay a couple of days and then go back. You would have to stockpile supplies. "Even old Muuni," he said, referring to the missionary at Cape Bedford, "when he killed a **buligi** ['bullock'] would salt most of the meat for storage."

"When this tide goes out," observed Roger, "it will leave the rocks on the point exposed. The mangroves here to the west aren't like the ones we just walked through. They're only few. There's another little beach around the point. Don't worry." He pointed west, where a rocky hill jutted out into the sea. "We won't go hungry tomorrow. Those rocks are covered with oysters."

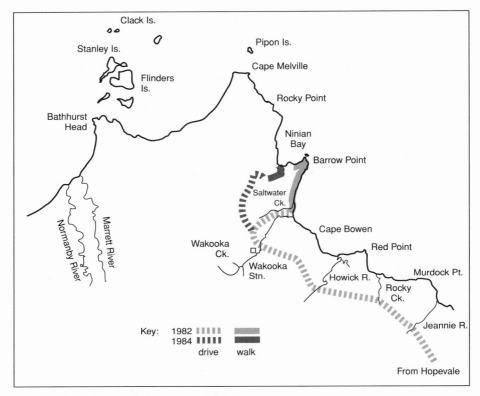

Map 3. The walks to Barrow Point

We threw out our lines to try to catch a couple of fish. We had only old bait, still clinging to the hooks. As we sat hoping for bites, Roger's memories began to sharpen. He was beginning to understand how our walk had gone wrong.

"I think these pandanus trees here are the only ones left. There used to be a good few standing here. The rest must have died by now. There also used to be a couple of coconut trees over there farther east."

"It's just as well we didn't try to walk right around the tip of Barrow Point. I thought that when people said 'Barrow Point' they meant our old camping place. But what they call Barrow Point is really over there to the east. Our camp was here, on this beach."

Tulo asked, "Doesn't Barrow Point have a name in language?"

"I think they call it **Wayamu.**[9] That little island out to the north is **Mulganhbigu.** This is all my country, from that point right through inland to the south." He had now decided that on the other side of the hill to our west was the old station where the white settler Instone had lived.

"There used to be a really good path across there, one time ago. The bama camp used to be on this side. Here to the south there was a big swamp." Roger promised that we would find fresh water there tomorrow.

"Very few people used to camp over on Instone's side," Roger went on. "They were mostly over here in this big camp, here at Iipwulin. This is where I was born."

Roger began to tell us about the old people in the camp, how they had been taken away to Lockhart. He checked himself, with an embarrassed laugh. "Don't say the names of the dead. They might come and grab us by the neck."

"They wouldn't recognize us," replied Tulo. "Anyway, I'm an Australian bama, too!"

Roger kicked at an old beer bottle, half buried in the sand on the beach, its label bleached white by the sun, silent testimony to strangers —perhaps fishermen off passing boats—who had camped here.

"How do you suppose this got here, thawuunh? Might be stockmen brought it with them from the south. Oh, it makes me sorry, this place."

A breeze blew up from the east. Roger launched into another story-memory from childhood.

"When I was a little fellow, thawuunh, it was blowing just like this out of the east. All the bama's camp was just over there, a bit farther west.

"You know that 'kerosene grass'? There used to be a lot of that growing around here—it might still be here. They told me to burn the grass.

"'Just go over there to the east and set fire to the grass, tidy the place up.'

"So I set the fire, but the flames blew up high on the east wind. They went rushing along and burned up all the humpies. Our houses used to be made out of tea-tree bark, and the fire just cleaned them out.

"I still remember that plainly. The place looks just the same to me." (See Pl. 11.)

Roger's enthusiasm about his homeland would have to wait until we had rested and found some water for a drink of tea. We prepared to sleep. Not to be outdone by Roger's memories, Tulo told his own story, aiming a bit of practical advice at me.

"Thawuunh, don't sleep out there on the open sand. There might be stray crocodiles around here, you know.

"I remember we once went out turtle hunting at Cape Flattery. We came up to the beach, with one big turtle we had speared. We laid it on the beach. Then we all went to sleep right there.

"The next morning when we got up we saw crocodile tracks—they were this wide." He stretched out his arms to their full span. "Truly! We had been sleeping here. The croc had come up right next to us, to pick up that turtle shell. Nobody saw him. He took the shell away. If there hadn't been a shell, he would have picked one of us."

When I awoke the next morning, Tulo was still asleep. Roger was nowhere to be seen. There was no sign of a rogue crocodile, but fresh pig tracks ringed our little camp. I surveyed the country. The sea was very calm, lapping at what seemed slabs of hardened clay at the water's edge. The beach stretched for 3 or 4 kilometers to the east, from where we had come the previous night. Mangroves darkened the far end of the beach, and a small island could be seen just north of Barrow Point itself. To the west, the rocky hill sloped down to the shore, projected big boulders into the water. It looked about one hundred meters high.

To the south was dense scrub. There, perhaps, lay the swamp that Roger remembered. As I looked, Roger himself walked into view, wearing a triumphant grin and carrying our water bottles, now full.

"A bit brackish, mate," he announced, "but still sweet."

Unable to sleep, he had set out early to reconnoiter. He had not found the freshwater creek he had remembered, but he had found the swamp. After a drink and a good wash, he had returned full of enthusiasm.

We roused ourselves, breakfasted regally on old bread and fresh tea, and set out to explore Roger's homeland.

Delousing

While Fog was making mischief with the giant dingo's head, the two Magpie brothers stayed behind to eat the rest of the meat. Once they had finished it all up, it was a long time before they felt hungry again. When finally they decided to go out hunting for more meat, they set out toward the south. (See Pl. 12.)

They were great hunters, you know, those two Magpie brothers. In the past, though, they never used to have to sneak up on their prey. They could just walk up to the animals, spear them, and kill them.

When the two brothers came to the south, they looked around. One brother spied a big mob of animals. They were red kangaroos, stacks of them, and wallaroos.

"Where's the minha?"

"Standing over there. Let's kill some."

They started over toward the kangaroos, which weren't feeding, you know, but just sitting down resting in the shade. The Magpie brothers walked straight toward them. When the animals saw them coming, they all got up and ran away.

The two brothers went hunting for another lot, now. But the other animals ran away, too.

The younger Magpie said, "What's wrong with all this minha? They seem to have gotten eyes just like people. They can see us coming."

His older brother replied, "Didn't you notice? We gave old Fog the head of that giant dingo dog. He must have put a spell on it. Now all these animals have good eyesight." (See Pl. 13.)

Well, it was no use. The two Magpie brothers gave up their hunting and headed back north. When they came to the beach, they set up camp.

Meanwhile, what had happened to old Fog? They wondered where he was. "He must be hiding somewhere. Who knows where? He told all these lies and caused all this trouble," they said. "He's afraid someone will spear him."

They were still hungry, so they decided to try their luck at hunting turtle. They got their canoe ready, and they prepared themselves for the hunt.

Now these brothers had two sisters, too, who had come to stay with them. They decided to leave their sisters at the camp, on the beach. "You two stay here," the brothers said, "while we go out for turtle."

All right, they set out in the canoe.

While they were out on the ocean, looking around for more minha, where do you suppose old Fog was? He suddenly sprang up out of the south, near the camp where the two girls were.

"There comes our grandfather, from the south," sang out one of the sisters.

"Oh, so he's coming," said the other.

"Hello, grandfather," they said as he approached the camp.

"Yes, it's me. I'm here," he said. "What are you two up to?"

They were delousing each other. "We're looking for lice," they said.

"Yes?" Old Fog looked at them. "But your eyes are no good," he said. (I'm going to have to use a few bad words, now.)

"Your eyes are no good. You ought to let me have a turn looking for lice. I have really good eyes," he said. "Give me a chance."

Figure 16. Delousing

He sat down and started delousing the two sisters. He started up on top, looking for lice on their heads. He picked all the lice off, **di di di.** All right.

"Well, these are finished."

Then he started killing lice from their armpits. He killed them and killed them and killed them, until the armpits were finished.

"Go on, go on," the sisters were saying now, "go lower, go lower!"

So old Fog kept going lower. He started picking the lice from their pubic hair.

"Yes," said one of the sisters, "please delouse our pubic hair."

So Fog kept killing and killing and killing lice. But he kept on running even farther down

(You know, I can tell this story to my grandchildren, but not to everybody.)

He kept going lower and lower, deeper and deeper.

"Wait there, one went inside farther down! Spread your legs wide, spread them wide," he told the one sister. The girl spread her legs wide, and that old fellow just jumped on top of her! He started to penetrate her, now.

The other sister jumped up then and ran off. Old Man Fog started

150

chasing her. She went to hide, crawling inside a hole in the rocks. But old Fog got on top and sent his penis down through the hole: down, down, until he stuck her from above!

Anyway, when he had finished with the two sisters, the wicked old fellow went off and just lay down to sleep.

After a while, the two Magpie brothers came back from hunting turtle. They had a lot of meat.

Old Fog was sleeping peacefully, playing the innocent—the old liar!

"There come our older brothers, from the east," said the two girls. "Let's go over there and have a look at the turtle."

They went east. "Oh, you've speared a really big one," they said.

Then they started to tell the whole story.

"Our disgusting old grandfather is over there to the west, asleep. He molested us. He interfered with us."

"What?"

"Yes."

"Well, don't say anything about it. Just keep silent. We'll see what we can do about it," they said.

The brothers went over to the canoe and took all the turtles out. They pulled the meat west, back to their camp. Then the brothers said, "Look. Go and gather some stones for the earth oven." They wanted some special hard stones, you see.

The girls started looking around for stones then.

"Is this one all right?"

"No, not that kind. Get another one. That stone is no good."

They picked up another stone. "What about this one?"

"No, get another one."

They wanted those hard, black, "bouncing" stones—big, round ones, very smooth. People used to make tommyhawks out of such stones—it might be granite.

"Get that kind! That's the one. Gather up those stones."

They picked up a heap of hard rocks. They brought them over to the fire and starting throwing them on, more and more, until they had enough. Then they piled still more wood on top, to make the stones very, very hot.

They were ready to prepare the turtle. They slit its throat and pulled out the guts. They pulled and pulled and pulled—that's how we cook turtle up in my country. They took out all the intestines and cleaned them, taking out all the muck from inside and washing them all very carefully. Once the guts were clean, they pushed them back down inside through the hole in the turtle's neck, filling up its belly once again.

By now all the stones had gotten hot. They took the stones from the fire and stuffed them down inside the turtle's body, too. Then they closed up the hole in the neck, so the hot air and steam inside couldn't escape.

They left one especially hard stone on the fire. They didn't put it inside the turtle. They kept that stone very hot.

Then they put the turtle back on the fire. They covered the shell with coals so that the meat would cook both inside and out. It cooked and cooked, and the special stone cooked, too. They kept it to one side.

Finally the meat was ready. They took the turtle off the fire and let it cool.

Guilty old Fog was still asleep.

Finally, they opened the turtle up. They threw away the stones and the coals. They opened the shell and cleaned it out. They took out the meat from the chest part, which was now well cooked. They took out meat, and more meat, and more meat.

They went to find a bailer shell. It was to dip the soup out from inside the turtle shell.

Finally, when everything was ready, they woke old Fog.

"Grandfather, come here! Come here, and eat some soup!"

Fog came over from the west.

They were still keeping that special stone hot.

The elder Magpie brother said, "**Ngathi,** come here." He covered Fog's eyes and made him open his mouth very wide. "Open up," he said.

Then he poured the soup straight down into the old fellow's mouth.

Fog said, "Aaah, I really like to eat this soup. Give me more, more, more."

So they got more soup, dipping it out with the bailer shell. Once again, they covered his eyes and poured the soup into his mouth, right down his throat. He drank that lot of soup, too.

"Come on, come on, one more time, one more time," called out old Fog.

The older Magpie brother went back to the fire, but instead of soup he got the hot stone. He brought it over. Once again they had covered Fog's eyes.

"Open very wide!"

Fog opened his mouth up, and they stuffed that hot stone right down inside his mouth. He swallowed it!

It was so hot, old Fog just blew up, right then and there. He exploded! Pieces of his body went flying around everywhere. There was nothing left of him—his bones were all smashed toward the south. Only one part of him survived intact: his genitals. They flew straight up in the air, heading north. They kept on flying **yii** . . . until they landed squarely on an island. They call it Stanley Island, *Indayin* in the Flinders Island language.

Old Fog's spirit is over there now, still living on that island. And the mark where his balls came down can still be seen today.[1]

On the Beach at Barrow Point

Early on October 2, 1982, after boiling up our morning tea from Roger's brackish swamp water, we were ready to start exploring. We gathered up spear, rifle, and fishing gear and set out across the hill that separated our beach camp from the old settlement. Roger hoped to locate several spots at Instone's old compound, relying partly on his own memory and partly on what he had heard from Hopevale stockmen.

The sun was hot, and the grass had grown up tall, scratching at our legs as we passed, promising snakes. Roger was not pleased. "Used to be really clean here one time ago," he said, fingering the matches in his pocket. In the old days, he told me, people would never have let the country get so overgrown. They used to set fire to the bush and then hunt comfortably over the resulting **thulngga**—the burned country where fresh shoots promptly sprang up again.

Coming over the top of the hill we found what seemed to be the remnants of wartime tracks, broken cement slabs. We made our way down to a short patch of beach, on the western side of the rocky hill, where Roger's memory told him we should find Instone's old wharf. Instead there were only sprouting mangroves, and the beginnings of a swamp. Here, too, everything was overgrown.

We started to explore. Roger first found a rotting wooden beam sunk into the sand, part of what might have been an old dock. We then discovered a line of termite-infested fence posts apparently leading back to one of Instone's yards. As we penetrated more deeply into the scrub, we chanced upon other remnants of the abandoned settlement, which Roger pieced together from the jigsaw map in his memory. Here were what looked like house posts, which would have put the well over there. There in another corner was a large rusty piece of water tank, not far from what looked like the remains of a wooden platform. Everywhere the bush had reclaimed the country. It was hard to imagine a working cattle station here, with supply boats in the harbor, stockmen riding about on horses, or children playing along an open beach.

By mid morning we had fought our way over most of what used to be Instone's property. Roger had found many of the landmarks he was looking for, but not all. He felt his memory was playing tricks on him. Where was the nannygoat yard? Hadn't it been close to the well?—if that really was the well we had found. Where was the old track heading back south into the hills?

Thirst had again overtaken us, and it was time to look for drinking water. We set out through dense scrub and swamp to the west, looking for the creek Roger remembered as Uwuru. We broke out onto a wide beach. Farther west, in the corner of the bay, a small, dark pool of water was visible behind a sand hill.

I was in the lead, anxious for a drink. Tulo was coming behind with his rifle. As I approached the creek I found myself staring into the eyes of a gigantic crocodile, floating motionless just under the surface of the water. I gave a little shout and gestured for Tulo to come and look. The crocodile, unchallenged king of Uwuru for decades, watched us for a moment without concern, then slowly submerged and disappeared from view.

We followed the creek upstream and filled our water bottles. On our return, Roger spotted several large silver mullet, near the edge of the pool at the creek mouth. Hurling his spear bare handed, without his wommera (which had been left behind in the abandoned Toyota), he speared one long silvery fish. We pulled it out, staying as far as we could from the water's edge. Once on shore it was plain that the fish was already wounded, a huge mouthful of flesh recently chomped out of its back.

Roger recalled another time he had been on this part of the beach.

"We never used to stop in one place, you know. Once we were camped just around here, and we went up toward Eumangin. We saw a big wallaroo, and we started to chase it around. I don't know how that animal happened to come right out on the beach—maybe a dingo had frightened it. The men were trying to spear it, and the dogs were barking after it. There's a big rock up there, and the kangaroo was running round and round. It was a big one, an old one."

"Did you catch it?" asked Tulo, throwing the wounded mullet back to its fate.

"We killed it, took it up to the camp, cooked it in an earth oven, and ate it for several days."

Figure 17. Spearing kangaroo

Too much talk about food. It was time to find Roger's promised oysters. We walked back through the swamp, more confident now of our path.

As we passed the site of the old station, Roger finally gave in to an urge that had been with him all morning. Starting with a couple of matches, and then more deliberately with a tea-tree bark torch, he set fire to clumps of overgrown grass. The wind swiftly whipped up a blaze, pushing the flames west across Instone's former property and back the way we had just come. "Never mind," Roger said to me, "this is **awurr aliinbi.**[1] Might as well clean it up."

We made our way through the mangroves and approached the rocky point from the west. The tide was out. Sure enough, the exposed boulders were carpeted with oysters, large and small, piled one on top of another. We each took a fist-sized rock and waded out into the mud for a feast. Roger showed me how to aim a glancing blow at the oyster clumps to loosen them. The oysters that broke open were eaten on the spot. The rest we dropped into my net bag.

Tulo built a small fire on the shore. When we had all eaten enough raw oysters to make our knees weak, we hauled the rest of our collection up onto the beach and tossed the oysters shell and all into the fire. We boiled up a billycan of Alligator Creek water, and Roger rolled a cigarette. I asked him more about the camping places nearby.

"People used to go to the south side of that big swamp where I went for water this morning. There's a big flying-fox camp somewhere there. But they didn't often climb those rocks on the top of Barrow Point. I think some early explorers heaped those rocks up—maybe in Capt. Cook's time. Bama didn't go there."

"What do you call **baarrabaarra** [mangrove] in Barrow Point language?" I asked, trying to remember.

"**Althaán.** And this pandanus tree is called . . . **ubiir.** The young men used to make armlets out of it: ***thambal ubiir-yi*** 'arm with pandanus' they called it. All the young fellows used to put that on. Oysters we call **waman.**"

Ours were beginning to sizzle as they roasted in their own juice on Tulo's fire.

"What do you call flying fox?"

"**Waguul.** But the old people didn't let us boys eat it when we were little. They used to go over here to the southwest, to the big sandhill, hunt lots of scrub turkeys there. They wouldn't let us have any of that, either.

"'Oh, go on, give them some, poor things,' a few would say. So they would give us a couple of turkey eggs, and we'd eat them shell and all.

"They'd go south a couple of miles, and then turn east a bit, come to another big marsh—not really a lagoon. There used to be lots of game there."

Roger was still thinking about Instone's well. "I was looking at the soil, see? I wondered if it was still hard, but it was half sand. So I went farther south, keeping the tank stand to the east. But that well got me beat. The wild pigs have probably covered it over by now."

"If Instone never put any fence or posts around it," observed Tulo, "no wonder they dug it up."

"The water just ran out of that well like a spring," said Roger. "From where we found those posts in the old yard, the well was off toward the west. There used to be a big mango tree there. It was good black soil.

"Instone had nannygoats, too, but I don't know what happened to them. I think when the department[2] sent a boat up here to shift the people away, they also took the nannygoats. They had brought the goats from Pipon Island. They had a shed for them here somewhere."

We pushed the roasted oysters away from the fire with a long stick and started to eat them, burning our fingers on the shells. Our long walk and the hungry night had left us with prodigious appetites. We ate several dozen oysters each, then had a brief nap, then ate again.

"A lot of bama who lived around that big swamp in the south used to come up to visit. They would set out at night from the east and get here about sundown. They would meet the people here, sit around and exchange news and stories, get some tobacco. Then late at night they would start back again, walk back to the east, get home the next day.

"Have some more oysters, thawuunh. It's the last chance. We won't eat like this anymore."

We made one last trip to the mudflats to pick up hermit crabs for bait, and then we clambered back over the rocky promontory toward Iip-wulin, to fish for our supper.

As we stood around the campfire late that night, Roger marveled at the passage of time.

"This place, thawuunh, it's like I was just here yesterday! Looking that way, it's like I was seeing Cape Melville when I was a boy. The only thing that puzzles me is how the scrub has grown up so fast around Instone's place. It used to be completely clear there."

As we retired for the night we watched the glow from Roger's bush-fire, spreading back inland from Instone's place, lighting up the night sky as it cleaned up the land of the Gambiilmugu people.

October 3, 1982. After the bounty of Roger's country the day before, we had cooked the fish we caught in a **gurrma**, a small earth oven filled with hot rocks and covered with leaves. We opened it to eat some of the roasted fish, before setting out on our return trip. Again Roger urged us to eat.

"Finish those fish, Tulo. My country is a long way from yours,[3] and we'll only find coconuts to eat on the way back."

Roger talked more about old Fog and his stories.

"Wurrey has two names, you know. He was also called **Wuurmba.** That was his name among the 'younger brothers' from the inland half of the Barrow Point nation."

Roger asked me to take some photographs, so he would have something to remember the place by if he never managed to make the walk back.

"What do you suppose happened to Instone?" I asked.

"After he left this place, Instone lived in Cooktown. He used to come out to the Eight-Mile bridge.[4] Once some of the other boys told me he was there. I badly wanted to get a look at him again, but he left too fast. I would have said to him, 'You know me?' By that time he might have been glad to see some of the bama from Barrow Point, but he was mighty cruel to the lot of them when they were up here."

Following Roger's urgings as host and owner of this fat country, we ate as much of the roasted fish as our bellies could hold. Then we rolled up our swags for the long walk back. We intended to strike out southeast and inland, to avoid the mangroves along the coast, the rocks of Barrow Point itself, and the swampy country farther south. Having great confidence in Tulo's directional acuity, we elected him to be the guide. "He never gets bush," Roger told me.

By late morning we had made our way back out to the long beach that stretched southward from Barrow Point to the mouth of the Wakooka Creek. We started off into the breeze, walking briskly. We reached the old camping place Roger had spotted on our walk up. There stood a lone coconut tree. We had no bush knife, and no one was game to climb up, so Tulo took careful aim and shot some coconuts down with a couple of his .22 bullets.

As we ate, Roger told a story he had heard from Bob Flinders, who had camped around here as a child with his family from Cape Melville. Old lady Yuuniji[5] was trying to cut Bob's hair, but he wouldn't sit still, and he ended up with a cut in his ear. People would camp here in large numbers, drinking water from the lagoon just inland from the beach, and catching freshwater fish and eels.

It was early afternoon when we reached the Saltwater Creek, about two-thirds of the way down the beach. The tide was beginning to come in, so we hurried across the still shallow waters of the mouth. We decided to fish with our Barrow Point bait to catch something for supper. The three of us fanned out along the southern edge of the creek, as the rising waters swirled around our ankles. The sun was hot, and we were all half asleep from the long walk. Only a few fish were biting.

Suddenly I felt something hard hit me on the leg. Looking down, I was astonished to find that it was an ancient wommera, carved from ironbark wood and black with age, floating half submerged in the creek.

I called out to Roger, "Gaw! What's this?" He and Tulo came over to examine it. Unlike the wommeras of the Guugu Yimithirr people around Cooktown, this one was very broad and thin, like a sword, carefully worked smooth on both sides. Tiny holes were still visible where pitch had once secured both hook and shells on the handle.

What could have brought me this wommera? No Aboriginal camps had been here for almost forty years, and the people who had made this

Barrow Point style of wommera were long departed. Perhaps it had been buried in the sand on the banks of the creek for decades and had chosen this propitious moment to stir itself in the currents of the creek.

"*Andula thamu ami,*" said Roger with a grin. "You found a ghost. Or perhaps a ghost found you."

We spent that night—our last before driving back to Hopevale—sleeping on the beach just north of the mouth of the Wakooka Creek. We dug fresh water from an abandoned spring on the beach, and we ate the last of our roasted Barrow Point fish. The next morning we found our old Toyota and set out south again, traveling fast, covering in one long day the same trajectory that Roger had taken weeks to walk sixty years before.

Wurrey's Ghost

After they had blown up Fog, the Magpie brothers and their sisters finished eating the turtle meat. "Finally, that awful old Fog has been killed," they thought. (See Pl. 14.)

A few days later the whole lot of them set out north in their canoe. By chance they arrived at that very same Stanley Island where Fog's genitals had landed. They didn't know that old Fog's spirit had flown all the way to that island, too.

After the Magpies had stayed for a good while on the island, one brother said, "Come, let's go out hunting turtle again. What do you say?"

The two brothers set out once more in their boat. They sailed along for awhile, and then one of them harpooned a big **ngawiya**, a green-backed sea turtle. They waited while the turtle raced around. The harpoon barb, tied to a rope, was stuck into its back.

All of a sudden—I don't know how it happened—old Fog appeared again. It was his ghost. There he sat in the stern of the canoe, on the west side. One of the Magpie brothers turned and saw him.

"What? Our grandfather has come back again!"

Old Fog didn't answer him. He only said, "Hey, what sort of minha have you harpooned?"

"It's a big turtle."

Figure 18. Fog arriving at Mack River

"Well, you two hold on to that rope, see? Just let me dive down and catch that turtle. I'll haul it back up to the surface for you."

With that, he jumped overboard and dived into the deep water. Soon he found the turtle. He grabbed it, and he pulled the barb of the harpoon out. Then he dived down even deeper. He found a big rock, and he tied the rope to it, tangling the rope up in the coral.

While he was still under water, he caused a great wind to come up. He made a terrible storm. Then he took that turtle and swam off again, leaving the Magpie brothers in the middle of the big storm, holding the rope that was tied to a rock. They nearly drowned, you know.

Fog headed south a long way, **yii,** under water. Finally he reached the shore at the mouth of the Mack River.

A big lot of people were camped there, too. They saw him coming.

"Oh, this fellow has popped up," they said.

"Yeah, it's me all right." Old Fog jumped up out of the water.

From there, he just kept running, a long, long way to the west. Up toward the west where the Mack River starts he camped with his relations. He stayed there for a good long time.

'All These People Gone'

Standing on the beach at Barrow Point, Roger Hart had remarked with the loneliness of a last survivor and the triumph of a little boy who escapes his tormentors: "All these people gone, **nhila wanhthaa-buthu**— now wherever are they?"

The ground upon which we stood, the surrounding rocks and hills, the swamps and springs, even the trees and animals, resounded with memories of his childhood, the friends and relatives with whom he had grown up, virtually all of whom he had, by now, lost. His ancestry and light skin had meant a lifelong banishment from his own country. The same accidents of genealogy had probably allowed him, alone of all his boyhood friends, to survive to see it again.

Once Roger embarked on the task of teaching me his language, it became obvious that his memories of his language were bound up with his homeland, with the camp at Iipwulin, and with the other places he had spent time as a child. All these places were populated by ghosts, the shadows of the people who had walked this country before Roger, with him, and after he had been taken away. The ghosts dogged our steps, shared our meals, and slept by our sides. Some of them were, like me, strangers to the country, brought there by circumstances of history that embraced everything from abduction and fictive kinship to foreign invasion and the search for food. Others were true owners of Barrow Point.

Untangling the identities of these ghosts from the past proved to be a complex and difficult task. Answering my repeated question, "Who was living here at Barrow Point?" pushed Roger Hart to the edges of his knowledge about kinsmen, country, European settlement, and time. Even putting names to the ghosts was far from straightforward. Aboriginal language names, of which individuals ordinarily had several, are interlaced with nearly forgotten traditions and totems, while their English monikers—both surnames and first names—shifted like the seasons, the economy of the region, and the camps of their bearers.

This is true of Roger Hart himself. His best-remembered Barrow Point name, preserved in the name of one of his grandchildren, is **Urrwun-hthin.** When he was living in the Barrow Point camps, he was known in English as Stephen, but also sometimes as Jackie. When the bigger boys came back to the camp after working on fishing boats, they would sing out, "Where's Stephen?" When he first arrived at Cape Bedford, other boys dubbed him *arrwala* "Come here!" the only word they knew of his

Barrow Point language. Then he was called Lex. The missionary's wife, Mrs. Schwarz, who doubled as schoolteacher, decided that there were already too many boys named Lex at the mission, so to avoid confusion she gave him the new name Roger.

Most Cape Bedford people got along without any surnames whatsoever until they were evacuated to Woorabinda during World War II. At that point to comply with the new settlement's registration procedures a few community elders handed out surnames to reflect different reckonings of people's origins and antecedents. It was commonly supposed that Roger's biological father was Maurice Hart, leaseholder of the Wakooka property where Roger's mother had worked as a young woman. Roger was thus entered into official Woorabinda records as Roger Hart. Though born long after his mother had left Wakooka, Roger's younger brother Jimmy was also called Hart.[1]

Many people were known by multiple names, reflecting at once both Aboriginal and non- Aboriginal ancestors, employers or owners of stations on which they spent time, places associated with their fathers or mothers, larger regions of which they were traditional owners or which they had assumed or adopted, and a multitude of other links, including those established by marriage and adoption or, in the case of some nicknames, by simple accident.

Shifting names were an index of shifting identities. The shifts were never more pronounced than in the period of Roger Hart's childhood when Aboriginal life in the hinterlands north and west of Cooktown was under shattering attack from the outside.

By the 1910s even camps remote from centers of European settlement had been profoundly affected by the approach of white society. Fertility was low;[2] disease was rife; many young men were away from camp working on boats. Violence and abduction were routine. People had fled far from their own countries, taking refuge with relatives in distant areas, or settling near whatever settlements offered employment and food. Whole clan areas were bereft of owners, and whole languages were left with few if any speakers. It appears that people might switch or adopt new territorial or clan allegiances in order to fill such gaps (Sutton 1993). These were the circumstances that shaped Roger's memories of people who were living in the Barrow Point camps where he spent his childhood.

Although the names of people from the past are ephemeral and liable to change, Roger Hart keeps careful track of two parts of their identities: their kinship relation to him, "what I call them," and their links to places, "where they belong to." Even these apparently immutable facts have undergone reinterpretations over time. Like the fates of many individuals of whom Roger has only early memories, they are matters about which he has actively consulted with his relatives and acquaintances in later life. Like other Aboriginal people of his generation, Roger prefaces almost all discussions of other people with a short genealogical discourse, often mixing Guugu Yimithirr or Barrow Point kinship terms with standard English labels for analogous relationships and always interleaving talk about the places that people "belong to." These are the important facts about other people in Aboriginal social order, for they determine not only how one should act with another person but also how one should feel: what one owes and what one can expect from the other.

"Joe Rootsey and I are like brothers," he says, for example. "Old Barney Warner, **Wulnggurrin,** he's really my **mugagay,** like uncle. Barney Warner and Ernie McGreen and them lot, they're my full uncles, all those *Muunhthi-warra* people. Well, this old man is Gambiilmugu-ngu, this old man Barney Warner, that's his tribe, on the west side, like old man Yagay. But King Nicholas and I, our country belongs fully to here, to Iipwulin. And then this country here to the east belongs to the **Wuuri-warra-wi,** straight through from there to the south."[3] Such a compact and casual summary represents a dense package of kinship, social history, and geography.

Roger here mentions five people by name. The first is Joe Rootsey, son of another man known as Albert **Wuuriingu,** the second word here being a clan or territory name. Both father and son appear on published genealogies with the surname "Barrow Point." Joe, according to Roger, had a Barrow Point language name, *Alamanhthin,* which was also attributed to his father's father. He was only a little baby when Roger was in the camps.

Second, Roger mentions Barney Warner and Ernie McGreen, both his "uncles." Barney, who also had the name *Wulnggurrin,* was one of the oldest of the full grown younger men in the Barrow Point camps during Roger's childhood. An experienced boatman, he ultimately came to Cape Bedford to work after Roger Hart had left school. He was responsible for the contact many young mission men had with the Barrow Point language and traditions, as he used to teach bits of his language to the boat crews. Roger considered him a close kinsman, a senior male of Roger's Aboriginal father's line, though he was from the "younger brother" half of the Barrow Point people. So, too, was old Yagay, another man who survived the demise of the Barrow Point camps and who reconnected with Roger later in his life.

Roger can reckon his kinship with these people in more than one way: he remembers he was taught to call Barney Warner **urrbi-thu**, 'my uncle'—i.e., father's brother[4]—and that old Barney called him **thurrbiyi**, 'nephew' in return. But Roger was also told to regard them as 'older brothers,' perhaps recalculating his relation on the basis of the relationship his childhood friend Toby Gordon had with them. This latter relation in some ways contradicted the pseudo-kin relation that obtained between the two halves of the Gambiilmugu-warra, the "Barrow Point people," as a tribe. The kin labels reflect the direct link between these men and Roger's father's lineage.

Ernie McGreen, on the other hand, was only an infant when Roger was at Barrow Point. He was the son of a native trooper known as Charlie or Chookie McGreen, who was associated with the same clan territory as Roger's mother. Roger calculated his kinship with the "uncles" from this lineage through his mother.

Finally, Nicholas, "king" of Barrow Point, was one of the people who, like Roger's Aboriginal father, laid direct claim to the territory at Ninian Bay, the "older brother" half of the Barrow Point people. He was thus also effectively in Roger Hart's own patriline.

Roger refers to three "clans," using Guugu Yimithirr expressions[5] that denote groups of people associated with a named place, showing the close link between person and place in his understanding of social identity. He gives the names of the two main groups of people associated with the area known in English under the label of Barrow Point, namely, (1) his own Gambiilmugu group, divided into "older brother" and "younger brother" tribes, to the west of Barrow Point itself, and (2) the coastal area to the south of Barrow Point associated with the Wuuri-ngu group whose name is preserved in the "surname" of Joe Rootsey's father. Finally, he names the clan area associated with old man Chookie and his own mother, Muunhthi-warra from around the Jack River. Roger's quick characterization of people and their genealogies also includes the Barrow Point language name for the area Iipwulin, where we actually found ourselves as he spoke, relating it in space to other unnamed areas associated with particular people.

Roger did not carry the social map of the Barrow Point universe with him when he was taken from the camps as a child. He has constructed it with great care throughout his life, placing new people he has met into an elaborate and shifting network of kinsmen and acquaintances. Born into the disintegrating world of Barrow Point, and removed abruptly from it, Roger's fate was to reconstruct a new social world for himself.

Thunder and Fog

After camping at the head of the Mack River for a long time, old Fog began to miss his family. (See Pl. 15.)

"I wonder how my children are, there in the south."

He decided he would go right down to Muunhthi. That's where old Thunderstorm was staying, you see, near the Jack River. He was Wurrey's son-in-law. He was married to the old man's two daughters.

Fog stayed at the Mack River for a little while longer, and then he decided to set out. He headed south, **di di dii**, camping all along the way.

When he had come a long way south, he passed through the area they call Tanglefoot. There old Fog came across Thunderstorm's farm. It was Thunder's private property.[1] No one else was allowed in that area, because Thunder had lots of yams growing there. That area belongs to us Barrow Point tribes. Those yams were ones Thunder had planted.

Well, old Fog didn't take all that food. He only dug up a couple of yams. But he said to himself, "When I come back, I'll dig the lot."

Then he set out southwards again.

When he finally appeared in the south, one of his daughters sang out, "Oh, our father has arrived. Our father has come."

"Yes."

"Come, then," Thunderstorm ordered, "come and build him a house, separate from our camp. Put it there to the east."

"No, don't put my camp there," said Fog. "Put it to the north."

You see, he didn't want to be upwind. He was a bit of a rogue, old Fog. He was afraid Thunderstorm would smell the yams, you see.

"Don't put my camp there to the east."

He was really thinking about the yams that he planned to cook later that night. He wasn't going to cook them openly, you see, since he had pinched them from his son-in-law.

So they put his house to the north, a bit apart from their own camp. It was out of the easterly wind.

Fog went to his camp, and he sat there on the north, wide awake. He was listening for old Thunderstorm to start to snore up.

"Oh, he's snoring now."

He took out one yam and buried it deep down in the fire, so that no smell would escape.

That food cooked and cooked until it was ready. Fog dug it up and set it aside for a while, to let it cool down. Then he got up and started to eat. He ate and ate and ate. When he was full, he sat down to wait for morning.

At dawn, they all awoke.

"**Ma,** right," said old Fog. "I'm going north. I'm going home now."

"**Ma,**" they replied. "Go on go back home, then."

"I'll come back again later, certainly."

He set out, and he traveled north, north, for a long way. However, he sat down again when he got to Tanglefoot, where the rest of Thunder's yams were. Tanglefoot is the mountain you can see if you look toward the south from Jones's Gap. That's where Fog dug up all Thunder's yams.

He dug and dug and dug, **yii,** until he had filled up a whole dilly bag. He lifted up the food and set out north again carrying it on his back.

As he was traveling north, he chanced to see a little lizard. It was a **duguulmburr.** He put a spell on it. He said, "**Suuu, suu, suu.** Turn into a child! Turn into a child! Then we two'll eat this food I'm carrying."

That lizard turned into a human being. Old Fog hoisted him up onto his shoulder and kept going north, still carrying all those yams. He kept going north. It was about mid-morning.

Just then a great wind started blowing up out of the north. We call that north wind a **walburr.** It's a hot wind, and it dried out the leaves of the yams that Fog had dug up. It blew them to the south. All those leaves fell down right in front of old Thunder.

"My food! Who's stealing it? *Anunda unyjay?* Who's trying to screw me?" He was using curse words, see? "Who is messing with my food?" But he used a deeper word than that. He cursed the thief properly.

Fog kept heading north. He went a long way. He knew he had done something wrong, you see, and he knew where to hide in the north. He came all the way up out of the south, and then he turned west, heading for Bathhurst Head. That's where he had his cave, and that's where he still stays even today. He entered the cave toward the south.

He settled down there, then, with his little son, the lizard boy. They ate the food, ate and ate and ate. But they never went outside, except in the daytime. Fog knew that Thunderstorm would come after him, see. They would go out only in the day. At night, they would return to the cave, to the south, to hide. They kept eating the yams.

Meanwhile, down in the south, old Thunderstorm had become very angry. Rather than travel by day, he set out at night, coming up from the south. He came all the way to Fog's cave. He sat down above its mouth. He waited for old Fog to come out of the cave so that he could jump on him.

He waited and waited and waited.

"Isn't that fellow ever going to come out from the south there?"

Figure 19. Thunder drops pebbles

He picked up some gravel and threw it down in front of the cave mouth. He kept dropping it, letting the gravel trickle down in front of the cave.

You see, Thunder thought he would trick old Fog into believing that a porcupine was crawling above the mouth of the cave, sending down little showers of pebbles.

But old Fog just stayed where he was. He couldn't be tricked that easily. He knew what Thunderstorm was up to. He saw the pebbles falling, but he didn't come out.

After a while, the little boy—the one that had been a lizard before—needed to relieve himself. "*liwadhu,*" he said, "Father. Take me outside for toilet."

"No, no, no. You can't go outside. Just wait," said old Fog. "Your brother-in-law is up there, waiting for us. He might spear us."

"No, you have to take me outside. I want to go for toilet."

"No, no, just do it here in my hand," said Fog.

But the little boy didn't want to, you know.

"Come on, just do it here on my chest."

"No, no. Take me outside."

167

Figure 20. Thunder kills the lizard boy

"Well, then, do it here in my mouth," said Fog.

But the little boy still said no. "I want to go outside."

"Well, all right, then," said Fog.

He took the lizard boy to the mouth of the cave. The little lizard boy jumped out to the north, with Fog behind him to the south. As Fog came near the entrance, his beard first came into view, just sticking out of the cave mouth to the north.

Now Thunder was watching, and when he saw that beard poke out, he thought, "There's Fog now." Thunder took his lightning bolt spear and threw it.

The spear killed the little boy straight out, and it cut off Fog's beard.

Fog ducked back inside the cave, still alive and unharmed. He stayed inside the cave, crying and mourning his little son. He couldn't go outside to get the body, since he was afraid that Thunder might still spear him. He waited, and he waited.

When daylight came, Thunderstorm departed, thinking he had speared his victim. He went home again.

Fog spied all around the place. "Nothing there—he has gone," he said to himself. He went outside, took the child's body, and prepared to bury him.

"I'll let the remains of that dead child decompose, first," he thought. When enough time had passed, Fog dug up the remains again. He made a kind of coffin. Then he took all the little boy's bones, and he put them inside.

Then he waited. "Let that fellow there in the south forget all about it," he thought. "Then I'll go to have my revenge."

Camping at Uwuru

In October 1984, two years after our first trip, Roger Hart and I walked back to Barrow Point, this time by ourselves. Our friend Tulo Gordon was now in ill health and reluctant to set out again. In the time since our previous visit to Barrow Point Tulo had completed a series of paintings about Roger's life and homeland, and about the adventures of old man Wurrey. The landscape was firmly fixed in his mind.

While Tulo was now content to stay home, Roger and I were eager to return to Roger's country. After the previous visit, Roger's memories had become more vivid, his reminiscences more complex. Even his confidence in reconstructing his language had grown. Now he wanted to explore the country with more care, to find other landmarks he had remembered at Instone's settlement, to walk over an area that he thought the protector of Aborigines had pegged out for a possible Aboriginal reserve, and to revisit sites of other newly recalled events from his childhood.

In the first half of the 1980s there was a general reawakening of interest in the bush areas north of Cooktown. Not only Hopevale people, thinking about their homelands or the country they had known in their youths as stockmen, but also non-Aboriginal tourists and fishermen had begun to explore wilderness areas long abandoned up the Cape York Peninsula. At the beginning of October 1984, Roger and I had accompanied a group of young Hopevale men and a few aging former stockmen on a combination fishing trip and exploration of the inland routes leading north toward Cape Bowen and Cape Melville. Our companions, missing the comforts of home, abandoned the trip before Roger and I could convince them to try to visit Barrow Point. We did spy a rough track, heading east across the sandhills north of the ruins of Wakooka

Station, which looked as if it might reach Roger's homeland by a route more direct than our previous trek up the beach.

Finding no one who wanted to accompany us on another expedition, Roger and I once again set out on our own, on 15 October 1984. Driving another borrowed Landcruiser, we again headed **guwa,** '(north)west' from Hopevale, camping along the road as we made for Wakooka. Early bush fires had begun, and we crossed smoldering landscape and lines of fire, watching through clouds of smoke as wild horses and terrified emus fled the flames.

On the third day, we rediscovered the traces of the old road we had noticed a month before. Carefully wiping away our tire tracks with branches, to discourage from following any Cairns fishermen who might also have braved the bushfires, we set off to the northeast into uncharted territory. From the top of the ridge we could make out in the distance the familiar contour of Barrow Point, some 10 to 15 kilometers away. The intervening terrain was thick bush, forest, and sandhill, traversed by a few rocky ridges.

We forded a couple of creeks, but in a few hours we were exhausted by hauling rocks and filling washouts. We found ourselves above a creek which we decided the Landcruiser could not cross. From here we would have to proceed on foot. To one side of our road we found a large patch of bush where the bushfires had already passed, a zone of charred grass and small trees still smoldering, where we thought it safe to leave the vehicle.

Anticipating a rough walk, we packed the lightest of swags, no rifle or spear, only fishing gear and makings for tea and damper. Without the benefit of Tulo's directional acuity, I also stuck a compass into my pocket. If we walked always northeast, we reasoned, sooner or later we would have to come out to the coast to one side or another of Barrow Point. We intended to follow the creeks we encountered down once again to Roger's birthplace at Ninian Bay.

The walk took us two days. Roger was suspicious of my compass, preferring whenever the surrounding bush was dense to trust his own sense of direction. He would send me scuttling up trees to try to catch a glimpse of the horizon. As darkness fell in the bush late on our first day of walking, we simply dropped our swags where we stood, built a fire, and stretched out to talk as we waited for the billy to boil.

LIGHT SKIN

There was a big sandhill south of the Barrow Point camp where people used to go to hunt echidna. The method was simple and dramatic: set fire to the bush and then explore the burned out ground, peering and poking into "porcupine" holes that were exposed to view.

There were what Roger remembers as "cork trees" growing on the sandhill. Children used to play with the burned bark from these trees, using it to decorate their bodies. Once Roger painted himself from head to toe with charcoal. Toby Gordon, his playmate, went running to the adults shouting, "Look, look, his skin's turned all black!"

The color of Roger's skin figures in many of his childhood memories. There were few children around, and women seemed to have great difficulties in caring for those they had. Settlers and native troopers alike were "chasing bama women," and the children of mixed descent put heavy strains on the social fabric of Barrow Point life.

Roger remembers meeting the native tracker, old Harry Moll, when he went with his mother on a trip to Laura.

"He told her to throw me into the creek. '**Wangaarrbi ganggal, thulawi thambarra.** It's a white man's child. Throw it into the flood!' he said."

One of Roger Hart's siblings suffered just such a fate.

"It was at Eumangin Creek. We had all gone out hunting, and they had left that little boy for someone to look after in the camp. I don't know who was supposed to be taking caring of him.

"The little fellow was crawling around. He crawled off to the north and fell into the water. They didn't run and pick him up. They just let him drown there. 'Leave him. He's a white man's child.'

"That was long before my brother Jimmy was born.

"When we came home that evening, we found out he was dead. He drowned.

"They didn't care. I think we put the body into a bark container and carried him with us for a couple of months. Then we buried him somewhere—I don't remember exactly, probably to the south around Jones's Gap.

"I didn't know how he died until after we came back from Woorabinda, after the war, when Toby Flinders told me the story.

"I was called **Urrwunhthin,** and my little brother's name was **Ugurnggun.** He was called Nicholas in English. My mother might have gotten him when she went up to Laura for tobacco—like that."

Roger and Toby Gordon often talked about what happened to lightskinned children who were removed by police, occasionally hearing of someone at Palm Island or Cherbourg who remembered his or her parents as coming **guwaalmun,** 'from the west,' around Barrow Point and Cape Melville.

"But the police didn't pick up **bama buthun.gu,** 'real Aborigines.' They wouldn't bother. They would just shoot them outright with rifles. It was a cruel time, thawuunh. It was very bad to take those children from their parents. Kids who were taken away just ended up lost. They learned a strange language, and they forgot their own. They didn't know where they came from."

Because of his Aboriginal father's "touchiness," Roger remembers a childhood of constant movement. The old man was reluctant to mix up with other families and was always on the lookout for police. Sometimes Roger and his parents would leave the main camp and hide out with just his family.

Once his parents and a couple of other women took the little boy to stay in a cave in the mountains above Cape Bowen, where they camped for several weeks alone. They were worried by a report that the policeman from Laura would be coming to the Barrow Point camps. (See Pl. 16.)

"We went south toward Cape Bowen, and we crossed a large salt pan there. I still remember. When we came to the end of the salt pan, old lady *Arniirnil* was bitten by a red-bellied black snake. The sun was already low in the afternoon sky. We had left the camp in the west early that morning.

"They cut the wound.

"'How are you?'

"'I'm all right,' she said.

"'**Ma,** come on!'

"We kept going south, and we started to climb. As we went up the mountain it started to rain. We went through the scrub and camped half way somewhere. It was still raining, but the rain stopped before morning. The next morning we continued the climb.

"When we got to the top, my old man said to me, 'We'll stop here. There's a good cave to camp in.'

"He went down and told the others. 'Come on up here, this is a good dry place.'

"Then we went inside.

"'You sleep over here to the east,' he told the women. 'We'll sleep here on the west.' My father slept to the north, I was in the middle, and my mother to the south.

"But I couldn't sleep. I had a bad spot. There was a rock sticking right in my ribs. The others had just managed to dodge it, where they were lying down. It rained all that night.

"The next day I went to get some coals from the fire. I wanted to see how they painted boats and other designs. I asked my mother to paint on the walls of the cave. She was starting to paint a ship, but I made her paint my hand, too.

"'Put your hand up here,' she told me, and I did.

"Then she painted her own hand.

"'What about the ship?' I said. So she drew a ship.

"When it wasn't raining, I used to climb around outside, playing on the rocks. The clouds would come over. The rocks had a strong smell, where the hot sun had burned off the rain.

"The women had a little bit of flour. They used to get paid with flour, when they did any work for Mr. Hart or the others. Then they would share it. When the food ran out they began to say, 'Let's go back now. Might be that policeman has gone back to Laura.' But they were really thinking about the flour, see? So we all packed up and walked down the mountain, back to the main camp."

On the second day of our trek Roger and I made our way onto a high ridge that sloped gently down toward the north. We began to follow a dry creek bed that promised to take us toward Ninian Bay. The country thinned out, and though we never had an unobstructed view of the sky, Roger began to sense the approaching coast. We came across the unmistakable remnants of an old water tank, its fragments rusted to the color of the dark red soil on which we walked. Although Roger couldn't identify the spot, it proved that we were near the former settlement. Perhaps this tank had been left by stockmen working the Starcke Station decades before.

Rock gave way to sand, and then to tea-tree scrub. Late on the second day, we finally emerged onto the beach just east of Uwuru. Ninian Bay was before us, the site of Instone's settlement and beyond it Iipwulin still farther east, to our right.

Clouds were gathering, and we needed fresh water and a feed of fish. We decided to camp nearby, in the sandhill by the creek, just upstream from its mouth. As we made our way to a sheltered spot, we found recent tracks of what must have been the same gigantic crocodile we had glimpsed here two years before: footprints a meter and a half apart, with a furrow down the middle where the animal had dragged its tail across the sand as it headed out to sea to hunt.

We built a large fire and stretched out our swags, well back from the edge of the water. Roger rose to face the creek. We knew that sooner or later the big *anhiir* 'salt-water crocodile' must return.

Back at Hopevale Barrow Point language did not always come easily to Roger's memory. He often had to think hard to dredge up a word, and

173

sometimes he seemed almost surprised when a particularly fluent phrase would spring from his lips as if of its own accord.

Now, however, we were in his homeland. Facing Uwuru, Roger launched into a fluent peroration in his native tongue—the first time I had ever heard him speak with such effortless fluidity. He addressed the giant crocodile as a kinsman, identifying himself as a long lost relative now returned to his own land. "We are countrymen," he declared, "and if you leave me in peace, I will also leave you in peace." Gesturing in my direction, he added, "And he's with me."

That night in our camp we were content with more stories and a meal of the remaining Hopevale food. Tomorrow we could look for bait in the mangroves and fish for our dinner.

"I know they used to pick up **waathurr** somewhere around there," he said, referring to a mud whelk with a long conical shell that inhabits the mangrove roots. "They would gather that for bait. They used to catch rock cod with it, and with the hermit crabs that live in that same shell.

"One night I was out hunting for bait with my mother. She was look-ing around for frogs. Not the long nosed ones, the fast ones, called *arriil-malin; arriila* means 'run!' I was carrying a tea-tree bark torch. I would shine it in the mud, and if she saw a frog she would club it with a stick. Then I was supposed to pick it up.

"She hit one frog, and there it lay dead. I reached out my hand to pick it up, and at the same time a **yigi**—a ghost—put out its hand and grabbed me on the arm.

"I let out a screech, gave us both a big fright. Well, we didn't do any fishing *that* night."

We stacked our bonfire high with wood. The breezes blew up from the sea, and the stars blinked. Despite Roger's eloquent speech to the crocodile, we both slept, as one says, with one eye open.

The next morning, when I awoke, Roger had already been out to recon-noiter. Down near the creek mouth he had found the tracks of **anhiirr** re-turning from a night's hunting sometime before dawn. We drank our morning tea on the beach, facing Ninian Bay.

As a little boy, Roger recalled, he liked to accompany his mother when she went fishing. Sometimes she would leave camp at the very spot where we now sat and go walking on the reefs at low tide looking for fish and lobsters.

"Once she set out east to that little reef just north of here—if the tide were low enough it would be sticking up there, look. I wanted to go, too, so I followed her. She wanted me to stay behind.

Figure 21. Roger hunting with his mother

"'You stay here,' she told me. But I kept on following her anyway. I was disobedient.

"Probably she was thinking, 'How am I going to get rid of him, make him stay home?' I was still following behind, even when she tried to chase me away.

"She headed out east along the top of the reef. Suddenly she pointed down and said to me, 'Watch out for that snake down there!'

"I froze. I just stood there. I was rooted to that spot for hours and hours. She kept on going, but I never moved from there. I stood where I was while she went hunting, and I never moved from that spot until she came back.

"Then I got a good flogging.

"It was my own fault, I suppose. She tried to stop me; but I just kept following her. I always used to hang around her when she went out hunting."

We decided to walk north up the coast toward Eumangin Creek before going back toward Instone's old place. We passed a freshwater spring, bubbling up out of the sand on the beach, just as Roger had remembered.

We climbed a hill that projected into the bay, and Roger pointed out the creeks along the beach that extended to North Bay Point and on to

Cape Melville. Near here Roger had camped when he saw an initiation dance. Near here, too, he had played with his childhood mates, Toby and Banjo Gordon. He also remembered little Billy McGreen, Jr., son of the tracker Long Billy McGreen who would come up from the Laura Police Station occasionally to stay with his relatives in the Barrow Point camps.[1]

A CHILD'S SPEAR FIGHT

We used to have spear fights. It was something like the young men during their initiation dance. They would have mock wars, pretending to spear one another. We used to do that, too.[2]

We would collect weeds—**muunun** in Guugu Yimithirr. We would make spears out of that, with little blobs of beeswax on the end of them. That's what we played with. Because of the wax tip, instead of penetrating the flesh the spear would just hit you and fall off. It wouldn't stick, and it didn't hurt much.

We only used to spear each other for fun, for play. That's how **bama** would learn how to throw spears and how to dodge them. We used to make a big heap of spears like that; but we wouldn't use wommeras.

Billy McGreen was a little bit bigger than we were. He used to come around with his mother, old lady Yuuniji. One time Toby and I were playing on the sandhill, just south of Eumangin Creek. We were practicing spearing bark on a tree.

Billy McGreen came along. He said, "Hooo, give me that spear." He took our spears and started to break them.

Toby said to me, "Go on, hit him."

"No, no. He's too big for us. Leave him. Next time we'll take care of him."

A few days later we were playing again. Billy McGreen came along. He did the same thing. He took our spears and broke them all. They were grass spears, *abulthabul,* made from the long stalks of the **bungga** palm.

But we were ready for him. I had another spear hidden in the grass. When he turned to go, I grabbed the other spear and speared him right in the back. That made old Billy cry. He started to howl and ran off to find his mother.

She came back and said, "Who speared my son?"

Then I ran away into the bush.

Roger wanted another look around Instone's place. Although we now knew the way, it was a long walk. Planning to camp again at Roger's birthplace at Iipwulin, we hauled our swags and fresh water through the overgrown scrub. The afternoon sun was hot, the clouds of the previous evening having blown away.

This time when we reached the place where Instone's compound had once stood, Roger did not hesitate. Rolling and lighting a cigarette, he set fire to the grass. The winds quickly set the blaze running up the gentle slope where the settler once had house and yards. We retreated to the safety of the water's edge to collect bait and let Roger, somewhat redundantly, finish his cigarette. The flames crackled in the distance as the bushfire spread rapidly, sending billowing clouds of smoke into what had been the blue afternoon sky.

TOBACCO AND TEETH

Some of the provisions of Aboriginal life during Roger's childhood had come directly from Europeans. Blankets, for example, were an annual government gift to each Aboriginal soul. Flour, tea, fishhooks, iron axe heads, and a variety of food rations were obtained from boat or stock work.

Then there was tobacco, which everyone smoked.

"We used to get a bit of smoke from Sam Malaya. I was already smoking as a little kid—I remember that even Mr. Bleakley gave me a stick when he came to Barrow Point. It was this long tobacco, they called it 'Rooster tobacco.' In the camps they would to smoke it in clay pipes.

"When the clay pipes broke, they used to make their own pipes out of wood—ironbark or some hard wood like that—so they could keep on smoking.

"When people ran out of tobacco, they might beg some off the people who were working for Instone. Those working men always had smokes, and sometimes the women would have tobacco, too.

"But if all our own tobacco ran out, well, that was it. We just had to carry on until we could get some more. Some people used to smoke bush plants: I forget the name, it had little leaves, all in a bunch, with yellow and pink flowers on it. The plant is like a hedge; it grows anywhere, even on the sandhill. They would gather those leaves and dry them. Then they would smoke it, but it tasted terrible.

"I didn't smoke all the time. One morning I got very sick. It made me almost drunk. I spewed up everything I had eaten. My mother threw water over me, and then I got better.

"Well, I kept smoking until they took me to Cape Bedford. I had to stop then. School children weren't to smoke at the mission. When I left school I didn't start smoking again until I went out on the boats. They used to say to me: 'Light my cigarette for me.' So I got stuck into the smokes again, since I had to keep on making cigarettes for the rest of them."

Memory of the poor tobacco substitute reminded Roger of another bush plant.

"I used to see those old people burning this other kind of wood and putting the gum from it on their teeth. Old Yagay was telling me that it was the blue gum tree. They call it **binyjin**—*ardamarda* in my language. I think the gum from that tree might be all right for toothache. If you get a bad toothache, thawuunh, you can't sleep, you know. It makes your head hurt.

"Of course, the old people had pretty good teeth. They were only drinking pure water and a little bit of honey. I don't think honey will give you toothache, eh? But they never brushed their teeth."

After setting fire to the undergrowth at Instone's station, we continued east over the rocky outcropping, coming again to the beach at Iipwulin. We set up our camp and prepared to fish for supper, after baking a bit of Johnny-cake in the fire. Hunger and place combined to produce another story.

CYCLONE TIME

We used to sleep in little humpies. But during cyclone season they wouldn't make round humpies like the ones bama make these days. Instead they would dig a hole: dig and dig until the hole was very deep. Then they would put their humpy down in that hole and cover the whole thing over, first with bark and then with sand.

One night we hadn't got anything to eat. It was cyclone time. We were all very hungry.

That night a big cyclone blew up from the north. There was rain! There was wind! Well, we were all inside our humpies, underground.

The next day I was the first one to wake up. I went outside the humpy.

This beach was just covered with crayfish and octopus. **Gurriitha.** Fish, too. They were everywhere. The beach was piled high.

I went back to the camp. "Hey, you people are all hungry. Over there to the north there is a heap of dead octopus. The cyclone killed them." Maybe the lightning and thunder had thrown them all up on the beach.

The people went out then and started collecting all that minha. They cooked it up and had a good feed.

There was more, too, because the winds had also driven some big trunks of **mungguul** up onto the beach, whole trees. It's like sago palm. Who knows where it came from? Maybe from New Guinea. The people chopped up the trunks, cooked it, and ate it. We had to eat that food because we were hungry; it was soft, a bit like damper without any soda in it.

The next days were spent walking over the freshly burned ground at Instone's old settlement, looking again for signs of the old well, the tank stand, the nanny goat yard, the buggy tracks, and the house posts that Roger thought he remembered. We combed the ground for bits of metal, old bottles, any sign of the early settlement.

Roger Hart's mind was drawn to details of camp life at Iipwulin. We fished and bathed in the freshwater swamp inland to the south of our camping place. We walked back east in the direction of Barrow Point to a narrow creek where Roger felt sure we could catch barramundi.

A SAND GOANNA

Once we were staying here at Iipwulin, in the main camp. But we boys used to come east from there to this little river. Upstream it was deep, but near the beach it was shallow, and we used to play around here. They wouldn't let us go any farther from camp. "Don't go to the mangroves," they would say, "**yigiingu,** because of ghosts, *ama gunyjiingu,* because of witches." They wanted us to play where they could see us.

Well, we were playing around here, and suddenly we flushed out a great big **manuya,** a sand goanna. I jumped up quickly and went chasing after him. All us boys followed his tracks, which went along and along. Then we saw him, lying down in the short grass.

He got frightened, and ran off that way, to the south. He was following this little creek upstream. We went after him until finally he jumped in the water.

We couldn't get him then. The creek was too deep. I think a crocodile used to be up there before.

So we never caught that **manuya.** It was too dangerous to go any farther, so we went back to camp. Soon after that we shifted away from there.

A tree, the contours of the land, or the call of a bird would bring an image to Roger's mind. Surrounding us as we explored were the spirits of the people who lived now only in Roger's thoughts.

Figure 22. Chasing the goanna

A BITTEN FINGER

We used to camp at Cape Melville, near the very tip of the point. There was a long line of **nguundarr** trees there on the beach. That's the wongai plum. Just to the east of the last fruit tree there used to be a big camp. People used to come there from farther west. My family would camp nearby, too, but we never used to mix up with them—they spoke a different language, you know. *Ama uwu yindu.*

While we were living there I got really sick. We had been over to the Mack River to collect **mayi mabil**—water lilies. You had to dig around in the swamp, and then come out into the hot sun. I got this whooping cough, I think, a terrible cough. And my head hurt all the time. Maybe it was some kind of pneumonia or something.

They tried to cure me in different ways. First, they crushed green ants and smeared them all over my body. But I didn't get better. Then they tried boiling hot water. They would dip a piece of towel or rag in it and warm my whole body that way. I still didn't get any better, and I was beginning to get very thin and weak, very poorly.

Well, after that they thought of another way to cure me. They collected a heap of rocks, and they heated them all in a large fire. It was just

Figure 23. Sick at Cape Melville

like a **gurrma,** an earth oven. When the rocks were really hot they went to bring a bucket of water. Actually, they filled an old kerosene tin—that was what they used in the early days. It was a square one. They filled it half full with water, and then they tossed those hot rocks in. The rocks made the water very hot.

They made a little frame out of branches and put the tin and hot stones inside. Then they spread blankets over the top and made me sit down at one side. They covered me with more blankets, one on top of the other, and they sealed the edges right around. Just like an earth oven. They didn't put dirt or leaves on top but only held down the edges of the blankets with sand so that the heat wouldn't escape and the wind wouldn't get in.

I lay down in there for about an hour, I think. The sweat came.

Afterwards they opened it up. Well, I didn't know, you see, I was too sick. I didn't remember a thing about it. Perhaps I was about to die from that sickness. But when I got up, I was feeling really good. They told me afterwards, "We put you in there."

I didn't walk around much for a while. I was really thin, really bony. I couldn't eat anything until they did that to me.

Little by little I started getting better. I didn't get sick any more after

181

Figure 24. A bitten finger

that. I started playing again. I was able to go around with my mother then.

The Flinders Island people used to come around these camps, too. They would come as far as Cape Melville, and I would see them there.

I saw old Johnny Flinders when I was just a little boy. He came right down to Iipwulin, right here to Ninian Bay. They had a camp down to the south there.

He was feeling really sick at that time. He was lying down in his humpy under a blanket, which had a hole in it. I kept poking my finger in to see if he was under there. I was trying to poke him in the eye.

He just waited while I jabbed around. Then he bit me on the finger! Ngaanhigay! He wouldn't let go.

I still remember the place where that happened.

Two days later it was time to walk out again. We had some dried fish to eat, and the last of our flour and tea. Roger's tobacco was growing short. We thought the walk back inland across the bare country left by the bushfire would be easier than following our earlier path along the coast. I had my compass in my pocket.

We sat on the beach at Iipwulin late in the afternoon, planning an early start the next morning. Roger again had stories to tell about the endless travel of his childhood. He remembered shifting with his family back to Ninian Bay after camping for months at Cape Melville.

"Too much **bama** there," he recalled, "but once we got back here, we only stayed about three weeks."

Then they shifted again to a new camp on the coast south of Barrow Point.

"It was just here to the east," he remembered, "and there was a river on the south side of the path. They were carrying me on their shoulders, and I could see **juubi** and raffia palms lining the southern bank."

When traveling from place to place, men carried their multi-pronged **banyjarr** spears for fishing and **banggay** or **muthin** spears, whose points were made of a single wire, used for spearing game. They also had general purpose "knife" spears, whose tips might consist of a flat piece of iron, perhaps made from a door hinge sharpened to a double edge and a point at the end.

"An animal dies quickly if you spear it with a knife spear. It loses a lot of blood and falls exhausted.

"We would carry our spears and a couple of government blankets. That was enough for traveling. Also the dogs. If the boys had brought any knives from the boats, they would take them along to cut up game. They used to have billycans for mixing up honey. No tea in those days, or only sometimes. Just honey, to mix in water.

"They never used to carry any clothes along. Just my mother and my old man—they had a few trousers or a gown. But not the kids. We didn't have hats. Only those few people who had worked for the white man wore hats.

"They had spoon and knife, but no forks. They sometimes had matches. When the matches ran out, they would make fire with fire-sticks. Very hard, you know: it makes your hands blister. Some people can make the fire come quickly, but not everyone.

"So they didn't have much gear. Some people were carrying bark containers with the remains of their relatives. But that wasn't very heavy, since they only took the bones. They would carry the containers around until they felt satisfied. **Ganaa wawu buliiga.**[3] Then they would leave the remains in a high cave somewhere."

We set out early the next morning, also traveling light. We followed the contours of the land back the way we had come, trusting to our memories and my compass to guide us over the blackened earth. There was no water to be had between the swamp at Iipwulin and our vehicle, aban-

183

doned somewhere along the overgrown track, so we took care not to get lost or to walk too slowly.

Late in the afternoon we stumbled out onto what Roger recognized as the same old track we had been trying to follow from the Wakooka turnoff. Sure enough, half a kilometer farther west we found the Toyota. We drank the last of the Barrow Point water and photographed ourselves, setting the camera in the crook of a tree. With my grimy hair standing on end I towered over Roger in his baseball cap. Covered with soot from the bush fires, our different skin colors had merged to a single, shared hue.

~~~~~~~~~~~~~~~~~~~~~~

Fog's Revenge

Fog waited for a few weeks after burying his little lizard-son, and then he got ready to set out again. He wanted his revenge.

"I'll just go and spear that son-in-law of mine, there in the south."

But first he needed a good spear. He decided to try the wood from several trees to make himself a **murranggal,** a bullet spear.

He chopped down the first tree and made a spear of it, but it was no good. Then he chopped down an ironwood tree and made a spear out of it. No good. He tried another spear which he made from black palm. But it, too, was no good.

Finally he made up his mind to go down to the sandhill. There he started searching in the scrub. He found the tree he was looking for: *yigu ithin.gal.* Cooktown people call it **mirrbi.** He made a spear from that wood. When it was ready, he threw it at another tree nearby. The spear went right through the first tree and lodged itself in another tree on the far side.

"Oh, well, this is the good one," he thought.

He made a stack of spears from *ithin.gal* wood.

Early the next day he got up and set out. "I really mean to spear that fellow there in the south."

He went south **yii,** and he camped half way. Then he set out again. He walked and walked. Finally, about three o'clock in the afternoon, he came to the place where Thunder lived.

He approached quietly, sneaking up on Thunder's camp. He looked cautiously over toward the south.

184

"Ah, they are killing his lice, then."

The two wives were delousing Thunderstorm, who was sitting between two trees. He had one leg leaning up against a tree on this side. The other leg was propped up against a tree on the other side. The younger sister was killing the lice on Thunderstorm's beard, and the older sister was delousing his head.

As Fog was spying on them, the birds came up. They started laughing at him, as he sat crouched down out of sight. They laughed and laughed and laughed. Fog just crouched down even further.

Thunderstorm sent the older sister to have a look. "Go," he said, "and see what sort of animal is over there. The birds might be laughing at a big python or something. Find out what the birds have seen."

She came up from the south. She looked all around under the tree where the birds had been making noise. A huge mob of birds had gathered in that tree, laughing at old man Fog.

The elder wife couldn't see anything. Fog burrowed down even deeper in the grass. He hid himself from his elder daughter, because he was afraid she might tell on him.

He waited and waited, hiding, and finally his daughter went back south. She sat down in the shade.

"There's nothing," she said. "Who knows what those birds are laughing at there in the north."

Still more birds came up, and they made even more racket laughing at old Fog. They were 'tit-tit' birds. This time Thunderstorm sent the younger sister to have a look. "You go, this time. Perhaps you have better eyes."

She walked northward, and she found her father there. Old Fog raised himself out of the grass and called to her. "Come here, my child, come here."

He told her about the lizard-boy Thunder had speared.

"Your younger brother is dead there in the north. Your husband is the one who killed him. That is why I have come. I want to spear him. So don't tell him about me, see?

"Now, don't you get too close to him. I'm going to spear him. You just go on killing the lice from his head."

Obediently, she went back to the south.

"Well, it's nothing. Who knows what in the world those birds are laughing at."

Old Fog began to sneak up from the north. He moved up as close as he could.

Thunderstorm was starting to snore loudly, as they searched for lice

Figure 25. Fog spears Thunder

in his hair. The younger sister knew that her father was coming to spear old Thunderstorm.

When the old man was close enough he suddenly stood up and threw his spear. It went right through one tree, and then through one of Thunder's outstretched legs. The spear kept going: it speared his other leg and went on to spear the tree on the other side.

Old Thunderstorm started to spin and roll. **Buuuu, du du du.** His legs were pinned to the trees by Fog's spear. Thunder tried to throw one of his own thunderbolt spears, but old Fog ducked under it. Thunder threw another thunderbolt to the north, but old Fog ducked again. For a third time Thunder threw a thunderbolt spear to the north, but again Fog ducked under it.

At last, Fog stood up there in the north, and he looked back out of the corner of his eye. At that same moment, Thunder threw his last spear, and this time it chopped old Fog's beard right off.

Fog started running then, all the way home. He ran **di di di diii,** until he came to the Mack River. He didn't stop with the people there. He kept running, turning west. He entered the same cave where the little lizard boy had been speared. He went in there, and that's where he still is today.

When I was a little boy at Barrow Point, we would go up to Cape Melville and look west to Bathhurst Head, where old Fog has his cave. Every morning we would see white fog around that mountain—old Fog's beard floating free, after Thunderstorm speared it.

And that's the end of the story.

AFTERWORD: BARROW POINT IN THE 1990S

Roger Hart and I made another, very different trip to Barrow Point in mid 1989. Times had changed. We drove direct to Iipwulin in a line of four-wheel-drive vehicles, tracking a caravan of Cairns fishermen who had hauled their motorboats right to Roger's birthplace. Luckily they had not—yet—discovered Roger's oyster beds.

Our party included a diverse bunch of people: a Hopevale community councilor, a Cairns Aboriginal activist, a young Sydney University law student from Hopevale named Noelie Pearson, who brought along a couple of **wangarr** 'white' friends and his mother, a Kuku Yalanji woman. Tulo Gordon, ill with severe emphysema, had sent his youngest son Reggie with us. I took my family, and we were also joined by the late Tim Asch, an American anthropological filmmaker who had long wanted to share an adventure in Hopevale and who insisted on swimming in what Roger told him were shark- and crocodile-infested seas.

Noelie, who had perhaps glimpsed the possibilities for Queensland Aboriginal land rights on the political horizon, had taken an interest in Roger Hart's language, a relative of his own tribal Jeannie River tongue, now extinct. There was talk about tourist development, ecological protection, putting rangers on the land. Noelie and Reggie, anxious to get their hands on a boat, offered to take the Cairns fishermen out to look for turtle, but brought back only a few stingrays. Once again, Roger Hart torched the bush to "keep it clean."

Since then Roger Hart has been back again to his homeland several times, as the senior claimant to various tribal territories and as a recognized expert on land and tradition. He has flown over his own country by helicopter, preparing to give evidence for the ultimately successful Flinders Island, Cape Melville, and Cape Bowen land claim,[1] which unfortunately fails to include precisely the area at Barrow Point he himself claims as his own.[2] Roger told me in early 1995 that he had begun to suffer from chronic back pain, the result, he thought, of being obliged to take white folks to visit so many sacred Aboriginal sites.

Since 1991, the Starcke holding, which grew in the 1930s to encompass all the land from the McIvor River to Cape Melville under a single huge pastoral lease, has been the object of intense land rights efforts on the part of Aboriginal groups with traditional claims to the territory. Under provisions of Queensland state law, those areas already gazetted as National Parks were available to claims by the descendants of their original owners, subject to the parkland's being immediately leased back to the government.[3] Other areas of the pastoral lease are being considered for government buy-back for the benefit of the tribal owners. Still other areas are disputed under controversial judicial and legislative provisions for a "Native Title" that predates even the crown's conquest of the lands.[4] In January 1998, Roger told me he had put a rough shack on the beach where he was born, planning to use it as a vacation home despite the facts of legal ownership.

How the history and stories of the Barrow Point people figure in the current discourse about land, ownership, and genealogy would take us far beyond the scope of the book Roger Hart, Tulo Gordon, and I set out to write almost twenty years ago. Roger Hart remains a central player in the drama, and his language lives on in maps, sites, and legal argument about legitimacy and tradition. Even old Wurrey still travels about the territory, as his adventures mapping the land are recounted by lawyers and judges.[5]

None of this will be enough to keep the language and traditions of Barrow Point alive. The dismantling of Aboriginal life throughout the north was cruelly effective and irrevocable. What survives is radically transformed. What were once moral tales for initiated adults have become "fairy tales" for children's books. What were once the special words for respect or intimacy have now become arcane counters in a calculus of claims for legitimacy and land. What were once elaborate social institutions for sharing resources, honoring the law, and educating human beings have been reduced to boundaries, titles, racial distinctions, and a decidedly European notion of "ownership."

Seventy years ago, the Cape Bedford missionary G. H. Schwarz pronounced a pessimistic prospectus for the Barrow Point people and their immediate neighbors to the north.

> In a few years time it may be said that there once were two tribes living between Cape Flattery and Cape Melville but that they have died out.[6]

Roger Hart's life shows Schwarz's epitaph for the Barrow Point people to have been slightly premature. Perhaps also our book will help leave a little something to remember them by.

GLOSSARY

Note: GY is an abbreviation for Guugu Yimithirr, the language of the Cooktown area; BP stands for Roger Hart's Barrow Point language.

anggatha	'friend' in BP language; *anggatha athu,* 'my friend'
bama	GY word for Australian Aboriginal person
baramundi	a large, especially tasty game fish
bêche-de-mer	a sea slug or sea cucumber, prized as food in certain Asian cuisines
billy, or billycan	a tin can or old milk tin, with a wire handle, for hanging over the fire to boil water
bull dust	a penetrating powdery dry dust in the Australian bush
dagu	GY expression, literally meaning 'thing,' used as an exclamation meaning, 'why' or 'well'
damper	Australian bush quick bread, made from flour, water, salt, and baking powder, and customarily baked in the ashes of a fire
dilly bag	a carrying bag woven from grass or other natural fibers
duburrubun	GY word for species of magpie
fair dinkum	Australian for "true"
fossick	to search for valuables in refuse, in dirt, etc.
Gambiilmugu-warra	GY name for the Barrow Point clan to which Roger Hart belongs
gaw	GY exclamation, or call for attention, "Hey!"
gin	an Australian term for Aboriginal woman, nowadays considered offensive
goanna	one of a variety of native lizards
grog	alchoholic beverages
guya	GY for 'no, nothing, none'
humpy	Australian term for Aboriginal bark shelter
larrikin	Australian for mischievous, troublemaking person
ma	GY expression used as a prompt to action: "OK, let's go . . ."
mayi	GY for edible vegetable 'food'
minha	GY for 'meat' or edible animal
muster	Australian verb for "round up (cattle)"
ngaanhigay	GY exclamation of pain
offsider	companion, assistant
round scrub	a discrete area of rain forest surrounded by less dense vegetation
scrub	Australian term for an area of rainforest
sugar-bag	a drink made from native-honey mixed with water
swag	the Australian term for one's bedroll
thawuunh	'friend' in GY

Glossary

wangarr	GY word for non-Aboriginal person, European, 'ghost'
wommera	the Australia-wide term for spear-thrower, derived from an Aboriginal word of New South Wales
yimpal	BP term for 'story' or 'news'

NOTES

HOPEVALE AND HOPE VALLEY

1. The following historical summary draws heavily on Haviland 1985; see also Haviland and Haviland 1980 for a general account of the founding of the mission at Cape Bedford.
2. See Haviland 1974.
3. Queensland State Archives Colonial Secretary's Files, A314, no. 2395 of 1881. Letter from St. George (police magistrate) to colonial secretary, 27 May 1881.
4. See Haviland and Haviland 1980.
5. Letter from Missionary Schwarz to the mission inspector, Archives of the Neuendettelsau Mission Society, Bavaria, Germany, 527, July 25 1906. Missionary Schwarz partially justifies the heavy losses in the mission budget for the year by saying that he thought it would be useful to get better acquainted with "new blacks" from Cape Melville. Subsequently he had kept them at the mission longer than he should have, having, he said, to feed them in the meantime.
6. For example, the elders actively discouraged intermarriage between Cape Bedford and Woorabinda people.
7. See Haviland 1993.
8. See Haviland 1979a, b.
9. The research in the 1970s and early 1980s was conducted jointly with Dr. Leslie Knox Devereaux of the Australian National University.
10. An Australian expression that suggests rummaging around through ruins, discarded waste, old mine sites, and the like, looking for something of value. This and other Australian or Aboriginal terms appear in the Glossary below.
11. This comment came from the late Bob Flinders, of Cape Melville, one of Roger Hart's countrymen and schoolmates from the early mission days.
12. Roger first refers to the late Billy **Muundu** Jacko, a man who took me under his wing when I first went to Hopevale to teach me the language. Muundu was a senior claimant of the clan estate at **Junyju** on the Starcke River. Because under normal circumstances, people from Hopevale avoid mentioning the names of the deceased, I have preserved polite usage in the text and largely moved the names of these departed kinsmen to footnotes.
13. Roger here refers to the late Tulo Gordon, of the **Nugal** clan area, co-author of Gordon and Haviland 1980 and the artist who painted the illustrations for this book.
14. Toby Gordon (**Urrguunh,** or **Wurrkuyn**), Roger Hart's childhood friend and later housemate at Mossman in the 1970s, was, along with his brother Banjo (**Udhaay**), from the same area as Roger at Barrow Point. He was photographed by the anthropologist Norman Tindale at Flinders Island in 1927, when he

appears to have been no more than about eight years old. He was later an informant for Peter Sutton in the 1970s (see Sutton 1993 for further genealogical details). He was a fluent speaker of both Barrow Point and Flinders Island languages.

15. See Haviland 1979a, 1979b for a description of some of these specialized linguistic forms and the social conditions that inspired their use.

WURREY

1. Throughout this and other translated narratives, cardinal direction terms abound, since directional insistence is characteristic of both the spoken Guugu Yimithirr and Barrow Point language. The terms should be understood not as Western compass points, but as directional "quadrants" rotated slightly clockwise from their compass equivalents. "West," for example, is a quadrant of the horizon centered slightly north of standard west. See Haviland 1993, 1998. The places named in Wurrey's story appear on Tulo Gordon's painted map of the Barrow Point area.

FOG VISITS GURAABAN

1. Literally, "thing,"—here, a rough equivalent of "gee!"

THE GIANT DINGO DOG

1. **Mayi,** or 'food', denotes an edible plant, and thus contrasts with **minha,** 'edible animal' or 'meat'.
2. Mischievous persons or troublemakers.
3. In Guugu Yimithirr storytelling, narrators often use such strings of nonsense syllables to denote the passage of time or distance.
4. According to Roger Hart, the head of an animal was customarily reserved for the hunter himself.
5. Aboriginal people.

THE STORIES: OWNERS AND MORALS

1. Parts of Roger's story have appeared in other guises. Dick Roughsey and Percy Tresize published a version of the Devil Dingo story (Roughsey 1973), without locating it geographically the way Roger does. Similarly, Tulo Gordon's collection of "Guugu Yimithirr" tales "from the Endeavour River" (Gordon and Haviland 1980) includes a somewhat expurgated version of the Thunder and Fog episode, recounted below, which Tulo learned growing up at Cape Bedford, where the story was widely known among older people. These stories were originally carefully fixed geographically, although there were probably variant versions associated with different Aboriginal groups.

2. A reference to the late Mary Ann Mundy, a woman who lived in the same camp as Roger when he was a child and who spent all of her life in close contact with the Barrow Point people.

3. Like all Guugu Yimithirr or Barrow Point language kin terms, the word **gami** denotes a classificatory relationship, implying both a genealogical link and a social category equivalent to a person "like" a mother's mother or a father's father. The **gami/gaminhtharr** relationship was perhaps the prototypical "joking relationship" (see Thomson 1935, Haviland 1979a) in this part of Australia. In Barrow Point language, the terms are reciprocal; thus, a man calls his paternal grandfather *amithu* and his grandfather calls him by the same term.

4. Literally, a 'non-salty, sweet, or bland' person.

SWALLOWED BY THE EARTH

1. These are the English words Roger Hart used to introduce this story, distinguishing it explicitly from some of the other tales that appear in this book. This version of the story of the demise of the Pinnacle mob is based on Roger Hart's telling on 18 September 1984.

2. Sutton 1992 lists this as clan area no. 10, including Barrow Point proper and the eastern side of Cape Melville. This is Roger Hart's own traditional country, inherited from his Aboriginal father. As the story indicates, the area extended considerably inland to the southwest and was divided socially into two halves.

3. Sutton 1992 lists the territory known by this name as clan area no. 12, described as "part of coast south of Barrow Point; Barrow Point to Cape Bowen," claimed as the traditional territory of several of Roger Hart's relatives named in later chapters.

4. There was evidently a basic similarity between the coastal and inland dialects of Barrow Point language despite different words in the two dialects for common objects and actions.

5. The Guugu Yimithirr word **yiirmbal** refers to spirits associated with dangerous or sacred places. **Yiirmbal** often take the form of gigantic animals, but they can equally well be manifested by powerful destructive forces, punishing everything from serious wrongdoing to simple disrespect.

6. Some residents of modern Hopevale worked in the 1950s and early 1960s as stockmen on the Starcke Station that ultimately grew to include areas as far north as Wakooka and Cape Melville. Older men with knowledge of these areas, including Roger Hart's childhood playmate Banjo Gordon, were still doing stockwork at the time and passed on scattered bits of local lore to the younger men.

7. Guugu Yimithirr–speaking people from the south used to refer to the northern tribes—including Barrow Point people—collectively as **Yiithuu.**

BARROW POINT AT THE TURN OF THE CENTURY

1. See Haviland and Haviland 1980 and Loos 1982 for the Cooktown area. Sutton 1993 gives 1890 as the date of the discovery of payable gold at Munburra on the Starcke River, and he mentions gold prospecting inland from Ninian Bay in 1884.
2. Sutton 1993, vol. 1, pp. 5–13, summarizes the historical record for the wider area encompassing Flinders Island and Cape Melville and extending south beyond Barrow Point to Cape Bowen.
3. Roth's report to the commissioner of police, "On the Aboriginals occupying the 'hinter-land' of Princess Charlotte Bay," 30 December 1898, MS. photocopy, Mitchell Library.
4. Ibid.
5. See "The Tragic History of Mrs. Watson," a booklet dated 24 January 1882 that reports on the inquest into the Lizard Island affair (whose date is set at 12 October 1881), also reprinting Mrs. Watson's diaries, J. C. M. Oxley Library.
6. Sutton 1992 shows this clan area (no. 21) as "Jack River, Battle Camp area."
7. Queensland Parliamentary Papers 1903 14 no. 1 / 1902, Roth's annual report for 1902.
8. Queensland State Archives (hereafter cited as QSA) Police records 13a/G1, pp. 68–69, 20 December 1910 (hereafter cited as POL). Bodman goes on to ask for reimbursement of £3 for the costs of the trip to Red Point on the boat *Seabreeze*. He excuses the failed mission by saying that he had had it on good authority they could get Chucky at Red Point, suggesting that some sort of a network of Aboriginal informers was already in place. QSA POL/13a/G1, p. 70, 3 January 1911.
9. QSA POL/13a/G1, p. 153, 5 April 1911, memo from Bodman to the inspector of police at Townsville, who had issued the warrant for Chucky's arrest.
10. QSA POL/13a/G1, p. 160, 18 April 1911, letter from Bodman to the chief protector Brisbane.
11. QSA POL/13a/G1, p. 172, 3 May 1911, letter from Bodman. During World War II, when Roger Hart and other young men from Hopevale visited Cherbourg on labor gangs, Roger was shown the graves of several men said to be his "relations" from Barrow Point who had been "removed" to the south decades before.
12. QSA POL/13a/G1 (Cooktown Police letterbook 1910–1912), pp. 4ff., 10 November 1910.
13. QSA POL/13a/G1, letter from Constable W. K. Aird, submitted by Sgt. Bodman, 10 November 1910.
14. QSA POL/13a/G1, letter apparently to the harbormaster. The boys' names and ages are listed in Mackett's index to the QSA Aboriginal papers, Mackett 1992, volume 36.
15. Archives of the Lutheran Church of Australia, 1, 28 November 1925, Schwarz

letter in reply to protector's inquiry of 19 December. "Sugar-bag" refers to the sweet drink made from water and native honey. Archives of the Lutherna Church of Australia are hereafter cited as ALCA.

16. Ibid.

17. "Island men" were natives of the Torres Strait Islands, Melanesians not considered to be quite **bama,** i.e., not true Australian Aborigines.

18. ALCA, 1, 28 November 1925, Schwarz letter in reply to protector's inquiry of 19 December.

19. In his reply to Schwarz's letter, Chief Protector of Aborigines Bleakley quoted "the regulation wages for mainland aboriginals" as " £2/5 to £2/10 per month and clothes, tobacco, food, and blankets, for Torres Straits men £3/15 to £4 with food and blankets, Torres Straits men in charge of boats £7 per month." QSA A/58682, letter from chief protector to Schwarz, 17 February 1926.

20. See Sutton 1993, 17ff.

21. King Harry was stepfather of the late Bob Flinders, of Hopevale, one of the biological children of the Danish lighthouse keeper mentioned.

22. The protectors of aborigines bestowed a crescent-shaped metal plate on the men they named "kings." Norman Tindale photographed King Harry with his plate at Flinders Island in 1927. See Sutton 1993.

23. From Guugu Yimithirr **milbi-thirr,** 'news-COMIT,' i.e., "bearing news."

24. The Abbey Peak property ultimately came to encompass both Occupation Licenses 394 and 395, whose histories were officially distinct but intertwined.

25. A Lands Ministry minute dated 12 April 1916 described the official situation as follows: "The land in the locality is part of a large area (4,500 sq. miles) which was opened for occupation license in May 1889 and remained open for over 26 years until the area not applied for was withdrawn last September." Lands OL 394 Cook, QSA.

26. QSA (Lands OL 394 Cook): 27 March 1916, letter from James Bennett, late 15th AJJ, c/o Cooktown, to Brig. Gen. Command 1st Military district, Brisbane, forwarded to Minister of Lands, 4 April 1916, including a map that shows OL 373 [Kalpowar] leased to Maurice Hart at £6/-, and Mount Hope to O'Beirne & O'Beirne for 30 years. Bennett visited the property and made an official application on 11 April 1916.

Maurice Hart is a recurrent player in this history. The O'Beirne brothers also reappear in local histories as landowners, as well as in the biographies of Aborigines to whom they gave their surname.

27. The annual rent was £4/16/6 for the two blocks. QSA Lands OL 394 Cook, entries dated 21 August 1916, 31 August 1916, and 6 September 1916 (no. 27920).

28. QSA Lands OL 394 Cook (no. 06064).

29. Applications from Allan Crichtley Instone of Cooktown appear in QSA Lands OL 395 Cook. On 11 June 1918, OL 395, Sapper Bennett's original property, was transferred to Instone. Instone applied to take over OL 394 as well (QSA Lands OL 394 no. 17405, 14 June 1918). Applications from Gordon and Stew-

art, the leaseholders of Starcke, appear in QSA Lands OL 394, 11 July 1918. The ubiquitous Maurice Hart's application appears in QSA Lands OL 394 Cook, 11 September 1918.

30. Government Gazette, 10 October 1919, p. 1208: Abbey Peak, 228 square miles, "Commencing on the coast at a point about 2 miles 40 chains N-Wly from Cape Bowen and bounded thence by Wakooka Holding, bearing west about 15 miles to Birthday Plains holding, by that holding bearing north about 10 miles 48 chains to the coast," inclusive of Ols 378, 394 and 395. (QSA LAN/AF run 1228).

31. Preference had originally again been given to a returning soldier, since Abbey Peak was leased to John Phillip O'Beirne, of the 12th Australian Light Horse Regiment, Moascar, Egypt on 10 December 1919. O'Beirne, evidently from the same family as the leaseholders of the original "Mt. Hope" occupation license, applied for the Abbey Peak property on 24 November 1919; the 228-mile property was gazetted on 10 December 1919 and sent for charting on 16 March 1920 (QSA LAN/AF run 1228). Instone's lease appears in QSA LAN/AF run 1228, 18 June 1920. The lease was to run for 30 years from 1 January 1920, at an annual rent of £85 until 1924, and £57 thereafter (QSA LAN N143).

32. ALCA, 1, letter dated 28 November 1925, Schwarz's reply to Protector Bleakley's inquiry of 19 November 1925.

33. Sam Malaya was reputed to have worked as a gardener for many other European station owners, and no one knew how he had come to Barrow Point. He had worked at Kalpowar, far to the south at King's Plain, and at Olivevale. While he was at Barrow Point he had no wife, but he was rumored to be the biological father of Hopevale resident Charlie Maclean, who was born in the area called **Jugun** at King's Plain. Malaya died in Cairns sometime after World War II.

34. QSA Lands OL 378 Cook no. 20561, 4 April 1916; Hart asked in an urgent telegram to be allowed to lease a 50-square-mile block adjoining Starcke to the north.

35. QSA Lands OL 378 Cook (no. 26902, 1 September 1916), telegram sent on 10 August 1916 from O'Beirne at Cooktown to "Hart, Grazier, c/o Donald, Laura."

36. The tract had been gazetted on 29 September 1916. QSA Lands OL 397 Cook, letter 8 November 1916. Government Gazette, 29 September 1916, p. 973.

37. A certain cowboy free-for-all atmosphere seems to have obtained in the area at the time. The official records pertaining to the Wakooka holding attest to a series of running battles between Hart and his neighbors, ostensibly over grazing rights. See QSA Lands OL 394, and OL 397 files, especially QSA LAN/AF 1247, Wakooka Run 2623 Cook, ranger's report dated 10 March 1920, QSA LAN/AF 1247, Wakooka 2623 Cook, letters dated 26 June, 12 July 1922; QSA LAN/AF 1238, Howick 2621 Cook, letter of 26 September 1924, QSA LAN/AF 1238, Howick 2621 Cook, letter dated 19 November 1924, from A. Wallace, Glenrock, to the Lands Commissioner, QSA LAN/AF 1238, Howick

2621 Cook, Land Ranger report 2 December 1924, QSA LAN/AF 1238, Howick 2621 Cook, minute 10 December 1924.

Roger Hart suggests that since these properties were vast in area and sparsely patrolled, cattle wandered freely from one station to the next. Maurice Hart believed that his neighbors were "duffing" (i.e., rustling) his cattle, and in retaliation when he came upon his neighbors' animals, he invited bama living on his property to dispatch them for food.

38. ALCA, 1, letter dated 28 November 1925, Schwarz's reply to Protector Bleakley's inquiry of 19 November 1925.

39. Ibid.

40. Maurice Hart had a large family of his own, and Roger Hart has kept track of some of the other descendants of his presumed biological father. Just before the war, when Roger and other Cape Bedford men were working to clear a mission outstation north of the McIvor River, at what was later to become Mt. Webb Station, they encountered a group of men shifting cattle south to Hughendon. "I seen his son there, Barney Hart . . . He was a young fellow—might as well call him **yaba**, 'older brother'." After the war while living in Mossman, Roger met a European woman from Port Douglas who identified herself as Hart's daughter. Another daughter, Madge, had a son Brian who operates bus tours from Moree, N.S.W., and who has visited Roger Hart at Hopevale. See Sutton 1993, p. 24.

41. A certain Mr. White had the sandalwood business, and he gave his surname to Tiger White—"the brother of old Charlie Burns"—who worked for him. He also employed a number of Aboriginal horseboys and other workers. Roger Hart identifies Jupert Bairy ("father of Lindsay Bairy") as White's horseboy, who took care of the pack horses, and old man Wulba, from Rossville, as another of his main employees. Jupert, from the Battle Camp area called **Balnggarr,** later worked at the Cooktown slaughteryard. Roger Hart remembers that he still recognized the former sandalwood worker when he saw him many years later in Cooktown.

42. Sutton 1993 records the spelling *Ipolyin,* from Toby Gordon, as the cover term for the Barrow Point area. He gives the Flinders Island equivalent as **Ipwolthan** and the Guugu Yimithirr name as **Dhibuuldhin.** (The latter appears transparently to translate as 'Place of Bats' < **thiibuul,** 'bat' + **thi(rr)** COMITATIVE), although Roger Hart remembers the Barrow Point equivalent of Guugu Yimithirr **thiibuul** as *mali:rr,* meaning 'bat'.) Sutton 1993 comments that "specific names refer to smaller parts of" the whole Barrow Point area. For Roger Hart, *lipwulin* is the proper name for the Aboriginal camp on the eastern side of the rocky outcrop that bisects the southern shore of Ninian Bay.

Variant pronunciations of place names, such as those for Eumangin or Roger's camp (Iipwulin, Ipolyin, Iipwolin, Ipuulin, etc.) attest to a complex vowel system in the Barrow Point language whose proper reconstruction is probably now impossible.

43. One nearby spot where people used to camp when traveling south and east—where Roger, Tulo, and I stopped to eat a coconut on our first trek to Roger's

homeland—is still remembered by name: *thulgumuway,* on the eastern shore south of Barrow Point itself. Sutton 1993 lists a Barrow Point language site called *tholkamoway,* which Toby Gordon identified as belonging to *ama Al-thanmungu* near Cape Bowen. Roger Hart puts the site squarely in his Gambi-ilmugu area. He translates *thulgu* as the name for a species of large flying fox, whose neck is ringed with white fur. The name *thulgumuway* would thus denote a place where such animals are plentiful.

44. Roger Hart glosses the word *uwuru* as 'deaf'. Sutton 1993 gives the name of this same creek, provided by Toby Gordon, as *Owuro,* 'Alligator Creek'.
45. Sutton 1993, following Toby Gordon, lists the Eumangin Creek, as it is known to stockmen, as *Yamaaynthin.*
46. Sutton 1993 shows this clan area (no. 11), "part of coast just north of Barrow Point," as beginning somewhat farther south on the coast than Roger himself remembers, in an area which Roger Hart identifies as still associated with his own Gambiilmugu group.
47. Several large shell middens are still evident in this area, attesting to sizeable Aboriginal settlement here up until the 1930s.

BUSH TUCKER

1. At Hopevale macromoieties, whose importance for social identity has faded somewhat before massive numbers of marriages, "crooked" by traditional standards, are alternatively identified by reference to totemic bee or bird species.
2. In Guugu Yimithirr two closely related species are the cognate **muunhthiina** and **mabil**. There are several other named varieties in both languages, but people rarely, if ever, collect these roots for food in modern times.
3. In Guugu Yimithirr, **babunh**.
4. In Barrow Point, *Warninil,* sometimes also known in English as "barra barra" nuts.
5. Nicholas Wallace, brother of Hector, and according to Roger, son of a Barrow Point man known as Barney.
6. Long Billy McGreen was later a native trooper, a tracker for the Cooktown police, the wardsman for the Cooktown lepers camp, and a celebrated victim of a witchcraft killing.

YIITHUU-WARRA

1. The reconstruction of the past has been further complicated by contemporary efforts to reclaim land rights for the descendants of the original Aboriginal owners of this part of Queensland. See, for example, Haviland 1997.
2. Literally, "they have a single intestine," i.e., they are both stubborn and easily angered.
3. "Old woman."
4. Roger describes Toby Gordon's wife Topsy—whom Toby married after being sent away to Lockhart—as a 'cousin' of Rosie, wife of King Nicholas.

5. Classificatory father's younger sister, i.e., a paternal aunt, who would normally be married to a man in the opposite moiety and thus be the mother of an appropriate cross-cousin bride.
6. Grandchild of the same moiety, e.g., a classificatory son's child, an appropriate joking partner but an inappropriate marriage partner.
7. The Guugu Yimithirr word for the practice is **gunyjil.**
8. The Lutheran church had founded another mission for the Aboriginal inhabitants in the Bowen-Proserpine area in the latter part of the previous century. Ultimately the mission failed for financial reasons, and a large group of former residents was sent to Cape Bedford in 1902. Most of these people were quickly returned to the south, since the Hope Valley missionaries found that they had been "spoiled" by inappropriately free contact with Europeans in their homeland. A small group of these "strangers" from the south, however, stayed on at Cape Bedford.
9. A Marie Yamba man who became an important leader at Cape Bedford and who was, coincidentally, Roger Hart's father-in-law.

THE PORCUPINE

1. The animal is actually an echidna.
2. Tulo Gordon remembered having heard another detail of this story, that the angry people from the camp also hit the porcupine-woman with their wommeras, leaving a hollow space at the base of where the modern echidna has its ears, thus rendering her not only "disobedient" (i.e., "without ears") but permanently deaf.

NGANYJA

1. Sutton 1992 gives the name as **Wurrkulnthin.** He mentions it as a "Carpet Snake" story place and cites as well a "Tiger Snake" story associated with the island. Roger Hart explicitly denies that his own **Mungurru,** 'Carpet Snake', story has an association with Noble Island, contrasting the owners of that island with the Cape Bowen, Barrow Point, and Cape Melville people that share his version of the story.
2. Roger contrasts the burial customs of his people at Barrow Point with the Guugu Yimithirr practice of keeping parts of bodies, especially the fingertips, in a small bag to use in hunting magic, i.e., to attract game. Barrow Point people would keep bits of skin and hair as "remembrances."
3. The Aboriginal people at Iipwulin used to call the European settler, Instone, by the uncomplimentary and somewhat terrifying name *damu munun urdiiga,* i.e., 'ghost with skin removed'.
4. The man was Toby Flinders, also known as Toby Cape Bowen, described by Roger Hart as a "paternal grandfather" of Mitchell McGreen.
5. See Dixon 1971, Haviland 1979a, 1979b.
6. In Barrow Point language, literally, 'name-with'.

7. Johnny Flinders was a Cape Melville man who, until his death in 1979, was a central figure in helping anthropologists to reconstruct Aboriginal territorial and genealogical ties in the whole Cape Melville area. Sutton 1993 gives two Flinders Island language names for him, **Wodhyethi** and **Orpayin.** According to Sutton's account, John Flinders saw his brother Diver Flinders initiated at Bathhurst Head around 1908. Sutton reports John Flinders's belief that this was the last initiation in the area. On the other hand, Roger Hart remembers John Flinders to have been about fifteen years old at the time the ceremony he describes took place.

   Roger's description of the **nganyja** is apparently based both on his own childhood memory and on accounts of others with whom he shared memories of the Cape Melville camps in later years. It is likely that the rituals he describes here were something less than a full initiation.

8. The two brothers, Nelson and Wathi (also known as Billy Salt, or **Nhimaarbulu**) were from the area called **Wuuri,** and lived most of the time in the Barrow Point camp at Iipwulin during Roger Hart's childhood. They were **thuway,** or 'nephew' to Roger.

9. Roger is reluctant to use the Guugu Yimithirr word **nganyja** for this ceremony, saying "that's what *they* [i.e., the Cape Bedford people] call it." The ritual Roger describes he identifies closely with worship and respect accorded to the Carpet Snake, whose spirit inhabited Cape Melville.

10. The reference is to the totemic bee species representing the two moieties.

WITCHES

1. One of the first children to be born to newly Christianized parents at the Cape Bedford Mission, Mickey Bluetongue is shown in mission records as having been born in 1886, son of "Mickey" and "Rosie," and later married to "Nellie."

2. McGreen was also known as Billy **Galbay,** "Long Billy" or Billy **Tharrathan**, after his father; taped conversation with the late Tulo Gordon (80:45) and Sutton's genealogy, Sutton 1993, 2:18.

3. A man with the clan association known as **Yalnggaal-mugu,** inland south of Red Point, Burns was known to the young Roger Hart as a stockman working for Maurice Hart at the Wakooka Station in the late teens. His father was old man **Waarigan,** 'Moon'. Burns's brother Tiger White worked at Wakooka in sandalwood cutting. Burns later returned from Palm Island to Laura, and thence to Hopevale, where two of his daughters married Hopevale men.

4. Haviland fieldnotes; taped conversations with the late Billy Jacko (79:17).

5. The death of McGreen was reported to the protector of Aborigines in Cooktown by his brother, Jackson, in 1937; Queensland State Archives, Protector of Aborigines Occurrences Book.

6. This story was told by the late George Bowen, long-time master of the mission boat *Pearl Queen.*

7. The late Tulo Gordon remembered hearing this story as a young lad.

THE PROBLEM OF "HALF-CASTE" CHILDREN

1. Despite the fact that this term is in frequent use even at modern Hopevale, it is offensive to many Aboriginal people. I apologize for having been unable to avoid citing archival documents that make free use of the expression.
2. Queensland Votes and Papers, vol. 4, 1896, 723–36, 731, A. Meston's Report on North Queensland Aborigines.
3. Report of the Northern Protector of Aborigines for 1899, 1 July 1900. Roth also opposed suggestions that half-caste women be allowed exemptions from the provisions of restrictive legislation governing the status and employment of Aborigines, on the grounds that this could leave them without legal protection and relegate them to "nothing else than slavery."
4. Roth, Report of Northern Protector of Aboriginals, 2 January 1901.
5. Ibid.
6. Queensland State Archives, Police records 13a/G1, 20 April 1910.
7. Roth, Report of Northern Protector of Aboriginals, 2 January 1901.
8. ALCA, 1.2, tape no. 3, 24 April 1900, letter from undersecretary for Home to Pastor Rechner, condemning management at Bloomfield and mentioning a telegram in which the mission worker "has made a written and witnessed confession to having had connection with some of the girls at the Station" during the missionary's absence.
9. In a letter to the mission inspector, Schwarz said he first refused to accept the delegation of twenty-five Marie Yamba people who were transferred to Bloomfield (Archives of the Neuendettelsau Mission Society, Bavaria, Germany, 477, no. 2, 3 September 1901, and Kirchliche Mitteilungen aus und über Nordamerika, Neuendettelsau 1886–1907, nos. 2 and 3, p. 471, March 1902). Subsequently, in July 1902, twenty-four of the Marie Yamba people were allowed to move to Hope Valley, at Cape Bedford (Archives of the Neuendettelsau Mission Society, Bavaria, Germany, 488, no. 2, 12 July 1902, letter from Schwarz to mission inspector). Roger Hart's history is intertwined with that of the Marie Yamba people, since he ultimately married the daughter of one of them.
10. In one case, a European man who had admitted paternity of a mixed-descent child applied for her to be placed at Cape Bedford after protracted correspondence about who should be financially and morally responsible for her upbringing. See QSA A/58749. The European later became a friend of Missionary Schwarz and a periodic visitor to the mission. He was praised by mission authorities as the only white man in the region to accept responsibility for a part-Aboriginal child he had fathered.
11. Schwarz in fact furnished most of the ethnographic and linguistic information about the Aboriginal groups living north of Cooktown that Roth later published. See, for example, Roth 1984 (1901–6).
12. A large Anglican mission station near Cairns.
13. Letter from Schwarz to Roth, 2 February 1902. QSA A/58749 northern protector of Aborigines. The man called Matyi (Schwarz's rendition of the Guugu

Yimithirr word **mathi,** 'rain') was still remembered by the oldest people at Hopevale in the early 1970s; photographs of him taken by the early missionaries show a grizzled sorcerer with white hair and a formidable nose-pin. Matyi's picture appears in Pohlner 1986.

14. QSA A/58749, letter 24 February 1902, from office of the northern protector to undersecretary.
15. QSA A/58749, letter from Kenny to his superior officer, 26 June 1902.
16. QSA A/58749, note from Kenny to Inspector Garroway, Laura, 30 June 1902.
17. QSA A/58749, letter 23 June 1902, from Wallace, Glenrock, to the home secretary.
18. Roth, as the northern protector of Aborigines, had of course ordered the removal. Despite Wallace's appeal to Roth's opinion, Roth himself was not well viewed by the settlers in the Cooktown area because of his interventions on behalf of local Aborigines. Wallace also wrote to his parliamentary representative complaining about Roth's attempts to have the girl Dora removed, and the legislator in turn forwarded the letter (from "an old and respected squatter in the Cook District") to the home secretary, with the comment that in a similar case "Dr Roth's action in forcibly taking a young gin from a comfortable and respectable home where she was treated by the whole family as one of themselves resulted eventually in the gin becoming a prostitute." QSA A/58749, letter from J. Hamilton, Brisbane, to home secretary, 8 July 1902.
19. Ibid.
20. Guugu Yimithirr, **Binhthi-warra,** a clan group whose traditional tribal estate included both the properties Glenrock and Elderslie on the McIvor River.
21. Protector Roth, later reviewing his own correspondence book, finds "that on 19th June 1899 I had to write to this same Charles Wallace as follows: 'I have just returned from a patrol along the coast and lower McIvor. At the 'landing' an Aboriginal named Jimmy whom I examined and found suffering from recent marks of violence, complained about your having whipped him, giving me full particulars and asking me to take action. I should be glad to hear what you have to say.' I remember distinctly his replying to the effect that he fully admitted it and would do it again"; QSA A/58749, letter of 22 August 1902, signed by W. E. Roth, northern protector of Aborigines, to home secretary. Wallace was frequently in dispute with the neighboring Cape Bedford mission over boundaries and cattle rights in the area.
22. QSA A/58749, report from J. Martin Kenny, Constable 419, Eight-Mile [Cooktown], to Subinspector Garroway, Laura, 15 August 1902.
23. QSA A/58749, Roth's letter of 22 August 1902. Roth requested that the settler Wallace not be told that Dora's situation had been raised by the Cape Bedford missionary, since "were Charlie Wallace ever to know that the Missionaries had first drawn my attention to the case I fear that something might happen to the latter's cattle on the [Aboriginal Mission] reserve."
24. QSA A/58749, letter from Wallace at Glenrock to home scretary, 20 September 1902. The removal orders from the under secretary for home affairs, W. H. Ryder, was dated 8 September 1902.

25. QSA A/58749, Kenny's report dated Eight Mile, 23 October 1902. This and subsequent correspondence in the case originally appeared in a separate file of the correspondence of the northern protector, with ID numbers 748/1902 and 945/1902.

26. QSA A/58749, letter from Wallace, Glenrock, to the home secretary, Brisbane, 14 December 1903. "Constable Kenny I hear caught the father of this gin and threatened to send him away to another country unless he came over and took the gin away from me."

27. QSA A/58749, Kenny's report to Garroway, Laura, 22 October 1903. The home secretary's telegram authorizing Dora to stay at Cape Bedford was also dated 22 October 1903.

28. QSA A/58749, letter from Wallace, Glenrock, to the home secretary, Brisbane, 14 December 1903.

29. Theile here refers to three women of mixed ancestry, considered "sisters" by the Hope Valley community, who went on to raise important families at Hopevale; one of them became a main schoolteacher at the mission.

30. Report from Theile, based on a letter from Schwarz, Deutsche Kirche-und Missions Zeitung, Tanunda, SA, 1885–1917 23 May 1916.

31. Removal records of the Queensland Department of Aboriginal and Islander Advancement (computer notes from Prof. Bruce Rigsby), 604 REM & DEP for 1912, include a reference to the removal to Cape Bedford of the late Dolly Wallace with her brothers, Ned and Harold, from Mayneside, at the recommendation of the protector from Hughendon. I am grateful to Bruce Rigsby for a copy of the relevant records. See also Pohlner 1986:85–86.

32. Sutton 1993:16–18. See also Pohlner 1986:171.

FROM BARROW POINT TO CAPE BEDFORD

1. Roger has heard details about only one of his maternal uncles, a big burly man who was said to have died in Cairns after signing on to a boat crew.

2. German Harry was the father of Helen Rootsey, whom Roger considers to be a classificatory sister-in-law, since he counts her husband Joe Rootsey as "like a brother." German Harry's Guugu Yimithirr nickname is a vulgar reference to his unusual hairiness.

3. Some material in this section is drawn from Haviland 1991.

4. Roger's reminiscences frequently mix languages, as in this example, in which he puts Guugu Yimithirr, rather than Barrow Point, words into his Aboriginal father's mouth.

5. Late elder claimant for the tribal area at Cape Flattery known as **Dingaal.**

6. Dabunhthin was a mission-educated mixed-descent man from the **Binhthi-warra** clan who was one of Missionary Schwarz's most trusted Aboriginal leaders, in charge of the mission outstation on the McIvor River. Rather than stay at the mission, he ultimately chose to go voluntarily to Palm Island, to accompany his "full-blood" brother whom Schwarz had ordered removed from the mission and deported.

7. Willie Mt. Webb is one of the senior claimants to the clan known as **Daarrba-warra,** whose traditional estate includes the area at Mt. Webb near the Morgan River.
8. The late Leo Rosendale, from the Maytown area, and the late Bob Flinders, the part-European boy taken some years earlier from Cape Melville, were both old hands at mission life by this time.

A SUNSET GLOW

1. Deutsche Kirche- und Missions Zeitung, Tanunda, SA, 1885–1917, 30, no. 11, p. 425 June 1898, report from J. Flierl on the Cape Bedford mission.
2. The two kings mentioned were government-recognized leaders of two groups of Guugu Yimithirr–speaking people, King Johnny (**Ngamu Binga**) of the McIvor River, and King Jacko, originally of Munburra on the Starcke River and later of Cape Bedford Reserve. Both men had been given their brass plates, symbols of office, in 1911, with the justification that with such authority the men "would be of great assistance to the police when any occurrence" of interest to the authorities ocurred in their respective areas. (QSA POL/13a/g1 Cooktown Police letterbook 1910–1912, pp. 278–79, dated 25 October 1911.) Both kings left many descendants at modern Hopevale.
3. ALCA, 3 no. 1 27 July 1926, Dr. F. O. Theile, "Report on Visit to HV July 1926."
4. Official mission policy was also to educate children in English, but the mission authorities considered Guugu Yimithirr a necessary instrument for religious instruction.

THE SCRUB PYTHON AT CAPE MELVILLE

1. This is the range called in English Altanmoui. Sutton 1993 notes a Barrow Point name for the mountains as **Althanmughuy,** corresponding to the clan name Roger Hart gives as **Althanmugu-ngu** for the area on the coast just to the north of Cape Bowen.
2. Roger Hart associates the area where the granite outcroppings stand today with the clan of the late Johnny Flinders, a group referred to in Guugu Yimithirr as **Yuurrguungu.**

THE BARROW POINT PEOPLE VISIT THE SOUTH

1. ALCA, Schwarz letter to chief protector, 20 November 1919 (quoted in Pohlner 1986:104).
2. Pohlner 1986:104.
3. In January 1924, the chief protector informed Schwarz that he was exploring the matter with both lands and marine authorities, but that for the moment only land at Cape Flattery and Lookout Point, at the northern extreme of the mission's boundary, would be reserved. ALCA, letter from chief protector to Schwarz, 14 January 1924 (quoted in Pohlner 1986:104).

4. Old man Jujurr, Roger Hart's relation on his mother's side, belonged to the tribal area around the Jack River, called Muunhthi.

5. See QSA A/58682, letter from chief protector to protector, Cooktown, 23 September 1925, suggesting that McGreen could give information about possible violations of the Aboriginal protection laws by Instone at Barrow Point.

6. QSA A/58682, note from chief protector to Schwarz, 19 November 1925.

7. QSA A/58682, letter from chief protector to protector, Cooktown, 17 August 1925, quoting cable from Mullins, the protector at Laura.

8. QSA A/58682, Chief Protector of Aborigines series (restricted), letter from Protector Mullins, Laura, to chief protector, 1 August 1925.

9. QSA A/58682, letter from chief protector to protector, Cooktown, 17 August 1925, quoting cable from Mullins.

10. QSA A/58682, chief protector to protector, Cooktown, 23 September 1925.

11. QSA A/58682, letter from chief protector to protector, Cooktown, 17 August 1925.

12. QSA A/58682, letter, 25/4948 from chief protector to chief superintendent, Palm Island, 23 September 1925. The results of the interrogation were inconclusive: in a letter to chief protector, 13 October 1925 (QSA A/58682), the Palm Island superintendent wrote that the Aborigine "states that he was employed by Mr Instone but never received any wages from him, only clothes. He uses the launch to convey food to and from Cooktown to his own station. The boy also states that he was sent to work for Mr Wallace, but never received any wages."

13. QSA A/58682, letter from Sgt. Guilfoyle, protector, Cooktown, to chief protector, 14 September 1925.

14. Sgt. Guilfoyle had written, in response to the chief protector's question about changing the supply depot to the McIvor River, a walk of several hundred kilometers from Barrow Point, that "the aboriginals referred to by the Laura protector could easily come to Cape Bedford outstation on the McIvor River for their supplies. The strong aboriginals are always willing to carry out anything to weak or old aboriginals and they think nothing of walking 50 or 100 miles at blanket time"; QSA A/58682, letter from Sgt. Guilfoyle, protector, Cooktown, to chief protector, 14 September 1925.

15. QSA A/58682, confidential letter from the chief protector to Schwarz superintendent, Cape Bedford, 24 September 1925.

16. QSA A/58682, 29 October 25 telegram from protector to Allan Instone, Cooktown.

17. QSA A/58682, letter from Instone, Abbey Peak station via Cooktown, to chief protector, 29 October 1925. In a marginal note Instone adds: "while I have been here the boys have been contented and well behaved, as they have been looked after, and Nicholas King of BP has aided the police in tracking and holding boys who had run away from boats on several occasions." Such policing of Aborigines under contract to European and other employers was one of the main reasons the government instituted the system of "kings" in the first place.

18. Ibid. The chief protector replied to Instone that "it is the desire to draw these people into the care of the mission where already some of their friends have taken up residence. The numbers of them that in the recent [past] have had to be treated in Cooktown for venereal disease also emphasizes the wisdom of this course"; QSA A/58682, letter from chief protector to Instone, 19 November 1925.
19. ALCA, letter from Schwarz to Bleakley dated 28 November 1925.
20. Ibid.
21. This is the late Bob Flinders, who in 1919 was transferred to Cape Bedford from Laura, where he had been taken the previous year.
22. Namely, Roger Hart.
23. A probable reference to Banjo and Toby Gordon.
24. Probably that of **Wanhthawanhtha** (Tommy Cook), whom the late Tulo Gordon remembered from his earliest childhood.
25. This is a reference to the Starcke Station, which included the area **Junyju** at Manbara, which was King Jacko's original tribal territory and where he was officially appointed king in 1911.
26. Possibly a reference to Nelson and his wife.
27. This may have been the late Mitchell McGreen, who despite reporting his birthplace and date as the same as those of his older brother Billy, Jr. (i.e., Laura in 1918), was remembered by all to be have been several years Billy's junior, having been born when Billy, Sr., was already living in the Cooktown area.
28. A reference to Yuuniji (Lizzie), Long Billy's wife, whose tribal territory was **Thanhil** in the Point Lookout area.
29. A reference to Roger Hart's mother.
30. A reference to Roger's half brother Jimmy Hart, who Roger believes was born at the North Shore camp.
31. ALCA, letter from Schwarz to Bleakley dated 28 November 1925.
32. Ibid.
33. QSA A/58682, report from Schwarz to chief protector, 12 January 1925.
34. ALCA, 1–2, letter dated 14 December 1925, from Schwarz to Theile, director of Lutheran Board of Foreign Missions. Throughout the 1920s and 1930s Shwarz was in a constant (and ultimately unsuccessful) battle with the mission board to procure an appropriate second missionary who could both adapt to the conditions at Cape Bedford and get along with Schwarz—a tall order.
35. ALCA, letter from Theile to protector, dated 10 March 1926. The mission strategy was apparent in Theile's letter to Schwarz, 10 March 1926 (ALCA), in which he described his negotiations with the chief protector: "I wanted to put the application [for a fishing boat] in writing without referring to the Cape Melville and Point Barrow blacks at all. Because I hold that the Cape Bedford aboriginals are quite entitled to help on the part of the government just as well as other similar groups of Natives further north. But he thought if I would mention these natives it would be of great influence with himself or with someone else who has to pass on the matter. At any rate I told him that

I would bring the matter into my application only in the manner which I did now. We would not get the Cape Melville natives first and then apply for the boat, we would apply for the boat and see what we can do with regard to the Cape Melville blacks afterwards."

36. ALCA, no. 2 (also QSA A/58682) letter from Bleakley to Schwarz, 17 February 1926. The government further imposed severe legal restrictions on Japanese who attempted to recruit Aboriginal boat crews from camps on the east coast of Cape York Peninsula (ALCA, letter dated 17 February 1926, from Chief Protector Bleakley to Schwarz). Bleakley asked Schwarz whether the new restrictions had brought any more of the Barrow Point people to Cape Bedford in search of rations.

37. ALCA, 16 no. 3, Theile, Report on Visit to HV July 1926, 27 July 1926.

38. On occasion Roger has reported that ex-tracker Charlie (Chookie) McGreen was the one who brought his brother Jimmy to the mission.

THE SECOND TRIP SOUTH

1. Schwarz reported that the group from Barrow Point arrived for rations at Cape Bedford on 5 February 1926. Roger Hart remembers the date 9 May 1925 carved on a **gabagarr** tree at Cape Bedford when his kinsmen were camped there. Perhaps some people from Barrow Point visited Cape Bedford on more than one occasion in this period, although Roger remembers only this one, final visit.

2. The man known as "Charlie Chookie."

3. Barney Warner's older brother.

4. This was Roger Hart's Aboriginal father, Charlie Lefthander.

5. Possibly Billy McGreen's brother, also known as Jackson.

6. The Barrow Point king.

7. Perhaps this was the sorceror "old man Johnny," **Ngamu Wuthurru.**

8. **Walbamun,** Toby Flinder's mother.

9. Probably Albert **Wuuriingu.**

10. Probably Toby Flinders.

11. The list accompanied QSA A/58682, letter from Schwarz to chief protector, 1 March 1926.

12. QSA A/58682, letter from Schwarz to chief protector, 1 March 1926.

13. **Barrbaarr,** or Bridge Creek, was the site of the main camp of "heathen" adult Aborigines living on the Cape Bedford reserve. Most of these people were Gu-ugu Yimithirr speakers from local clans. Many of them had children at the mission school, and they were often called upon by the missionary to do odd jobs or agricultural work in return for rations.

14. Barney and Yaalugurr were one of the early couples at Cape Bedford, whose sons, Yoren and Baru, became the heads of two large Hopevale families.

15. William, from the area around Cooktown, or **Waaymburr** was the father of Johnny, in turn father of Joseph and Alick Johnny, later of Hopevale, with descendants at Palm Island.

POINT LOOKOUT

1. QSA A/58682, Cooktown protector's annual report, minute dated 17 March 1927.
2. That is, Jackie Red Point.
3. QSA A/58682, letter from Guilfoyle, Cooktown protector, to chief protector, S. Brisbane, 3 May 1927.
4. Gordon was the owner of Starcke Station.
5. QSA A/58682, letter from Allen C. Instone, Abbey Peak, to protector of Aborigines, Cooktown, 24 February 1927(?).
6. QSA A/58682, letter from Schwarz to chief protector, 2 April 1927.
7. QSA A/58682, letter from Schwarz to protector, Cooktown, 2 May 1927.
8. As always, Schwarz was worried about his limited finances and inability to feed all the people living on the reserve. He wrote:

   Amongst the lot on the place now there are only about five or six men able to do some work. The rest are old men, women and children. We allow those who wish to do so to help occasionally at our beche-de-mer business but naturally we cannot on account of so few helping when it suits them supply the whole camp with food regularly. I do not think it necessary nor advisable either. (ibid.).

   Schwarz further asked Chief Protector Bleakley to supplement his food allowances and to help prevent Japanese boats from contracting young Aboriginal men from these groups who might otherwise join the mission fishing operation at Point Lookout.
9. QSA A/58682, letter from Schwarz to protector, Cooktown, 2 May 1927.
10. QSA A/58682, letter from Guilfoyle, Cooktown protector, to chief protector, S. Brisbane, 3 May 1927.
11. QSA A/58682, letter from Bleakley to Schwarz, 29 June 1927. He also requisitioned khaki uniforms and felt hats to outfit the new policeman; QSA A/58682, requisition dated 1 July 1927.
12. QSA A/58682, letter from Guilfoyle, Cooktown protector, to chief protector, S. Brisbane, 3 May 1927.
13. QSA A/58682, Schwarz to chief protector Brisbane, 11 July 1927.

ESCAPE FROM WAWU NGALAN

1. QSA A/58682, letter from Schwarz to chief protector Brisbane, 22 August 1927.

THE MISSIONER'S REVENGE

1. ALCA, 1 no. 2, report from Schwarz to Bleakley, dated 18 January 1927 (yearly report for 1926).
2. Ibid.

3. It is unclear whether King Harry and King Charlie are the same man or two different men; current Hopevale memory gives the name associated with Cape Melville as King Harry.

4. QSA A/58682, letter from Schwarz to chief protector, Brisbane, 22 August 1927.

5. QSA POL/13a/G1, p. 144, memo from Bodman to chief protector, Brisbane, 25 March 1911. The same Aboriginal Occurrences Book shows that Protector Bodman recommended that King Johnny (known as Mechan Euchan) be named king in October 1911, and a brass plate was issued the following month; QSA POL/13a/G1, Cooktown police letterbook, p. 279, 29 October 1911.

    Queensland removal records show that a King Johnny (Mechan Euchan) was removed from the McIvor to Barambah in 1913; the records describe him as "a troublesome character, a notorious sorcerer, spreads dissension and quarreling among other natives, [and] seriously interferes with mission life."

    Hopevale memory suggests that **Ngamu Binga** was deported because he was unwilling to send his mixed-race social children to the mission for school. Ultimately, **Ngamu Binga** escaped from Cherbourg and returned to his own country on foot. He later was speared near Cooktown and was buried at Four-Mile.

    Schwarz continued to have people officially "removed" from Cape Bedford right up until World War II.

6. QSA A/58682, chief protector to protector, Cooktown, 17 February 1927.

7. QSA A/58682, letter from Bleakley to Laura protector, D. W. McConnell, 22 September 1927.

8. QSA A/58682, letter from office of protector, Laura, to chief protector, 28 September 1927.

9. Ibid.

10. Roger Hart's **gami,** same side grandparent.

EXILE

1. Authorization for the surprise raids on fishing vessels suspected of illegally harboring Aborigines was requested in a letter from chief protector to under-secretary, Home Dept., 26 July 1927 (QSA A/58682).

2. QSA A/58682, doc. 28/6839, a letter from Guilfoyle, acting sergeant 1064, Cairns Police District, Cooktown, dated 21 November 1928. The police intended to use a mission boat for the expedition, but the local protector was "of opinion the mission lugger *Pearl Queen* is not a suitable boat to use on the patrol herein referred to owing to it having to be made at the most likely time to find the Japanese luggers anchored near where the Aboriginals are camped and this is generally when the weather is too rough for the luggers at the reefs which then compels them to sail back to the mainland or islands for shelter and it is then the illegal employment of Aboriginal women would take place. I understand the *Pearl Queen* is not a fast sailing lugger and if the Japanese or others sighted her approaching their luggers when they had any Aboriginal

women or male Aboriginals who are not signed on under agreement with them on board they could easily hoist their sails and sail away from the *Pearl Queen*."

3. In his report for 1928 to the chief protector, dated 25 January 1929 (ALCA, 1–2, 26–185, also QSA A/58682), Schwarz makes it clear that he wants more land for these non-Christian adults to hunt on. He also argues that he has moved them into closer proximity to their younger Christian relatives in hopes of some spontaneous evangelization, although mission memory suggests that the non-Christian adults were expected to do heavy agricultural work for the newly established mission farm.

4. Ibid., ALCA, 26–185.

5. QSA A/58682, report of superintendent, Cape Bedford, 21 November 1927.

6. QSA A/58682, memorandum dated 5 March 1928 from Chief Protector Bleakley, to Superintendent of Cape Bedford mission via Cooktown.

7. The only official documentation of this removal we have discovered is a handwritten note, appended to the front of the Cape Bedford file QSA A/58682, which reads "11 Cape Melville Natives removed to L.R.M [Lockhart River Mission]" with the apparent date 5 December 1929.

8. QSA 181 Starcke Pt 1 (also Lands OL 378 Cook), 8 September 1915.

9. QSA LAN/AF 1247, Wakooka 2623 Cook: Stewart obtained Wakooka on 5 February 1932. Further changes in the percentages of ownership appear in QSA LAN N143, 19 July 1932; see also QSA 181 Starcke Pt 1, 20 April 1933, 31 December 1935; QSA LAN/AF 1228 Abbey Peak, 5 April 1936.

10. The Lands Department inspector's report for 1928 on Abbey Peak remarked that the lease was "not subject to personal residence" as the actual leaseholders lived on distant properties (QSA LAN/AF 1228 Abbey Peak, 31 July 1928). In 1930, Abbey Peak showed a holding capacity of 3 head of cattle per square mile, with a total count of 684 head (QSA LAN/AF 1228 Abbey Peak, 11 July 1930). Land Ranger Charles Gordon reported that on his visit to Abbey Peak from 13 to 16 August 1931 he observed a large dwelling, outbuildings, 7 tailing yards, a horse paddock and bullock paddock with 1600 head of mixed cattle and 40 head of horses, branded QAK and RX9. He went on, "The lessees reside on other properties held by them but visit this holding fairly regularly" (QSA LAN/AF 1228 Abbey Peak, 7 September 1931).

11. He told Roger Hart that he had worked for one Sam Carlson, a man who later owned a property at Streamlet near Cooktown.

12. Bendie's father, Long Jack, was associated with **Wunuurr-warra,** the clan area around the headwaters of the McIvor River.

13. The Cooktown Police Occurrences Book for 1937 contains the following two entries.

> "Const. Costello left 9 AM 28/7/37 on Patrol to Starcke Station to serve summons on Manager Mr. Hales for Breach of Aboriginal Protection and Restriction on Sale of Opium Act, and to bring back two boys Bindy and Freddie who are to be sent to Mission."

"Const. Costello returned from Patrol to Starcke Station at 3:30 PM on 2nd. Freddy and Bindy brought to Cooktown"; QSA POL/13a/N6, 28 July 1937 and 5 August 1937. "Freddy" here was Fred Grogan, later of Hopevale.

ROGER HART AT THE CAPE BEDFORD MISSION

1. South from Cape Bedford, on the coast.
2. The late Jellico Jacko, **ngathu warra biiba,** was son of King Jacko of Cape Bedford and a senior claimant to the tribal country called **Junyju** up the Starcke River near Manbara.
3. This was Albert Lakefield, another of Roger's brothers, whose Aboriginal stepfather was Albert Lakefield, Sr., also called **Mayi-ngandaalga,** from Jeannie Tableland; Sutton 1993:24.

WARTIME

1. ALCA, no. 1 (27-11), 16 June 1932, Official Cape Bedford report enclosed in letter from Protector Bleakley to Dr. Theile of the Lutheran Church of Australia.
2. One such man was the late Billy **Muundu, ngathu warra biiba,** who arrived back at Spring Hill to find his wife and children gone, along with everyone else. Unlike the people from the bush camps, who merely fled farther into the bush, **Muundu** embarked on a solitary odyssey to find his family in the south, arriving on his own in Woorabinda many months after the main group had been evacuated.
3. Roger Hart had this news from Helen Rootsey and the late Mary Ann Mundy, who recounted having taken part in the burial.
4. Roger Hart still smarts with the memory that he was never allowed to visit his childhood playmate while she was ill in Cooktown hospital, since in those early days it was difficult for Hopevale people to get permission from the mission superintendent to travel freely. Barney Warner, who was "closely trusted" by the then Hopevale pastor and superintendent Wenke, visited Leah several times in Cooktown before she was transferred to Cairns.

IIPWULIN

1. Sutton 1993 shows clan area no. 9, corresponding to "part of the coast between Barrow Point and Red Point" by this Guugu Yimithirr name, called *Ama Alth(a)nmungu* in Barrow Point language. By Hopevale reckoning it is the area "north of Red Point." The mountain range known in English as Altanmoui (*Althanmughuy* in Barrow Point language) rises inland from Cape Bowen, in a clan area known as **Manyamarr,** the starting place for the giant Scrub Python who escapes to Cape Melville in Roger Hart's story.

2. A clan area associated with the coast between the mouth of the Starcke River and Point Lookout, including the area now known as Twelve-Mile (clan no. 64 in Sutton 1993).

3. Guugu Yimithirr **thawuunh** and Barrow Point *anggatha,* both meaning 'friend', are terms of address Roger Hart frequently uses with people whose exact kinship relation to him is not clearly established. Having considered the fictive kinship relations more carefully, we now call each other 'cousin'.

4. Bruce Rigsby (n.d.) identifies both these men as follows: "The Wallace family are Lakefield claimants by descent from Hector, Nicholas and Kathleen Wallace, who were Mbarruyu and/or Mbarrubarram clan members and Koko Warra by language and tribal identity." By contrast, Roger Hart associates Nicholas and Hector Wallace (also known as Hector Lai-Fook) with the area called Muunhthi (clan no. 21 in Sutton 1993), the Jack River area, where Thunder lived in the Fog story.

5. The late Jack Harrigan, of Cooktown, was a traditional owner of **Balnggarr,** an area around Battle Camp. The common core of shared social knowledge in this part of Aboriginal Queensland extends over both traditional and modern Aboriginal communities. The wide-ranging interaction of Aboriginal people in traditional times has its analogs in the period of disruption described here as well as in the present, when conversation typically concentrates as much on genealogy as on events.

6. Barney Warner belonged to the southern or inland half of the Gambiilmugu people, along with Yagay.

7. See note 4.

8. **Thuway** means classificatory nephew, or sister's son.

9. On first memory, Roger Hart mistakenly called the mountain by the name Wuuri. Toby Gordon gave Peter Sutton the name *Wuri-thamol* for a mountain range inland from the coast about halfway between Barrow Point and Weigall reefs, citing it as his mother's birthplace. Sutton 1993 gives **wuri-warra** or **wuriingu** as clan area no. 12, the country belonging to, e.g., Joe Rootsey. For Roger Hart the word Wuuri rightly describes a tribal estate between Barrow Point and Cape Bowen, starting somewhere around the mouth of the Wakooka Creek.

DELOUSING

1. According to Roger Hart, women were not allowed to visit *Indayin* at all. Roger recalls being told that men visited the island for ceremonial purposes and that they went about totally naked while they were there. See Sutton 1993, on *Yindayin.* There remains some confusion about whether the landing place for Wurrey's genitals was Stanley Island or the nearby Clack Island. Roger Hart remembers the episode as told here.

ON THE BEACH AT BARROW POINT

1. 'Our [dual] country', i.e., 'the country belonging to the two of us'.
2. Department of Aboriginal and Islander Affairs, although at the time the actual government office was that of the chief protector.
3. Tulo Gordon was senior claimant to the Guugu Yimithirr–speaking estate called **Nugal,** inside the Hopevale reserve itself. Like Gambiilmugu, Nugal was traditionally divided into two "nations," in this case called "younger sister" and "older sister."
4. The Eight-Mile Bridge on the Endeavour River was near a Cape Bedford Mission outstation established just before World War II. Young men from the mission worked on a farming operation there. Eight-mile is the site of the present-day Cooktown airport.
5. Wife of tracker Long Billy McGreen, Sr.

"ALL THESE PEOPLE GONE"

1. By contrast, the Cape Bedford elder who oversaw this process of supplemental christening, George Bowen, took his own surname from his community of origin; he had originally been sent to Cape Bedford as a young boy from the failed Lutheran mission at Proserpine, near the town of Bowen.
2. Roger Hart believes that women intentionally treated themselves with bush medicine in order to prevent pregnancies, so that, as he puts it, "they could easily get away," i.e., escape from native police. His explanation for why so many of the women from his area had no children contrasts with the received wisdom of the time that attributed low Aboriginal fertility to introduced venereal disease and malnutrition.
3. This little exemplary passage is translated from a short explanation Roger Hart recorded on 2 October 1982, as we sat gorging ourselves on the oyster beds at Ninian Bay.
4. The same term includes also father's sisters.
5. The Guugu Yimithirr form combines a place or area name, like **Wuuri,** with a purposive case suffix, e.g., -:**ngu** (thus, **Wuuriingu,** 'for the area Wuuri'), or with a derivational suffix -**warra**, 'people from the area' (thus, **Wuuri- warra,** 'people from Wuuri').

THUNDER AND FOG

1. In Guugu Yimithirr, the word **daman** denotes an area rich in food resources reserved for the tribal owners of a specific tract. The owners had first rights over such resources, whether deliberately planted or wild, whether explicitly tended or merely exploited on a seasonal basis.

CAMPING AT UWURU

1. Tracker McGreen's sons both went to school at Cape Bedford, and Billy McGreen, Jr., died at Hopevale in the 1980s. His younger brother, the late Mitchell McGreen, was probably too young to have visited Barrow Point as a child.
2. Another version of this story, told together by Roger Hart and Toby Gordon, was recorded by Peter Sutton in Mossman in 1970 (see tape in the Australian Institute of Aboriginal Studies (now AIATSIS) Archive LA4947a).
3. Literally, until they are "satisfied [and their] soul falls."

AFTERWARD: BARROW POINT IN THE 1990S

1. "Successful" under the provisions of Queensland's 1991–92 legislation rather than under still disputed provisions for Native Title.
2. See Sutton 1993, Land Tribunal 1994.
3. See Rigsby 1995.
4. See Bartlett 1993, Rigsby 1996, and Haviland 1997.
5. Land Tribunal 1994.
6. QSA A/58682, report of superintendent, Cape Bedford, 21 November 1927.

BIBLIOGRAPHY

Bartlett, Richard H. 1993. *The Mabo Decision.* Butterworths: Sydney.

Dixon, R. M. W. 1971. "A Method of Semantic Description." In Danny D. Steinberg and Leon A. Jakobovits, eds., *Semantics,* 436–471. Cambridge: Cambridge University Press.

Gordon, Tulo, and Haviland, John B. 1980. *Milbi: Aboriginal Tales from Queensland's Endeavour River.* Canberra: Australian National University Press.

Haviland, John B. 1974. "A Last Look at Cook's Guugu Yimidhirr Wordlist." *Oceania* 44 (3): 216–232.

Haviland, John B. 1979a. "Guugu Yimidhirr Brother-in-Law Language." *Language in Society* 8 (3): 365–393.

Haviland, John B. 1979b. "How to Talk to Your Brother-in-Law in Guugu Yimidhirr." In Timothy A. Shopen, ed., *Languages and Their Speakers,* 161–240. Cambridge, Mass.: Winthrop.

Haviland, John B. 1985. "The Evolution of a Speech Community: Guugu Yimidhirr at Hopevale." *Aboriginal History* 9 (1–2): 170–204.

Haviland, John B. 1991. "'That Was the Last Time I Seen Them, and No More': Voices through Time in Australian Aboriginal Autobiography." *American Ethnologist* 18 (2): 331–361.

Haviland, John B. 1993. "Anchoring, Iconicity, and Orientation in Guugu Yimithirr Pointing Gestures." *Journal of Linguistic Anthropology* 3 (1): 3–45.

Haviland, John B. 1997. "Owners vs. Bubu Gujin: Land Rights and Getting the Language Right in Guugu Yimithirr Country." *Journal of Linguistic Anthropology* 6 (2): 145–160.

Haviland, John B. 1998. "Guugu Yimithirr Cardinal Directions." *Ethos* 26 (1): 1–23.

Haviland, Leslie K., and John B. Haviland. 1980. "How Much Food Will There Be in Heaven? Lutherans and Aborigines around Cooktown before 1900." *Aboriginal History* 4 (2): 118–149.

Land Tribunal. 1994. *Aboriginal Land Claims to Cape Melville National Park, Flinders Group National Park, Clack Island National Park and Nearby Islands.* Report of the Land Tribunal established under the Aboriginal Land Act 1991 to the Hon. the Minister for Lands, May.

Loos, Noel. 1982. *Invasion and Resistance: Aboriginal-European Relations on the North Queensland Frontier, 1861–1897.* Canberra: Australian National University Press.

Mackett, P. J. 1992. *Queensland Aboriginal Papers,* vol. 36 (computerized index to QSA papers), April 14, 1992, Brisbane.

Pohlner, Howard. 1986. *Gangurru.* Adelaide: Lutheran Church of Australia.

Rigsby, Bruce. 1995. "Aboriginal People, Land Tenure and National Parks." Address to Royal Society of Queensland, draft, 3 October.

Bibliography

Rigsby, Bruce. 1996. "'Law' and 'Custom' as Anthropological and Legal Terms." In J. Finlayson and Ann Jackson-Nakano, eds., *Heritage and Native Title: Anthropological and Legal Perspectives,* 230–252. Canberra: Native Title Research Unit, Australian Institute of Aboriginal and Torres Strait Islander Studies.

Rigsby, Bruce, n.d. "Queensland Genealogies, Lakeland Land Claim." Computer files. 1992.

Roth, Walter E. 1984 (1901–6). *The Queensland Aborigines,* vol. 2. Victoria Park, W.A.: Hesperion Press.

Sutton, Peter. 1993. *Flinders Island and Melville National Parks Land Claim.* Vols. 1–2. Aldgate, S.A.: Cape York Land Council.

Thomson, D. F. 1935. "The Joking Relationship and Organized Obscenity in North Queensland." *American Anthropologist* 37: 460–490.

INDEX